The Method of Equality

D1231384

The Method of Equality

Jacques Rancière

Interviews with Laurent Jeanpierre and Dork Zabunyan

Translated by Julie Rose

polity

First published in French as *La méthode de l'égalité*, © Editions Bayard, 2012

This English edition © Polity Press, 2016

Polity Press
65 Bridge Street
Cambridge CB2 1UR, UK

Polity Press
350 Main Street
Malden, MA 02148, USA

ISBN-13: 978-0-7456-8062-0
ISBN-13: 978-0-7456-8063-7 (pb)

Library of Congress Cataloging-in-Publication Data

Names: Rancière, Jacques, interviewee. | Jeanpierre, Laurent, interviewer. | Zabunyan, Dork, interviewer.
Title: The method of equality : interviews with Laurent Jeanpierre and Dork Zabunyan / Jacques Rancière.
Description: English edition. | Malden, MA : Polity Press, 2016. | Translated from: La méthode de l'égalité. | Includes bibliographical references and index.
Identifiers: LCCN 2015030102| ISBN 9780745680620 (hardback : alk. paper) | ISBN 9780745680637 (pbk. : alk. paper)
Subjects: LCSH: Rancière, Jacques–Interviews. | Philosophers–France–Interviews. | Political science–Philosophy.
Classification: LCC B2430.R274 A5 2016 | DDC 194–dc23 LC record available at http://lccn.loc.gov/2015030102

A catalogue record for this book is available from the British Library.

Typeset in 10.5 on 12 pt Sabon
by Toppan Best-set Premedia Limited
Printed and bound in the UK by Clays Ltd, St Ives PLC

The publisher has used its best endeavours to ensure that the URLs for external websites referred to in this book are correct and active at the time of going to press. However, the publisher has no responsibility for the websites and can make no gua rantee that a site will remain live or that the content is or will remain appropriate.

Every effort has been made to trace all copyright holders, but if any have been inadvertently overlooked the publisher will be pleased to include any necessary credits in any subsequent reprint or edition.

For further information on Polity, visit our website: politybooks.com

Contents

Foreword

Jacques Rancière is one of a generation of French philosophers who, in recent years, have been unstinting in giving interviews to people from all kinds of different fields. While this is noteworthy, it is no accident. As Rancière explains here, an interview is not to be confused with the research work it's always in danger of short-circuiting or over-simplifying, but it does nonetheless represent a non-negligible part of the 'method of equality' that provides the present work's title. It's a title chosen by the philosopher for a process he has tirelessly defended since the 1970s. The activity of thinking is no less effective in an interview than in a written work, and one of the characteristics of the method in question is to posit that 'there is no proper place for thought. Thought is everywhere at work.'[1] But why add another book-length interview to past interviews, some of which have already been brought together in book form?[2]

Two objectives guided our approach here. This long conversation, divided into four phases, is meant to provide an introduction to the thought of a present-day theorist who is abundantly read and commented on. The point was to spell out the origin, function and

[1] This is a claim Rancière made in the closing lecture of the conference devoted to him at Cerisy in 2005 and which was entitled 'The Method of Equality' in the annals published subsequently. See *La Philosophie déplacée – Autour de Jacques Rancière* (Lyon: Horlieu, 2006), edited by Laurence Cornu and Patrice Vermeren, p. 519.
[2] Jacques Rancière, *Et tant pis pour les gens fatigués. Entretiens* (Paris: Editions Amsterdam, 2009).

definition of certain concepts and catch phrases (the distribution of the sensible,[3] dissensus, the ignorant schoolmaster, disagreement, the part of those who have no part ...) that are sometimes taken up by readers automatically and used without thinking. Beyond these now routine expressions, we asked Jacques Rancière to go into details on several issues in a bid to deepen or clarify certain elements of his thinking. That aim squared with our second goal, which was to restore the unity of Rancière's philosophical project, given that that project continues to be misread almost universally as being split into a so-called 'political' moment followed by a moment described as 'aesthetic'. Ever since his masterwork, *The Nights of Labour*, came out in 1981, the whole of the French philosopher's *œuvre* has consisted, on the contrary, in contesting that opposition along with all a priori demarcations of fixed fields of competence, by working on regimes of interaction and circulation between different ways of seeing and thinking, different ways of coming together and doing battle. This also allows us to define a method of equality that is fleshed out in a reconfiguration of territory and capacity and in the shift in the meaning of words and things that follows from this. If Rancière's work is all of a piece in its perspective and its method, it has shown, and continues to show, different inflections, moments and reworkings, which are also dealt with in the pages that follow.

The first part of the book, 'Geneses', revisits the elaboration of Rancière's intellectual programme via the education he received, born as he was in 1940, as well as his early writing. The first known text that Rancière published under his name was a contribution to *Reading Capital*, edited by Louis Althusser and published in 1965. In 1974, the publication of *Althusser's Lesson* ratified a methodological and political break, obvious as early as 1969, with the Marxist philosopher of 'the rue d'Ulm' (the École normale supérieure). In 1980, under the supervision of Jean-Toussaint Desanti, Rancière defended his thesis, which was called *La formation de la pensée ouvrière en France: le prolétaire et son double (The Formation of Working-Class Thought in France: The Proletarian and His Double)*. This was published the following year as *The Nights of Labour*. The problems orchestrating Rancière's thinking as a whole seem to have crystallized around that time. They also arose out of all he learned from the events of May 68 and the new diagnosis that ensued concerning the task of intellectuals and how far their knowledge and their discourse might extend.

---

[3] '*Le partage du sensible*' has been translated in a number of ways but is now usually translated as 'the distribution of the sensible', as 'distribution' manages to capture both senses of *partage* as a parcelling out or sharing and as a division. *Translator's note*.

The second part, 'Lines', tests the hypothesis that Rancière's *œuvre* is all of a piece by suggesting various ways of reading it that are internal to Rancière's research. It is not so much a matter of summing up or reiterating his thinking and its main categories, or of tracing its contours and compartments, as of seeking – as Rancière invites you to do in other forums – the transitions and various subterranean circuits. This sometimes happens by exposing the work to classical problems of philosophy. Particular attention has been paid to the philosophical utterance as such and this represents a way of raising a whole set of questions about Rancière's *œuvre* that Rancière has himself put to other producers of official discourses. More than a general philosophy, what we have tried to capture is a theoretical style.

The following phase of our interview, 'Thresholds', consists in comparing Rancière's work with that of other thinkers of the same period and subjecting it to some of the recurring objections it attracts, or, indeed, to new critical investigations. The possible connections or distinctions we could make between Rancière's *œuvre* and other significant bodies of work produced in his time are numerous and no doubt other researchers will work through these more systematically and precisely in future. For our part, we deliberately limited references to other authors, preferring to underscore, without attributing them, some of the controversies, misunderstandings or differences that have arisen. We locate ourselves here at the outer foothills of Rancière's conceptual mountain.

The last part of our interview, 'Present Tenses', aims to project Rancière's thought on to the current scene and the available possibilities. Various themes are dealt with, but the relationship the philosopher maintains with them is emphatically not one based on expertise or science, thanks to the method of equality. So the challenge is to isolate a way of viewing the times by posing a few unavoidable questions for contemporary liberation practices. This overview notes one thing in particular, which is the multiplicity of present tenses running through the current moment. As coherent and unified as it is, Rancière's intellectual programme continues to be endlessly renewed through the discordance between these various versions of the present.

The four moments of our interview describe one possible reading of this book. But nothing would be more in keeping with a theoretical approach that has stood from the outset for 'rejecting hierarchical thinking' than to work through them any way you like.

Laurent Jeanpierre
Dork Zabunyan

Part One

Geneses

Childhood and Youth

Let's start with your formative years and the building blocks of your thinking, up to when The Nights of Labour *was published in 1981. Tell us firstly what you remember of the period before you went to the École normale supérieure.[1] Whether we like it or not, for most of us in France the years of preparatory classes for the* grandes écoles *and exams often remain important elements in our intellectual trajectories. Maybe that means something to you too?*

I got into the École normale sort of 'automatically', even if you had to sit for the exam and pass. When I was twelve, I wanted to be an archaeologist. I was told that, for that, you had to prepare for the École normale, you had to do Latin and Greek, so I started off in the Latin-Greek stream. I went off archaeology, but I forged ahead anyway. I was good at arts and I took the supposedly royal road. In the end, those years of preparation weren't especially traumatic for me apart from a few serious health problems, it was just a little strange as an experience. We had a fairly amazing number of bad teachers. I discovered for the first time that the pinnacle of the teaching hierarchy had nothing to do with any level of

---

[1] The École normale supérieure (ENS) is the prestigious *grande école* for top-tier teachers and researchers. The *grandes écoles* are tertiary institutions specializing in professional training; entrance exams are rigorous. *Translator's note.*

competence or ability to teach. I also discovered the strange law of exams and competitions, which is their ritualistic quality, both in terms of setting you up and then humiliating you. I remember this bigwig at the Sorbonne who cut me off at the first sentence to say, 'Monsieur, this is a classic example of poor analysis,' after which I got my certificate with second-class honours. But that's a part of my experience that only played a role much later on. Because, once I got into the École normale supérieure, I was able after all to quite easily slip into the character of a person who'd passed a very hard exam and so could speak in the name of knowledge, of science. You could say there was a certain contradiction between my experience as a student doing exams and competitions, confronted by all the mechanics of getting in and being humiliated, and then, later, my fairly unproblematic support for the Althusserian struggle of science against ideology.

Did you go to school in Paris?

Yes, I left Algiers at the age of two. I lived in Marseilles between 1942 and 1945. After that, I spent my whole childhood in Paris, more precisely at the Porte de Champerret, which played a certain role because it was the border between several worlds. Right at the Porte, there was a bit of the *zone*, the rough area, that hadn't been completely destroyed; and after that, on the left, there was Neuilly, the bourgeois town, and, on the right, Levallois, which was still a working-class town at the time. I went to school in Neuilly, but there weren't many children from Neuilly in the local *lycée* since the whole of the north-western suburbs went there, including suburbs that were still very working class. I lived my childhood in an atmosphere that was very IVth Republic. By that I mean in an immediate postwar atmosphere, with rationing and power cuts, blackouts and strikes (those days we went to school in a military truck) and in a social world that was still extremely mixed. There were communist councillors in Neuilly. At Pasteur, the local *lycée* of that posh suburb par excellence, people came from everywhere. And at soccer matches, on the Île de Puteaux, which was another kind of *zone*, you would go, from one week to the next, from the posh kids from Janson de Sailly to teams from the technical colleges. I lived in that world, which was both conflictual and mixed at the same time, though its memory has been crushed under the weight of the clichés about the *Trente Glorieuses*[2] and the baby boom.

[2] *Les Trente Glorieuses (Thirty Glorious [Years])*, originally the title of a 1979 essay by French economist Jean Fourastié, has been used ever since

My experience was filtered through a vaguely progressive Catholic conscience. I was in the Jeunesse étudiante chrétienne (JEC), the Christian Youth Organization, and I first came to Marx because the school chaplain showed me a book he was enjoying reading, Calvez's book on Marx (*La Pensée de Karl Marx*, 1956). That means I first got interested in Marx through all the themes that Althusserism later brushed aside, notably the critique of alienation. I also discovered Marx through Sartre, since my first way into philosophy was Sartre via Sartre's novels and protest plays. I'd read him as a philosophical writer before my final year of high school. Those were the days when people still engaged in the great philosophical debates about existence, its absurdity, commitment, and so on – the heyday of Sartre and Camus, if you like. The first book of philosophy I ever read was Sartre's *Existentialism is a Humanism*. When I got to the philosophy class and I was subjected to courses on attention, perception, memory, etc., I was in complete despair. Luckily, the following year, in *hypokhâgne*[3] at Henri IV, I had Etienne Borne's philosophy courses. That was a revelation for me, the discovery of the 'great philosophers' in a form that was at the same time very impassioned. Because of an essay I happened to have to do on the distinction between the body and the soul in Descartes, I threw myself into his *Metaphysical Meditations* and *Objections and Replies*. My philosophical culture, like my culture generally, has always been cobbled together in fits and starts; it's been local, localizable, sporadic, never encyclopedic, and very often developed either alongside official school courses, or based on specific projects I had to do for school but which I immediately took a lot further than was required.

You managed to reconcile those two things? After all, there is the entrance exam ...

At first, I didn't understand how it worked. When we were in Henri IV, they made us think we were the best, that the rest were plodders, losers. Result: the exams were a bloodbath. When I got to Louis-le-Grand, where the teachers were very grey, where even the students mostly looked grey, I realized the problem was first and foremost to somehow manage to translate any random extract from Homer off-the-cuff. In the oral exam in Greek, there was a text you prepared

---

to refer to France's boom years between the beginning of postwar reconstruction in 1945 to the oil crisis of 1973, years marked by full employment and record growth. *Translator's note.*
[3] *Hypokhâgne* is the first year of the two-year preparatory course for the École normale supérieure. *Translator's note.*

and afterwards there was the killer question where you were given ten lines of Homer to translate – just like that. I understood that the great philosophical and literary production numbers were one thing, but that studying for the exam was a precise gymnastic exercise and you just had to do it. I did it, despite everything, and apparently I remember it, whereas all the people who now give fiery speeches about the republican education system and the great themes – being steeped in a humanist culture, learning to think, learning to be critical – have forgotten that, like me, they sat for their exams on the basis of a culture of lecture handouts (at the time the history syllabus meant lecture handouts) or index cards listing the meanings of all the Greek particles, and what was called at the time minor Latin and minor Greek, meaning daily drilling so as to be able to translate any text whatever off-the-cuff.

Before you penetrated the 'fortress' of the École normale, we should perhaps go back over your family background, which you glossed over so quickly. Was it a milieu in which people had already had careers in teaching at school or university?

No, my family had nothing to do with any university or academic milieu. My father had started studying German but gave it up for a career as a government official, but he was killed in France in 1940. I never knew him. And my mother was in the public service. My father had been in the public service, my uncle was in the public service, and my mother joined the public service when she had to go out and work. I didn't have an academic or university background at all.

Did you father die in combat?

Yes, in June 1940, just before the armistice. My mother never remarried. She had all the strength it took to raise three children on her own. I grew up in a very protective, close and loving environment. I didn't have a father, but I was never an unhappy child. The only time I felt miserable was when I started high school because, at home and at primary school, I'd lived in an essentially feminine world. The discovery of the masculine world was the main traumatism of my youth.

You mentioned Algiers. Well, before you went to the École normale, there was the Algerian War. Did that mean anything to you?

Let's say I had a split conscience when it came to Algeria. I lived surrounded by objects and documents from Algeria, books, postcards with coloured Algerian landscapes: Bougie Bay all in pink,

Chréa all in blue, Timgad dun-coloured ... I had a vision of Algeria as a kind of dreamland, as far as that went. Otherwise I lived through the Algerian War, after the war in Indochina, just as I was waking up to political life. But I didn't live through it as a native of Algeria. I lived through it as a young man of the times who read *L'Express*, with a mix of admiration for Mendès France and disgust for Guy Mollet. The Lycée Pasteur was pretty right-wing; I remember seeing extremely violent tracts for the defence of the Christian civilization of the West passed around in class. I wavered a bit, I have to say, but the kind of Catholic circles I hung out with were pretty progressive.

Later, when I was at the École normale, it was the days of the OAS[4] and the big demonstrations against them. The year 1961–2 was vital from that point of view. One of the first demos following the violent attacks on North African immigrants started off from the École normale; there were a few dozen of us, a few hundred demonstrating in the boulevard Montparnasse the next day or the day after that. Before, I didn't belong to any political group. I was in various Catholic youth movements, but they weren't political even if there was a fairly left-wing sensibility. Once we were at the *École*, there was constant agitation, rallies. The people who organized the rallies were communists who would say the word and, after that, we'd either follow or not. So that was my experience and it wasn't linked to the fact that I was born in Algiers, except that when Algeria became independent I said to myself, why not go down there? I even put in a request to go to Algiers as a teacher, but that wasn't till 1965.

Education

By the time you got into the École normale supérieure, your dream of becoming an archaeologist was a thing of the past, but had you already decided on philosophy?

I hadn't decided. I started first year at the École normale supérieure without knowing whether I'd do literature or philosophy. I was enrolled in arts; I went to see Althusser, who didn't exactly wildly encourage me to do philosophy. So I hesitated for a long while and then, in my second year, I took the plunge, I had to make up my mind and I opted for philosophy. We went to the Sorbonne to enrol and to sit the exams. Otherwise we never set foot in there, with one

[4] The Organisation armée secrète was the French terrorist organization that opposed Algerian independence in the 1960s. *Translator's note.*

exception: if you were doing arts, you went to the philology classes there, as that's something you can't make up and it takes up a lot of time if you want to do it without teachers. The first year, when I was still enrolled in arts, I took the courses for the grammar and philology degree, but otherwise we hardly ever went to the philosophy courses at the Sorbonne. There were no courses at the ENS either. Those were the days when there was no teaching profession. There were just the 'crocs',[5] like Althusser, who was either there or not there and hardly ever gave classes, though he'd invite other people to give classes, seminars, but we weren't forced to go to them. I hardly followed any philosophy classes at the Sorbonne and very few at the ENS. I didn't do that much philosophy at school, except in my *agrégation*[6] year, the year I did the teachers' exams.

That was also a time when figures who are sometimes at the outer limit of philosophy, like Bataille or Blanchot, shot to the fore. Did you follow the literary debates?

Absolutely not. I don't know when I first heard of the existence of Blanchot or Bataille, but I think I was already a qualified teacher by then. I'm exaggerating a bit, but that was completely outside my world. Once again, my horizon, at seventeen, was Sartre and maybe the people he talked about, the great novelists of the 1930s, like Faulkner and Dos Passos. He also talked about Blanchot and Bataille, to tell you the truth, but I must have skipped those chapters. Otherwise, my world was Rilke, since the first philosophy course I ever heard was Jean Wahl's course on Rilke. That was the Sorbonne open course, which I'd listen to on the radio when I got home from school. Otherwise, I knew there were things like the new novel; I read a few of them. I knew the Barthes of *Mythologies*. My culture, when I was twenty, was a modernist culture, which could possibly be called structuralist already, but let's just say that I saw myself more generally as being part of a culture we could describe as 'avant-gardiste' – even if it was only avant-gardiste for me, without necessarily being so historically. My references were the new novel, new-wave cinema, the concerts put on by the *Domaine musical* society, and abstract

---

[5] A crocodile, or *caïman*, is a senior master at the École normale supérieure.
[6] The *agrégation* is the prestigious teaching degree that allows *agrégés*, those who pass its difficult exams, to get well-paid and highly respected jobs as secondary- and tertiary-level teachers in France. It was, and is, extremely important in France's intellectual hierarchy. The *Capes* (*Certificat d'Aptitudes à l'enseignement secondaire*) is the much less prestigious secondary-school teaching certificate. *Translator's note.*

painting – to cut a long story short, the modernity of the 1950s and 1960s, excluding all the offshoots of surrealism which weren't part of my world at all.

In philosophy, did you see yourself as having any masters, such as Hippolyte, Canguilhem or Alquié? They were still alive then.

We knew Hippolyte as the school director at the ENS, but he'd stopped playing a role as a philosopher or master. There was Althusser, but he wasn't a teacher. He inspired us more with conversation or certain texts more than any actual lessons. There were the people Althusser invited in. I remember some of Serres's lectures that were pretty brilliant. I also remember Foucault, who came and announced a seminar but never came back to do it. So in those days I hardly followed any philosophy at all. In second year, I started on an essay on the young Marx. It seems to me that as soon as I chose to do philosophy, I decided to do the *diplôme d'études supérieures*[7] on 'critical thought' in the young Marx. I'd gone to see Ricœur, who asked me if I wouldn't prefer to work on alienation or fetishism. I said no, I wanted to work on critical thought.

I didn't want to work on a philosophical theme; I wanted to work on a practice of thinking. I read a lot of the young Marx. I began my philosophical career by doing a talk on Marx's essay on the law on the theft of dead wood. That was in the winter of 1961–2. It was pretty funny because, just a bit before this, I'd gone to see Althusser and he'd said to me, 'Listen, I can't guarantee you success in philosophy, but if you want to do it, do it.' Then he launched his seminar on Marx, at the end of 1961 I think, and I gave the paper on the theft of dead wood and, at the end of the paper, Althusser came to see me to tell me I'd get the *agrégation*, no problem, I wouldn't have any trouble with philosophy. For two years I basically concentrated on that piece. At the same time, I did a degree in psychology, with social psychology, the psychology of the child, etc., which involved a certain amount of practical work. Since I wanted to work on issues to do with ideology and representation, I hit on the idea that it might be interesting to go in that direction. But it didn't help me at all.

I didn't do much history of philosophy; there was no reason to once you got your history of philosophy certificate at the Sorbonne,

---

[7] The *Diplôme d'études supérieures spécialisées* (DESS) is a one-year post-graduate degree roughly equivalent to a master's, although it then required students to write a longer and much more thorough thesis than today's masters require. *Translator's note.*

unless maybe you wanted to learn more about a particular philosopher if a course or seminar had excited you. I only began working
– or working again – on the history of philosophy after the *khâgne*[8]
for the *agrégation* year. I remember the beginning of that year, when
Canguilhem was president of the board of examiners. As a result,
the class on the history of the sciences where there were usually only
five or six people – Balibar, Macherey and two or three others – was
full from then on. Everyone was there. Canguilhem said not to have
any illusions, the die was cast, you either knew the history of philosophy or you didn't. I said to myself, 'No, listen, you don't know
the history of philosophy, but at the end of the year, you'll know all
you need to know.' I spent the year reading all of Kant and, at the
end of the year, I was able to answer any even remotely thorny question on Kant.

Reading *Capital*

*You were talking about the young Marx, your DESS project, but
did people really already say 'the young Marx' at the time? Wasn't
it an effect of Althusserian reconstruction – distinguishing between
the 'young' and the 'old' Marx?*

Althusser's essay on the young Marx dates from 1961 and it was in
response to an issue of an orthodox Marxist review on Marx that
tried precisely to reappropriate the 'young Marx', who was then
inspiring the theologians after having inspired the social democrats.
So I don't know if people actually said 'the young Marx', but there
was already a surge in interest in all the young Marx's essays, especially the *Manuscripts of 1844*. That was notably the case with the
books that introduced me to Marx, books written by the Jesuits,
Father Calvez and Father Bigo, who made the essays on alienation
the very basis of Marxism. So the young Marx existed but it was
Althusser who said, 'No, that's not the real Marx.' At the ENS we
thought alienation was a joke; we laughed at Lefebvre, Morin or
whoever, but without having read them. The world of the left-wing
traditions of Marxism was totally unfamiliar to me, since they held
sway in circles that were completely separate from ours.

So I began my DESS on the boundary between two worlds of
thought, since, on the one hand, I was already more or less part of the

---

[8] In school argot, *khâgne* is the second year of the two-year arts course
students need to do as preparation for the École normale supérieure. *Translator's note.*

enthusiastic uptake of the essays of the young Marx with all that was lyrical about essays like the *Critique of Hegel's Philosophy of Right*, which sort of corresponded to my idea of the time, to a philosophy that emerges from itself and becomes a way of life, a world. So I had even less reason to spend a lot of time studying the history of philosophy as it felt like the thinking I was involved in spelled the end of philosophy. I started working on the young Marx with that particular impetus. Meanwhile, that impetus was mitigated by Althusser and his critique of the 'young Marx'. My masters thesis turned into an essay in which I tried to prove the existence of an 'epistemological break'. The third part was on *German Ideology* and Ricœur told me it was truly sad: the first two parts sparkled and then this third part just reiterated Marx's 'let's start with the facts; it is a fact that …'. He felt this descent into the world of facts was truly dismal.

In 1964–5, while Althusser's seminar dealt with reading Capital, *you did an essay on the concept of a 'critique' in Marx. What made Althusser decide to publish that exchange? The other seminars weren't published, were they?*

Yes, in 1964 there was the seminar project based on *Capital*. Althusser had said that Marx's philosophy was there in practical form in *Capital*, but still needed to be identified and put into theory. It was all a bit *Hic Rhodus, hic salta* – 'Prove what you can do, here and now'. What we had to do was try and dig the philosophy from out of the guts of *Capital*. I didn't really have much to do with the core group that discussed the seminar and its role, etc. My job was to demonstrate this 'epistemological break'. As a specialist in the young Marx, I was given the job of showing the difference between the young and the old. It was a strategic job, since if I hadn't got started on it, nothing would ever have happened. No one knew what philosophy we were going to be able to find in *Capital* that we could identify and extract. What I extracted wasn't necessarily what should have been extracted, but someone had to take the plunge, even if it was completely mad.

Summing up the *Manuscripts of 1844* and showing why they weren't scientific was relatively easy, but showing how *Capital* changed everything was much more complicated. First of all you had to read *Capital*, which I'd never read. Like everyone else, I knew the first chapter of the first book, and that was all. I threw myself into it, did my first paper and then normally I should have done the next one a week later. I went to see Althusser to tell him I had another two books of *Capital* to read, that it wasn't possible to work out its philosophical rationality in such a short time. So I got a bit of an extension. But it was still a completely mad process for me in which I poured out what I discovered as I went along without getting any distance on it, except for bearing in mind the seminar on structuralism that had taken place two years previously, in 1962–3, when the whole thing took off with several papers on Lacan. In the years before that, all I'd done was a paper on *The German Ideology* for the structuralism seminar, but I'd never done anything on Lacan or on any of the great structuralists. Michel Tort was the first to talk about Lacan, followed swiftly by Jacques-Alain Miller. I was trapped into having to do a synthesis as fast as I could of what I was reading in Marx and what was already in the wind at the time, what was going on in our minds after the structuralism seminar. I spoke four times as there was no end to it.

At the time, there was absolutely no question of publishing; it was originally planned as a seminar, and then it became a series of public lectures, which meant certain individuals, like Miller, who wanted it to be a seminar, pulled out. At the end of the year, Robert Linhart told me he wanted to turn my essay into a manual for theory training since this was the time when the Ulm Circle was becoming very vocal and was involved in organizing training in theory for the militants in the UEC (Union des étudiants communistes).[9] There was still no question of a book. I only found out quite late in the piece that it was going to be turned into a book. That was part of Althusser's politico-theoretical strategy, which I didn't have any kind of hand in.

Were the essays touched up or were they published as they were?

The essays were published as they were, or mine was anyway. Althusser didn't edit my essay for the original edition. Everyone handed in their essay and it was published just as it was. Mine was really a lecture and that wasn't a problem for a course in theory training whereby it would have been distributed to the militants as a handout. Afterwards, it turned into a book without people like me having any control over the process.

What was happening in 1968 when your essay was removed from the new edition of Reading Capital? *Were you driven to react or did it happen behind your back?*

Early in 1967, Althusser wrote to us saying there'd be a second edition, that it would have to be abridged but that at the same time

---

[9] The Communist Student Union. *Translator's note.*

we could take advantage of this to correct any errors in theory we might have made, rework the texts and so on. So I rewrote my essay, taking out the rather naive thoughts of the young structuralist discovering *Capital*. I made a lot of changes and I sent it off to Maspero and a few days later I received a letter saying that, in the end, for cost-cutting reasons, it had been decided that the second edition would be the same as the English edition, which had already come out and which only kept Althusser's and Balibar's essays. *Voilà*. Basically, it never was explained. They must have discussed it among themselves, but I was completely out of the loop. They must have felt that some of the essays weren't what was required theoretically and politically, and mine, which was a bit of a rallying cry for structuralism, was really a bit behind the times by then. They didn't say anything to me at the time. Althusser just told me that that's how it was; he'd decided there would be just the two essays. I didn't say anything. I sort of couldn't have cared less; I didn't say a word. I wasn't all that happy about it because, after all, I'd worked on it for two months and, what's more, I'd been coming out of a concussion, but in a way I was almost happy not to be associated with the whole thing any more. The real clash happened in 1973 when the decision was made to publish the complete set of essays again.

That was when you published that hostile article in Les Temps modernes ...[10]

... which was the preface I'd written and they'd cut. I'd sent the text to Maspero and he'd obviously started working on it, since I got my manuscript back all formatted, and then one day this note arrives saying that, despite the initial agreement for the preface, there were new problems and that, consequently, the first edition was to be published as it was, without any changes. I don't know exactly now how it happened that I sent the text to *Temps modernes*. André Gorz accepted it and saw to it that it was published.

And the idea for Althusser's Lesson (1974) *took shape then?*

No. It took shape when Althusser's *Réponse à John Lewis* was published in 1973 because I told myself that the fact that an essay as hopeless as that could cause such a stir was symptomatic of something. I told myself that apparently everything was reverting to how it was before. There was an outward show of moving further left but basically things were not only just the same, they were actually going

---

[10] 'Mode d'emploi pour une réédition de "Lire le Capital" ', in *Les Temps modernes*, 328 (November 1973): 788–807.

backwards – even to the point of negating what had happened, that is, the political effects of Althusserism. I decided I had to put my foot down and say my piece: say exactly what, from my point of view of course, its effects had been, what Althusser's so-called 'conversion' to politics in 1973 actually represented.

Speaking of the effect of *Reading Capital*, it was profoundly ambivalent. On the one hand, it had the effect of tidying things up, since all the somewhat dissident tendencies, all the interrogations going on all over the place, were suddenly stopped dead, as Althusser asserted that all of that was mere ideology, idle chatter, that what we needed was science. Said science had been put to work in the service of the communist orthodoxy. That said, the second thing was equally true: the autonomy of theory proclaimed by Althusser had sort of made Marxism available to everyone. Well, not to everyone, but at least to people who weren't part of the party machine. It had created something like a Marxist theory party – a party in the broadest sense, of course, not an organized party.

In actual fact, Althusserism was both completely dogmatic and ultimately in thrall to the classic idea of the workers' movement – the direction it was headed, the science behind it, etc. – and at the same time it had created an unidentified object, the theory of Marx, with all that that implied, including the move of wresting Marx from out of the clutches of the people who were his authorized agents, a way of extricating Marx from the legacy of the official Communist Parties and allowing us to draw all the logical conclusions from it. In 1968 there was this twin effect, starting with the critique of the movement as petit bourgeois, and then most Althusserians were marked by May 68, after all, a number of them permanently, others temporarily. Anyway, Althusserism had one unpredictable effect, which was to initiate a break with the whole system of allegiances Marxism was based on. You could do whatever you liked with Marxism. Althusser and his movement actually produced this rupture, which meant that other people could take up Marxism and work on it in a way that was different from what the traditional small groups did. All of a sudden, something like a Marxist authority was created and it eluded the party system, including all its appendages, the different varieties of Trotskyism or whatever ...

Attitude to Communist Engagement

Since you brought it up earlier when you were talking about the Althusserian environment at the ENS, were you part of the Ulm Circle or of the UEC?

I joined the Ulm Circle in 1963, when it was being reorganized. The Algerian War was over and the old team that was so tough on party positions had gone – people like Jean-Pierre Osier, who's since become a specialist on Jewish and Hindu thought but was in those days still very solid on the dialectics of nature. After that there were people like Roger Establet; he was the most rousing in general meetings. Then the Ulm Circle fell into the hands of my generation and we didn't really know what to do with it. That was the moment we sort of got going, Miller, Milner, Linhart and I, and tried to make something of the Circle. That something was necessarily connected to the Althusserian enterprise – let's say it was a matter of fighting against the spontaneous ideology of the students, against *Clarté*, which was the organ of a new-look and somewhat rebellious student communism. Serge July published articles in it on Le Golf-Drouot, the nightclub, interpreting what he saw as the symptoms of a youthful 'romanticism' ...

We really joined the UEC as a result of Althusser's essay on *student* problems,[11] which I critiqued afterwards. Althusser defended the idea that we needed to set up training in theory, to combat ideologies that perverted thinking and the student struggle. I was fairly active in that – I was even the person who was sort of behind the *Cahiers marxistes-léninistes*, including the title, since some people wanted to call it the *Cahiers marxistes* to flag the fact that it was anchored in theory; others, the *Cahiers léninistes* to underscore the fact that it was all to do with militant politics. I suggested *Cahiers marxistes-léninistes*, which was purely a compromise, only it then became an even stronger militant emblem than *léniniste* in the Maoist period. I wrote the article 'On the pseudo-Marxist concept of alienation' for the first number and, in number three, an article on the concept of relationships of production. I think that was my main contribution to the *Cahiers marxistes-léninistes*, apart from my contribution to the actual dynamics of the thing. For me, it was supposed to just act as a sort of bulletin, but it began to attract people's interest. Students bought it. On top of that, the PCF (Partie communiste français) and its faithful followers in the UEC saw that it could be good for them because it attacked the leadership of the UEC, and of *Clarté* – what was called at the time the 'Italian tendency'. A special issue of a communist magazine reprinted the essays that were in the first issue of the *Cahiers marxistes-léninistes*, seeing all that as a sign

[11] 'Problèmes d'étudiants', in *La Nouvelle Critique*, 152 (January 1964): 80–111.

of a revival of Marxist thought, of thought that positioned itself in opposition to the eclecticism of the student leadership of the day. But it was nonetheless put together by a small group of people who belonged to a fairly closed circle with pretty strong personal ties, such as I had with Miller and Milner at a certain point, or else ties of camaraderie with people I'd gone through *khâgne* with then cohabited with at the ENS, like Balibar. They were, after all, people who lived at the ENS, who saw each other every day through militant or other activities. So it was all very in-school, even if there might have been a few antennae tuned to the outside world.

By then, wasn't it embarrassing to be so intimately linked to the fate of the Communist Party? Hadn't anti-Stalinism gained your ranks? Or other ranks at the ENS who might have attacked you on that basis by emphasizing that you were young intellectuals who belonged to the party?

You have to understand we couldn't have cared less about Stalin in the 1960s. We weren't looking to the USSR at all. The outlook then was both all the movements in what was known as the Third World, and it was Cuba, the idea of a sunny, smiling revolution. It was the whole boiling over of the Italian Communist Party; it was Frantz Fanon prefaced by Sartre, and then it was Althusser, the idea of Marxism as the one theory in step with all that was new: structuralism, Foucault, Lacan. We had the idea that a new world was getting going, that a new Marxism was being created and that it would be the theory of this new world that was just getting going. The USSR really wasn't something we could do anything about. Then China arrived and support for Maoism, but we were basically Marxists who had the idea that everything was there to be done, that it was up to us to recreate Marxism. There was the working-class tradition, the working-class world and the labour movement but otherwise, for us, Marxism as a theory didn't yet exist in France. We scarcely registered that the radical libertarian group *Socialisme ou barbarie* or the review *Arguments* existed. Trotskyism existed at the Sorbonne, not at the ENS. To cut to the chase, Maoism was an ideology for *normaliens*, and Trostkyism was an ideology for *sorbonnards*.

Anyway, being a communist student wasn't at all stigmatizing at the time. Quite the opposite, it was more a form of aristocracy. As for the party itself, I hardly had anything to do with it. At the end of my first year at school, the secretary of the PC decided I ought to pay for his stamps since he'd found out I was a communist. I paid for them, that was my one action, and then I told him I was going to the Fondation Thiers[12] and didn't know what cell to go to. He told me about a neighbourhood cell and said they wouldn't ask me any-thing, wouldn't give me any trouble. In spite of everything, there was this idea that the PC was all about workers.

How was your first year teaching after the agrégation *in philosophy? Did it bring back memories of your disappointing years in high school?*

I taught for a year at the Lycée Carnot. That year was a catastrophe for me, I didn't know a lot about philosophy and I knew nothing about these young people, who lived in a completely different world from mine. They had interests, including cultural and theoretical interests, which were completely different. It was a world that had nothing to do with the one we'd sort of shut ourselves away in at the École normale. I turned up with my Althusserian certainty that I owned 'science', and I discovered that I really didn't know much at all. Consequently, I was forced to do the same hopeless courses that I'd sat through when I was young, since I didn't have time to come up with anything better. I realized at the same time that I had no real knowledge of the world I lived in. That experience was impor-tant to me later, during May 68. The people who did 68 were sort of the same people I'd dealt with when I was teaching at high school – people I basically didn't understand and who didn't understand what I was telling them either, even if some of them were happy because the rigour of Marxist theory appeals to some people, after all. That year I really felt that science as an emblem and a stance was one thing, but that the reality of knowledge was something else altogether.

May 68, Vincennes and the *Gauche Prolétarienne*

What did you do in 68?

Not a lot. In fact, the year before I'd had a serious accident, then a serious illness, and I was living on the fringes of society. I was half at the Fondation Thiers, which was a kind of oasis, and half in the country. I had no links with any militant group. When I saw what was happening at the beginning of May 68, I didn't really know what was going on, apart from the fact that all the slogans were

---

[12] The Fondation Thiers in Paris gives scholarships to promising students. *Translator's note.*

'ideological' and not at all 'scientific'. I was in the country not far from Paris; I had a sort of split consciousness. When I was coming back from the country, as you were emerging from the Saint-Cloud tunnel, you could see a big factory on the other side of the Seine with red flags on it and I was very happy to see those red flags. But in the beginning, that didn't mean that I was a player or a militant, I didn't build any barricades; I wasn't in the big demos. I was surprised by it all and I tried to hang on to what seemed to me to be really important, meaning, of course, what was happening in the factories. When the Sorbonne reopened, when we saw militant workers and all sorts of people at the Sorbonne, I told myself there was something positive about it, the encounter between students and workers. One of the rare things I did in 1968 was taking part in the discussions at the factory gates or a few meetings inside the factories. That movement ran completely counter to Marxism, both as we'd learned it and as we'd taught it. That's why I especially got involved in what seemed to me important, that is, meeting workers.

In the months and the two or three years that followed, you often returned to the event and the surprise factor. There is after all an interpretation and an analysis of the event that isn't just negative.

There were several phases. A negative interpretation to start with, because, for us, it was a petit-bourgeois revolt. Then I gave my positive support to that world where things were being decompartmentalized, especially with the student–worker connection and the possibility of free access to this working class that had till then been a matter for the party. And, in a third phase, Vincennes was set up ... Even if the buildings didn't yet exist, the department of philosophy already existed. As early as 1968, there were meetings about the department's programme, and the issue was, in the parlance of the day, whether we were going to let ourselves be 'recuperated' by the bourgeoisie or not. That was the word we used at the time to designate the enemy. There were meetings that paved the way for setting up the philosophy department at which Foucault asked Balibar to do a syllabus, and that syllabus was very much oriented towards epistemology. I said it was out of the question, that that was reactionary. Balibar was the only one from the PC on the team. One of the courses he'd planned was called 'The Philosophy of Work'. There were a few of us there and I leaped up and said, 'What do you mean, "Philosophy of Work"?' And he said, 'Yes, yes, "Philosophy of Work"; I like it and I'm sticking to it.' All of a sudden, I told myself that that was beyond the pale. I'd been behind in relation to the event, but the more time passed, the more I believed in 68. It's from that point that I started developing the thinking that led to the 1969 essay on the theory of ideology and then to *Althusser's Lesson*. I began to react in a way that was the complete opposite of what I'd been part of till then – the struggle of science against ideology, the theory of a rupture. It's based on this initial confrontation that I really started to question Althusserism, the famous essay on student problems and the whole trajectory we'd been on before that. Anyway, I'd never been very closely involved with the Althusserian enterprise. For the seminar, I'd been recruited as a specialist in 'rupture', but I never took part in the meetings of the inner circle – the Spinoza Circle – or other things like that. Never. The last time I saw Althusser was in 1967.

In 1969, I was really in a militant Maoist milieu with no ties to the old Althusserians, except the ones who'd become Maoists. Of my generation or later, Miller and Milner become Maoists, Badiou too in his own way, since his original family wasn't the Communist Party but the PSU, the Parti socialiste unifié (Unified Socialist Party). There were sympathisers like François Regnault, but it was Judith Miller who was the great militant Maoist at Paris-VIII. Vincennes militancy was an echo of the great battle between the PCF, for whom Vincennes was a model university, its university, and, opposite them, the lefties who said, 'Let's destroy the university'. I was dragged off to the Gauche prolétarienne[13] by the students. At the start of the year, I had a mix of students from the PCF, since we were dealing with Marxist theory after all, and students from what was starting to be known as the Gauche prolétarienne. But for the Gauche prolétarienne the main thing was playing out elsewhere, inside the factories, while the university was seen as a 'rear base'.

More generally, at Vincennes there was little investment in the idea of any new or revolutionary form of education; that was not what mattered. Or, if there was some notion of a new form of education, it was bound up with the PCF, with a new kind of university that was more about renewing different forms of knowledge than about a new teaching university. As a university, it could be called new in the sense that it had everything going for it that was considered hip: structuralist linguists and arts teachers, Althusserian philosophers, Lacanian psychoanalysts, sociologists who followed Bourdieu. And there were also all the people from the PCF who'd been passed over in their careers and who'd finally landed

---

[13] The Gauche prolétarienne, or Proletarian Left, was a Maoist political party, formed in France in 1968 and dissolved in 1974. *Translator's note.*

jobs. On the one hand, there was this university that had been overhauled and, on the other, all the people for whom university was a stop-off point or a rear base, but not the essential thing, which for them was to end the division of labour, the intellectuals vs manual workers divide. But the idea that workers were going to turn up en masse as students at Paris VIII turned out to be completely misguided. I remember we had great hopes for the evening classes in the beginning, but we hardly saw any workers turn up for those classes. There was no real new student audience. The first few years we got the slightly radical students from the Sorbonne who came over to us. Then, when the philosophy department lost its accreditation, after just a year, the students who wanted to study left Paris VIII and then we essentially got militants. We didn't make people sit for exams. So the PCF denounced us and we had our degree taken away.

Among the students, there were also lots of people who'd been driven out of their homelands, like the Chileans, for instance, and the Brazilians, quite a few Latin Americans, who came through Paris VIII. There was a fairly militant run that was different from what we saw at Paris VIII at the end of the 1990s, when the philosophy department got its degrees back and we saw students coming from the four corners of the globe to get a degree in the department where Foucault, Deleuze and Lyotard taught. A degree that they were able to turn to their profit to get jobs back home, which was unimaginable in the 1970s.

What form did your teaching take in the early days at Vincennes – what were the contents? It wasn't epistemology, as you've just said, but, according to the archives, you were giving courses on Marxism all the same?

The first year I taught a course on German Ideology, but that course turned more and more into a critique of Althusser's theory of ideology which ended in the 1969 essay on the theory of ideology.[14] After that, I gave courses that went back over the history of the communist movement, the USSR. That was a time when I discovered texts that were part of a critical tradition we knew

[14] Jacques Rancière, 'Pour mémoire: sur la théorie de l'idéologie', reprinted as an appendix, 'On the Theory of Ideology: Althusser's Politics', in *Althusser's Lesson* (London and New York: Continuum International Publishing, 2011, translated by Emiliano Battista; originally published by Gallimard, Paris in 1974).

nothing about, such as Castoriadis's essays. I tried to rethink the history of the USSR to come up with a critique of Leninisim. There was an introductory course of the 'Marxist-Leninist theory' type. But that was actually critical work in which I took up all the issues of the 'relationships of production and power in the USSR' kind, using a model that was sort of a mix of *Socialisme ou barbarie* and Maoism.

Didn't you ever think of leaving Paris VIII? You made your whole 'career' there, in the end. Was being there self-evident for you?

It wasn't self-evident, but there was a time when it was pretty exciting. After that, it was impossible to leave. When I called on the CNRS[15] and the EHESS[16] in the 1980s, I came up against a real brick wall. It was the same with the CNU.[17] In fact I got a job as a teacher at that university thanks to the art-and-aesthetics committee of the CNU, not thanks to the philosophy committee, who wouldn't give me a job. For people like me, anyway, there was no hope of going somewhere else even if you wanted to. In the beginning you didn't think about it. There was the feeling of being a political collective. There wasn't really a studies board in the department, and the general assembly of students and teachers was the supreme authority. For the rest, every teacher did what he liked and that continued to be the case, furthermore. Around 1974, there was a clash between we assistant professors and the professors (Châtelet, Deleuze, Lyotard) over a murky issue to do with part-time lecturers, following which we dissociated ourselves from the business of the department. François Châtelet ran it for a long time. He would phone Deleuze and Lyotard to find out what they thought, then he'd call us and say: this is what you have to do, do you agree with that? We agreed. In any case, we couldn't have given a rat's. But once the militant period was over and after the move to Saint-Denis, the 1980s were pretty depressing. There were practically no students left in the department

[15] Centre national de la recherche scientifique, France's national multidisciplinary research organization. *Translator's note.*
[16] École des hautes études en sciences sociales, the School of Advanced Studies in the Social Sciences. *Translator's note.*
[17] Conseil national des universités, the national committee that decides the careers of university teachers; to become a maître de conférence, a teacher, or a professeur des universités, a full-time university professor, you have to have its agreement. *Translator's note.*

apart from the external public who'd come to hear Deleuze or Lyotard.

What were your militant commitments at the time? Were you even remotely part of the Groupe information prison (GIP)[18] set up by Michel Foucault and others?

From 1969 to 1972, I was active in the Gauche prolétarienne essentially as a grass-roots militant, one of the ones who go to the factory gates and into workers' hostels to hand out leaflets, stick up posters in the early hours, transport various kinds of things and take part in collective action. It was grass-roots activism, but in an organization that was very small and where the bottom was thereby constantly rubbing shoulders with the top. After that, I was moved to a group that was charged more specifically with liaising with prisoners and preparing political trials. That was when the dynamics that created the GIP were triggered.

The problem was that the people in the GIP weren't necessarily available to go and investigate and hand things out at the prison gates. They needed to set up a specifically militant corps. I told Daniel Defert that my wife, Danielle, who'd been cut off from militant work after having a baby, was available. Daniel Defert and a few others did the bulk of the GIP's militant work with Foucault. But I didn't personally collaborate with the GIP. I might have lent a hand occasionally, since I'd already had contact with prisoners for a while. Otherwise, as far as militant work goes – but this was a very different matter – I'd directed the 1972 issue of *Temps modernes* that was called 'Neofascism and Democracy'. That was a bit like the politico-theoretical manifesto of the Gauche prolétarienne, which notably included the interview Foucault did with Benny Levy. That's what I did as an activist in the GP, but the GIP just wasn't me.

Did these militant activities take up much time?

Yes, it all took up a lot of time, but between 1969 and 1972, I wasn't involved in philosophy at all; I've only been involved in it at precise times in my life. Most of my life then, beyond looking after my son, was taken up with militant work. In a sense, the work on the archives followed on from the militant work. At a given moment, I found myself out of all militant work with the clear prospect of never finding anything satisfying on that front again.

---

[18] Prison Information Group. *Translator's note.*

Turning Points

Was that linked to the fact that you were writing as well as teaching? How did you go about teaching every year, every term? Did you start off by linking the teaching to some kind of exploration with a view to getting a book out of it, or was it a parenthesis in the personal writing work?

Actually, the main thing for me wasn't teaching or writing; it was research. I became less involved in the job of teaching at Paris VIII pretty quickly. In the years 1972–3, what I was interested in was delving into the workers' archives. Teaching was consequently pretty secondary for me. At the time, the university year started at the end of November and ended around the beginning of May. It was completely different. We were free to do what we liked with our time. In the years 1972–3, what very quickly came to matter to me was not necessarily writing a thesis, since I didn't have any idea what I was going to do; what mattered was the research work in the workers' archives, guided by the notion that 68 had shown us that there was a big difference between the Marxism we'd been taught, the Marxism we'd taught, and the reality of the working-class world. I needed to look more closely at that.

So around 1972–3 I started going to the library every day. I started off at the one in the Musée social. It was directed by a formidable person, Colette Chambelland, who was the daughter of a revolutionary trade-union militant. She was one person – there weren't many – who welcomed me straightaway and encouraged me and liked what I did. But the Musée social had very limited funds. I worked a lot at the Bibliothèque nationale on brochures and newspapers and then at different archives: the Archives nationales, the Saint-Simon Fund at the Arsenal, the Gauny Fund at Saint-Denis, and so on. After the end of the really militant period inside the Gauche prolétarienne, where militant action took over from all other activity, I launched into the research work without having much of an idea at first of where I was going, actually with the naive idea at the time that I'd find the 'real' working class, the 'real' workers' discourse, the 'real' labour movement, the 'true' workers' socialism, all that you could imagine and hope for as authentic. That meant my timetable was completely determined by the work.

Your critique of Althusserism was extended just before this in several ways. Several figures whose authority derives from their knowledge crop up: the figure of the official social critic or the party intellectual, the figure of the scientist and then this figure of the spokesman who confiscates speech. Don't these figures tend to blur into a single power in your work of the period?

I think that the critique of the spokesman is cyclical and is not the most important thing. If you take the famous interview Foucault did with Deleuze,[19] you can see that what matters isn't simply the fact that prisoners speak for themselves and aren't spoken for by spokespeople; it's the fact that people who didn't speak now speak, and that these people who didn't speak have a theory about prison. Basically, the important thing is challenging the parcelling out of the whole set of social practices and discourses that are bound up with ideology, on the one hand, and science, on the other. What Foucault says in that interview, for me, is that any theory about prison is always a theory about prison, whether it's delivered by a prisoner or by a lawyer. There is no hierarchy between different types of discourse, and the fact that people who didn't speak are now speaking assumes its importance in relation to that.

We very quickly saw the limits of attacking the spokesperson, and of the demand for authenticity, of the demand that only those who are authorized to do so can really speak. In those days, we already felt that there was this duality: on the one hand, the challenge to those who spoke in the name of science, who spoke in the name of splitting the world of speech in two, but also, on the other hand, something that was very big at the time, namely the tyranny of the authentic. Anyway, the PC had always played around with the two registers: science, on the one hand, and the people who are 'really' workers, on the other. In 1968, to keep people quiet, there was this summary expression which consisted in saying, 'Go and tell them that in the factories'. In that sense, the critique of the spokesperson had regressive sides to it such as the fact of asking 'where' you were speaking from, which was sort of the killer question in those years. It's not that the question didn't have its validity. But, after all, the main thing about this 'where are you speaking from' is not finding out what your parents do for a living, but what world of speech, what division of speech you're talking from. The main thing for me was to question that division of the world between the subjects of science and subjects that are the objects of science.

[19] 'Intellectuals and Power: A Conversation Between Michel Foucault and Gilles Deleuze', in *Language, Counter-memory, Practice: Selected Essays and Interviews by Michel Foucault* (Ithaca, NY: Cornell University Press, 1980, ed. Donald F. Bouchard, 1972), pp. 205–17.

*Neither Althusserism nor new leftism – that seems to be your posi-
tion, because the cult of authenticity or of true speech as opposed
to confiscated speech is also a potential sin of the New Left.*

The communist duality I've just been talking about was appropriated
in different ways in the years after 1968, with the Trotskyists grabbing science and awareness of the avant-garde for themselves, and
the Maoists grabbing authenticity, in the sense of 'it's the workers
who said that'. For me, there were two aspects that marked my later
research: I wanted firstly to get back to the words that were the actual
words exchanged, that were spoken in the workers' struggles, the
workers' texts, the manifestos. But it very quickly became important
after that to disengage these workers' words from any labels identifying the real worker, the person who is justified in speaking, who
expresses his class, his being, his ethos.

*In the early 1970s, the issue of the autonomy of working-class
culture and, with it, the quest for the authenticity of 'real' speech
was effectively the prospect that seems to have got you going. But,
after 1975, we get the impression that you're more interested in
problems to do with circulating, with crossing borders, like the
problems you described when you were talking about growing up
at the Porte de Champerret in the 1940s and 1950s. These are heterogeneous situations capable of provoking a self-abandonment [à
la Foucault], a kind of dis-identification, which you seem to feel it's
very important to analyse. So we get the impression that your work
then switches definitively from the problem of working-class identity
to an interest in forms of desubjectivization.*

Yes. There are three elements for me. On the one hand, there's the
critique of the theory of ideology, of a certain status and position
of science. The search for working-class speech that isn't what was
transmitted by the Marxist tradition is not simply a quest for
authenticity. It's the idea of knowing what was really said, what
really circulated in words, how speeches, ideas, hopes, plans were
constituted. It's not just a matter, then, of finding real workers, but
also of finding the real dynamics of establishing a certain common
working-class world. With that initial objective, there was a target:
to do away with the thesis that science was imported, with the
idea that social practice necessarily produces illusions and that
science is there to correct those illusions, without its being clear
where that science comes from, how it is produced, how it itself
escapes the social necessity of illusion. That was the first important element.

The second element was that, as soon as I started working on workers' texts from the 1830s, I was struck by what we might call the performative dimension of those texts. Instead of an assertion of identity, there was a whole rhetoric, a whole performance based on playing around with identities, with the identity the other perceives. Because those were years when people were trying to track down an unplanned revolt and a working-class voice that would appear at the outset as different from or opposed to the official discourse of the labour movement – a voice that really came from the factory, the local neighbourhood, from a substantial working-class world. Instead of that, I found people who were extremely polite, a tad formalist, and who reasoned. The important thing for me was being faced with these texts, which in a way say, 'We are speaking as reasonable human beings and not as working-class brawn.' That was the second important moment. All these texts said, 'We are no rebels,' and forced you to read workers' discourse as a lot more complex, as going beyond the issue of identity.

The third important element was, *a contrario*, the 1974–5 craze for popular culture, crafts, folk festivals, the moment of Pierre-Jakez Hélias's autobiography *The Horse of Pride*, of Le Roy Ladurie's history *Montaillou: The Promised Land of Error*, followed by a whole host of film representations, like Tavernier's *The Judge and the Assassin* of 1976, or René Féret's film of 1977, *Solemn Communion*. It was sort of the end of hard-core militant leftism and people couldn't get enough festivals. They turned to a whole vision of popular culture – the idea that if leftism had failed, it was because it was authoritarian and because its authoritarianism was linked to the negation of the true traditions of the people and popular culture, folk festivals, popular speech. That was a big movement, one that also coincided with a moment when the 'new history' was visible – as the representation of a people whose every manifestation had its roots in the land, the *terroir*, in ways of being and in the movements and gestures involved in skilled work. Now, that was precisely the moment I started working on the Saint-Simon archives and on the Gauny Fund. And what leapt out at me straight away were these texts written by workers who no longer wanted to be workers, who couldn't give a hoot about traditional working-class culture, about folk festivals, but who wanted to appropriate for themselves what had been till then the language of the other, the privilege of the other.

From that moment on, what was important for me was attacking all ontologies of identity, the idea that it's not about working-class ideology versus bourgeois ideology, popular culture versus educated culture, but that all the important, explosive, phenomena in ideological and social conflicts are events that happen at the dividing line; they are phenomena that have to do with barriers that you see and that you transgress, crossing over from one side to the other.

In *The Nights of Labour*

How do you get your bearings in this mass of stuff when you're not a historian by training? In your early essays, you concentrate a lot on the period around 1848 before going back a bit in time. How did you organize this choice of time periods, the location of sources, your historiographical apprenticeship?

In the beginning my project was a pretty gigantic one, it has to be said, and it would have started with the origins of the labour movement in France and gone on to the constitution of the PC. The idea was to start from the meeting – and misunderstanding – between Marx and working-class political theory. My idea hinged on the *Manuscripts of 1844*. Roughly speaking, while Marx was writing these inaugural essays, what was happening down among the workers in 1844? What did Marx notice; what didn't he notice? That was always the idea: not to go back to the original origins, but to the origins of dispute and dissensus.

What about the conditions that made Marx's discourse possible?

Yes, indeed, what in working-class practice made Marx's discourse possible and what, in this discourse or that practice, was impermeable to Marx – what did Marxism more or less have to suppress? My idea was to start with that and then go through the whole history of revolutionary trade unionism and anarchism up to the beginnings of communism. I worked on a number of different areas, for example on the files of the insurgents of June 1848, without ever doing anything with it. I did interviews with former militant communists, people from the days when the Parti communiste was founded. Finally, I focused on the period 1830–50.

But I didn't follow any historian's advice; my relationships with historians have never been very good ... apart from one person who treated me extremely warmly, Michelle Perrot. She really embraced my work, and defended it and got it out there, but she didn't give me any leads because she'd never worked on that period. Historians are after all very stuck on the fact of being specialists in whatever period. In the beginning, the first texts and the first directions were given to me by Alain Faure, with whom I did *La Parole ouvrière*, and he was a history student. Alain Faure more or less drew up my very first bibliography. I ran into him outside my class one day in 1972, but there was a strike on and so there wasn't any class. We went off to have a bite to eat together and we became friends.

After that I'd say I let myself be guided pretty much systematically by the connections the material itself would offer me, with one source leading to another, Jean Maître's dictionary leading to a source I'd then follow to see if it took me anywhere or not. I worked the opposite way to how a historian works, which means you first draw up a bibliography of general works, and then, when you have the overall framework, you go off and look at pamphlets, the details. I didn't do it that way at all; I just threw myself into it, starting with a heap of fairly scattered leads that came at me from all sides.

I spent a lot of time in archives, but the decisive element for my method stemmed from the fact that I worked in the old Bibliothèque nationale, that is, in a place where everything was centralized and where, while you were waiting for someone to bring you Grignon's pamphlet on the tailors' strike, you could take out a Budé of some Late Latin author, or a volume of the dictionary of patrology on the writings of the Fathers of the Church, or a volume of some treatise on law. That way I was also able to put together *The Nights of Labour* because I was working in that realm of absolute non-specialization with the ever-present possibility of drawing a diagonal line between a workers' pamphlet and various bits of literary, legal or religious material. What made that book conceivable was the possibility of constructing a sort of symbolic plot that had absolutely nothing to do with any chronology or any transition from cause to effect in the traditional mode of the historian. When I praise auto-didacticism, it's not simply from a higher vantage point; it was for me a way to work. Of course, I learned a heap of things by heart at school, like Greek conjugations and the meaning of all the particles. But all the key points in my work are linked to a personal quest in which I learned things by immersing myself in unfamiliar material, with one source leading to another and the contours being constructed little by little by feeling my way along. That was already Jacotot's method, even if I didn't know its name: learning something and then relating all the rest to it.

Was that work well received in the university as an institution? How did your thesis exam go?

'Institution' means several things. I didn't have a problem proposing it as a thesis topic, and I didn't have a problem with Jean-Toussaint Desanti, who was supposed to be my supervisor but instead gave me carte blanche and didn't get mixed up in seeing what I was up to.

Then, the day I had to go before the jury, there were people who were a bit goggle-eyed, and there was a historian, Maurice Agulhon, who felt obliged to play the real historian, the serious historian, so he wasn't going to let some joker take charge of these working-class histories and put down the great republican social tradition of France. Next came my relationship with the corporations. When it came to publication, there was my relationship with the historians in power in the publishing industry. Gallimard didn't want it unless I transformed it into an anthology of archives; Le Seuil took it with so many restrictions and such an air of disdain that I withdrew it. And when I confronted the philosophers on the National Council of Universities a long while later, the first question they asked me was, 'Monsieur Rancière, what is your philosophical body of work *in*?' That work was neither philosophy for the philosophers nor history for the historians. It was a UFO – and ultimately not accepted by any corporation as such. Certain individuals read it and appreciated it, but only after a certain incubation period. The reaction was delayed, including overseas. People are interested in it now, after having read much later books that look more classically philosophical, like *Disagreement*. All of a sudden, people can see that that's the work that subtends more doctoral books.

In 1980, the perspective of hope, in terms of the history of the labour movement or the issue of the theory of emancipation, was already blocked off – and not just by disciplinary divisions ...

It was a doubly barred perspective. On the one hand, there was the beginning of a great offensive by François Furet against the whole revolutionary working-class tradition. On the other, there was a hard-line neo-Marxist discourse being peddled by people in the CERES[20] which decided the ideology of the PS, the Parti socialiste, around Chevènement. On the one hand, no one wanted to hear any more talk of such histories. On the other, people wanted theory, well, what passed for theory ...

---

[20] The Centre d'études, de recherches et d'éducation socialiste (Centre for Study, Research and Socialist Education) was originally the intellectual wing of the French socialist party and is now independent. *Translator's note.*

Birth of a Method: Ways of Reading and Writing

You just said that your way of working, of doing research, especially in the years between 1972 and 1981 when The Nights of Labour *was in the pipeline, was piecemeal. You also insist, in essays from that period – and this is not only aimed at historians but also at the discourse on science kept up within Althusserism – on the idea that the pursuit of causality in the social sciences reproduces a representational scene comparable to one politics sometimes produces which divides representatives from those represented. Your ambition is to construct a discourse in which the writing of the storyline is not governed by this kind of epistemology in which the search for causes takes precedence – meaning, for you, the representation of causes by effects. So you come to the aesthetic tonality, which you feel is a potential and undoubtedly desirable alternative in the discourse of the social sciences. Was that idea already clear to you at the time?*

There's a lot going on in the idea of the relationship of cause to effect, but if you think of the type of rationality common to the practice of historians and to a whole political tradition, including the revolutionary tradition, the classic causal model not only implies searching for the cause of an effect; it is always a way of identifying the cause–effect relationship as a relationship of one level to another level. So it's an inherently hierarchical principle. There is a world of causes and a world of effects. What happens in the drama of causes and effects is that the closer you get to the surface, to what people do and say, the more you move away from an original cause and the less it makes sense. The ordinary historian who had to deal with my material looked for the profound causes subtending this or that discourse. The historian's model was the Labrousse model: economics, then society, then politics and, finally, ideology. That's something that remains very powerful. If you look at Noiriel's bibliography of the labour movement, *Les Ouvriers dans la société française, XIXe–XXe*, published in 1986, and you look up *The Nights of Labour*, you'll find it under the heading 'workers' cultural and religious problems' …

That's how we learned history – with subheadings such as 'the causes of the revolution'. For every revolution, there was a structural cause: an economic crisis. Yet, as we now know, no economic crisis has ever led to revolution. A revolution is a matter of words, of demonstrating; we can see this still today despite all the clowns who say there is no revolution in Tunisia because there is no revolutionary plan, as if a revolutionary plan has ever made a revolution. You can always provide conditions, which will be conditions for some kind of convergence, but what happens in 1848 has much more to do with what happened in 1830 than with the economic crisis of 1847. You even get revolutions that work the wrong way round. Take what the workers said after 1830. Before, business was going well, then there was the revolution – that's terrific, the people are on the streets and taking power. But then the workers are out of work, there is no more work. This means that workers are dual creatures; they are labourers who've lost their jobs or their customers, and they are the working class who have won, but whose victory is then stolen from them. We really need to see that a social actor is always a multiplicity of social actors. Naturally, the search for causes can establish correlations but, at bottom, the question that remains central is what you think people are capable of. It's from that point of view that I was gradually led to follow a principle of non-hierarchy. And that principle was later summed up in the idea of 'the distribution of the sensible': it's not the case that there's a material world and an intellectual world in a potentially reversible hierarchical relationship. There is an actual relationship between a sensible world and what we can decide it means. In short, it's a matter of constructing a plot.

Hence the importance, obviously, of the writing, which fixes a certain relationship between different meanings. Hence my choice, essentially intuitive at the time, not to link a speech scene to a so-called real scene that is supposedly its basis or that the words reflect or express, but to try to link a speech scene to all the ramifications it has for itself or that can be linked to it through storylines that are no longer stories of causality between different levels, or even simply before-and-after stories in terms of history. That's sort of what I once said about the term 'proletarius', the fact that I understood the proletarian issue the day I came across Aulu-Gelle's essay, in which he explains that 'proletarius' is an old Latin legal term, completely out of use now, which means 'he who makes babies'. I found it long after *The Nights of Labour*. But after all, I've always sort of worked like that, by demolishing the causal hierarchy twice over to bring out a sensible world that's unstable: on the one hand, I took workers' texts as being the same as any other texts, to be studied in their texture and their performance and not as expressions of something else. It was a lacunary speech world that had to be kept lacunary to express the way of life the words were the work of – and not just the expression. On the other hand, it was a matter of extending the ramifications to see what was really symbolic in that experience, not in the sense of 'a symbol of' but in the sense of a distribution of the sensible, of the place you occupy in a sensible order which is also an order that divvies up places and possibilities. So I had to place the words in relation to scenarios and textual performances that normally belong to other registers, to worlds that supposedly bear no relation to working-class culture.

In the plotting of *The Nights of Labour*, there are a lot of opera references that are practically invisible but that allow me to mark an intense moment. So I conceived of the story about the break-up of Cabet's Icarian commune around two of Verdi's then-contemporary operas, *Sicilian Vespers* and *Simon Boccanegra*. In 1856, the Icarian workers divested their 'father', Cabet, of the presidency of the Commune. This business of the father was very important at the time. It was central in Saint-Simonism. A year before Cabet's divestment by his rebellious sons, the first version of *Sicilian Vespers* was performed in Paris. Well, the librettist on *Sicilian Vespers* was Duveyrier, an old Saint-Simonian 'father', and, in *Sicilian Vespers*, there is a moment when Governor Montfort grants his rebellious son pardon for the conspirators if he agrees to call him 'father'. Two years later, there's the first version of *Simon Boccanegra*, another matter of paternity played out against a backdrop of class struggle; in the finale, while his father-in-law is dying, the young Gabriele Adorno sings about the end of love's happy days (*Come passò veloce/ l'ora del lieto amore*). That allowed me to scan that historic moment: the end of the love stories between workers and bourgeois utopians. I don't know if I've really answered your question, but for me the issue of causality is an issue of hierarchy: in the dominant causal logic, there is a subterranean order that determines what's possible to perceive or think. With the aesthetics of plot-shaping, the question of what's perceptible and thinkable is always a surface matter, a way of carving up the surface.

Is it possible, in shaping a plot like that, to lay out, or rather weave, around a speech act the whole set of 'scenes' induced by, or correlated to, an observation scene, without organizing them into a hierarchy? Doesn't writing force us, regardless, if only in its syntactical structure and grammar, to introduce a cause where you don't want it, various 'fors', 'becauses' and 'therefores'?

In *The Nights of Labour* the 'therefores' are kept to a strict minimum – those that exist are often miscast, since they're used to refute a conclusion ('nothing to do, therefore, with ...'). I systematically avoided relationships of a hierarchical kind, the book being made up essentially of equivalences and displacements: a text cited, a commentary in the form of a paraphrase that displaces it and starts a movement towards another scene; lots of nominal sentences in the commentary, a sort of indirect free style that – at its humble level – seeks, in Flaubertian fashion, to 'unscrew' paragraphs so they can slide on top of each other. Obviously, that's not a formal principle of fluidity; it's a principle of egalitarian writing: doing away with the hierarchy between the discourse that explains and the discourse that is explained, and bringing out a common texture of experience and reflection on that experience which crosses the boundaries between disciplines and the hierarchy of discourses. It's a quasi-syntactical problem.

Then there is the problem of shaping the plot. *The Nights of Labour* set out two types of plot. There was a slightly Hegelian type of plot, which meant a division into three parts, like a circle of circles, where you go from the most abstract – the typical experience of the worker confronted by his problematic identity – to the most concrete, the formulations and experiences of the group as a group, via the mediation of an encounter with the other; as it happens, the encounter with the Saint-Simonians. And then there was a sort of biographical schema: I chose a slightly artificial plot, which was the story of a generation. What happened to these people who, in 1830, saw the sun and tried to remain faithful to that sun? Of course, the plot's ideal, even if I do have a character – Gauny – who lived through all that and who left me with the advantage of having his archives, from the 1830s to the 1880s. But anyway, it's exactly the kind of structure that tries to say what's at play within all that, how it's going to define these people as a particular kind of subject or actor, and how we can construct the intelligibility of a series of apparently disparate phenomena, situations and events as belonging to the same curve. It could have been extended into different areas. With the United States' Icarian archives, which I was only able to consult after I'd finished my thesis, I amassed a heap of elements as material for a book I'd never do but which would have been roughly the story of how a French communist worker became an American democrat farmer. That could have been a sequel, but there isn't going to be one.

Let's get back to your relationship with archives, which is something we come across again in other works of yours, like The Flesh of Words *(*La Chair des Mots*, 1998). In the chapter on Rimbaud, where you talk about his way of describing the times, you say you don't start out from any historic systematicity, and then you list a certain number of documents that may have belonged to Rimbaud and allowed him to write about his era. That's an approach that can be* *found in your way of working, no matter what the area under consideration, and it's close to what Walter Benjamin describes in* Unpacking My Library.

The important thing for me is to try to define a period of time, an era, a set of conditions, in an immanent way. My question, after all, is always: 'What can we perceive, what allows us to see this particular thing, what makes this particular word, this particular sentence make sense and acquire a value that's symbolic – whether limiting or liberating, either assigning you an identity and locking you into it, or allowing you to free yourself from it?' It's linked to the fact that I've always sort of worked on the margins, occasionally collecting scraps or remnants, the idea being that what defines the conditions for thinking and writing is never the times or the situation as they are described by the dominant discourse. There is a perceptible texture to experience that must be found and that can only be found by doing away completely with hierarchies between different levels of knowledge, politics, society, intellect or popular culture. I'd say it consisted in the things you feel by trawling a bit randomly, after stirring up a mass of papers and after consulting almanacs or the little pamphlets of mad inventors, or corny little vaudeville acts.

Basically I've tried to combine two things. One is transversality: I think the things that matter for theory turn up at crossover points, where the different jurisdictions disappear, when – in reality – the poet Rilke meets the young working girl, Marthe Hennebert, or when – in imagination – I try to make Emma Bovary's experience resonate with the experience of militant workers or with Saint-Simonian ceremonies in Mallarmé's prose poems. The other feature is precision. That's a quality that has been fostered in me by my constant practice as a gardener. With plants, you can't be vague. I've done the same thing with the texts. I've learned, more than some others have done, what the perceptible texture of the times was and thereby understood which acts and words, in those times, could make for consensus or rupture. This allows me to see, for instance, that a particular expression of Mallarmé's which others see as radically new was lifted wholesale from Banville or Gautier, and so I can substitute the process of spotting changes in history for the process of openly declared breaks.

We get the impression that, in your practice back then, the boundaries between philosophy and art are floating rather than absent. The absence of a hierarchy between different registers of inquiry and discourse only seems to appear later in your work.

Probably in practice, even if at certain times I had to suppress it. If you take the essay *Reading Capital,* or certain other essays where I have to explain at a conference what the police are and what politics is or the aesthetic regime of art, I'm in a bit of a bind, I'm forced to produce a discourse with signposts that are acceptable. You have to do this from time to time because people want you to; they want you to do 'theory' the way they understand it, meaning to start with a concept and then develop that concept, as I did in *Disagreement.* And even then I tried to hedge a bit there as well, since you find quite a few scenes in it: the plebians on the Aventine Hill; the tailors on strike in Paris. After all, what's important for me concerns all the essays in which I've been able to deploy a narrative storyline and bring out the perceptible texture of experience. What you're talking about started to be effective in *The Nights of Labour* and has continued through all the work on literature and cinema.

Another approach in your research in the 1970s appears between the lines in the texts that preceded and accompanied The Nights of Labour. *We are talking about an interrogation of ways of reading that is also bound up with the critique of Althusserism. You ask yourself the question of how to read a text. The attack on Althusserism in fact also works through a critique of internalist ways of reading philosophical texts like Marx's essays, but also through a critique of the Foucault of* The Order of Things *as well. What's more, you've talked about the 'performative' dimension of the workers' texts that you discovered in the archives and of your overriding commitment to their effects more than to their contents, all in all. You've also said, speaking about the beginning of the project that wound up producing* The Nights of Labour, *that the aim was to see what Marx's sources were. Can this manifest interest in performativeness and the practical nature of discourse constitute a sort of background to, or beginnings of, a method?*

One thing's for sure and that is that I had absolutely no method in the sense of a reading protocol. For me, the only worthwhile method is to see whether words suddenly have weight or resonance in relation to other words, if they establish a web in relation to another web. I knew nothing about performativeness and all that. And when I talk about it now, it's not in relation to some linguistic theory. It's to mark the way in which those words constitute a scene. In the 1970s, in any case, I didn't read any works of philosophy, or any works of linguistics or methodology. I was completely immersed in my material without having any interest in all the theoretical debates that were going on in philosophy and in the social sciences. It was only after I finished *The Nights of Labour* that I felt the need, for various reasons, to situate what I'd done in relation to a certain number of reference points. But at the time the only method I had was to look and see what I found interesting as a discovery and as a kind of connection between my discoveries.

To get back to the issue of an internalist reading, I think my method has always combined an immanent reading, one that looks for the type of relationship between different meanings that makes for a text's texture, with a reading of the unplanned connections that tries to capture the text's scope by making one text resonate within another, outside any question of whether someone has read someone else or not. If you take Marx, my problem is not what Marx read. I think he read very few workers' pamphlets of the day. All the things I've read – I don't think Marx read them. He read a few books on communism, then factory inspectors' reports, but I think he read very little of working-class literature properly so-called, and my problem was not finding out what Marx read and how he transformed it, but how we can underscore what Marx said by making other words resonate in it, words that basically talk about the same thing he talks about.

That's actually the fundamental problem of method: determining the common ground in thinking. The 'science and ideology' protocol that characterizes Althusserism and a good part of Marxism is made to show that the knowledgeable and the ignorant are not talking about the same thing; and even if there are workers' texts that apparently talk about the same things, they say that's not the case since, in those texts, it's ideology, lived experience, the realm of the empirical that is expressed, whereas, in Marx, it's concepts. There is always this notion that concepts are an absolutely autonomous world and that, as a result, even if a concept unfortunately has the same name as an empirical reality or as an ideological discourse, it's nonetheless completely separate. Whence the Althusserian notion of a 'class struggle within theory': if at a given moment Marx, in the pages on fetishism in *Capital*, uses 'humanist' themes such as the transparency of social relationships, we need to see this as the persistence of a sort of class enemy, hidden in the words themselves, and which we need to flush out. Myself, I think more simply that it makes sense based on a shared universe of words and practices in which the transparency of social relationships, trade between producers, the world of free producers, are themes that exist in a whole host of texts and projects of workers' associations. It's based on that universe that you can understand why Marx says what he says. Otherwise, if we get bogged down in the idea that science is a separate discourse, then by the same token we're obliged to look for the reasons it's contaminated either in the developments of science itself, or in the endlessly unfinished attempt to wrest science from ideology.

My idea was that there are resonances, and things you can feel and understand based on those resonances; there's no need to know if the workers read Jacotot or if Marx read this particular Saint-Simonian pamphlet or whatever. There are signifiers that circulate and crystallize historic experiences, situations, movements, projects, all sorts of things. There again we are outside any regime of strict causality, we have circulating words, images, signifiers, phrases, and meanings. My problem was not to say, 'Marx wrote that because the previous year there was an essay in this particular workers' journal.' Even if you can also do that. Susan Buck-Morss did a whole book on the Hegelian master–slave dialectic by strictly following the terms of the debates on the Saint-Dominigo revolution in the German newspapers. I've never done it. At a pinch, I might have dreamed of doing it, but I've never had the time. In terms of what interested me in all that, in questioning a mode of reading, it was enough to do what I did. A bit like what Foucault said, since we're talking about him: 'Listen to the rumble of the battle.' Think of a theory as something that hinges not on other theories or ideologies, which it would then be attacking, but on a whole world of discourse. That's what I thought of, sort of following in Foucault's footsteps, as effective thinking. Thinking occurs in a whole host of institutions, rules, social strategies and polemical discourses. And a 'theory' is something you have to think of as a particular organization of elements of that whole.

What conditions do you prefer for writing? A closed space? Do you prefer to write in the country? What kind of weather, what climate? Are things like that important to you?

I write preferably in the morning and sometimes till mid-afternoon. I like daylight, and having a table that faces the window with a view up to the sky and of trees if possible. There are books I wrote largely outside, but that was before computers. That said, the writing is always linked to research work. There was a time in my life when I got into the habit of going to the library or the archives every day they were open. Every day I'd set out, including when I didn't really have a goal, a bit like the film-maker Pedro Costa says: 'Every day I went to Fontainhas with my little DVD camera, the way you go to work.' In actual fact, after a while, I got into the habit of going off to work every day; for a very long while I went off to the library or the archives every day, and I continue to work every day.

For me the main thing is always to be able to discover something, read something I haven't read, reread, discover; for things to leap out and tie in suddenly with something else, to outline a trail, cause a harmony to ring out. It's important to give myself the possibility of discovering something new every day, the idea being that thought means things said and written down, that are there, that are never in your head but always in transit on the page, waiting to be transported elsewhere and expressed differently. Being close to the material is an absolute necessity in my work, whether I'm dealing with an essay or a film or a work of art. I've never been able to work the way you do in history or the social sciences, where you amass data and then process it. I just can't do that. The way I work is not by gathering data that I then process afterwards, but by managing to attain a certain level of intensity. Something leaps out, as Deleuze would say, 'forcing you to think'. You always have to have some kind of material that you weren't expecting. There's a dynamism in thinking if you constantly allow yourself to be surprised by the material, by a provocative jolt that comes from somewhere else. I've always worked in a complicated relationship between, on the one hand, this daily process of putting myself at risk of a possible surprise and, on the other, demands that are suddenly made on me that come from elsewhere – demands I've responded to, including talking about things I knew nothing about beforehand, the idea being that it was going to be necessary for me to immerse myself in something for three weeks, a month, two months, to be able to respond.

This also means that I'm endlessly forced to go back over the point of intensity or the moment that leapt out at me. If I'm writing about cinema, I absolutely cannot do so without taking a fresh look every time at the films and shots I'm talking about, or without having constantly to assimilate things I hadn't assimilated. I'm always in the process of stripping back the canvas and redoing it. That's sort of my way of working: having a kind of sedimentation, which means that at certain moments there are flashes, things that pop up in spite of everything. All of a sudden a landscape emerges and you can try and draw it. That's what I'm able to say about how I work, a bit ideally, since, after all, I'm often subject to different constraints and they aren't all constraints that make me think.

Michel Foucault

You brought up your relationship with Foucault in the 1970s. Did you go to his course at the Collège de France?

I sat in on a few of his courses but not all that much as I didn't have the time. That said, I had all sorts of opportunities at the time to be aware of what Foucault was doing politically and theoretically. I must also have had something more or less to do with his seminar at the Collège de France in those days. At a different time, our group, which later produced *Les Révoltes logiques* (1975–81), was supposed to be one of the groups associated with Foucault's seminar at the Collège de France, even if, in fact, it was completely autonomous.

Yes, Foucault was important for me because all of a sudden, with Foucault, we took philosophy completely out of the philosophy books, out of the institution of philosophy. That was something I didn't see at the time of *The History of Madness*. I didn't really see what he was getting at. But when he started tackling the issue of prison-based incarceration, that whole period when he developed *Survey and Punish*, it all became clear to me and it was a bit of a model for me. You turn your attention to thought wherever it's genuinely at work. Foucault saw thought at work in the techniques of power. But where he was interested in power, I was interested in resistance; I wanted to see thought as also being at work in the practices of those who resist power, in polemical practices, in political struggles. That's sort of what I synthesized in that little essay, 'La Pensée d'ailleurs'.[21] This thinking about an elsewhere – elsewhere than in the institutions of thinking – is both thinking as it is realized in instruments of domination, but also thinking as it is realized in forms of struggle, words of struggle. That was an essential model for me, even if I didn't see it straightaway, this de-stratification of discourses that wasn't perceptible to me at the time of *Words and Things* but was completely perceptible by the time of *Survey and Punish*, or in the 1972 interview with Deleuze in *L'Arc* that we've already talked about. It was something I was able to be sensitive to, especially through the history of prisoners' speech. Prisoners have speech, they know very well what prison is, they have theories about prison. The idea is always the same – that people don't wheel science in from outside but that theories are produced everywhere. A discourse on exploitation is always a discourse on exploitation. At the same time, there is the idea of distinct planes. That's why I was able to feel close to Foucault at the time – there was this close relationship between militancy and theory work that was at the same time beyond any notion of applying a theory to a practice.

---

[21] 'La Pensée d'ailleurs', in *Critique*, 'La philosophie malgré tout', 369 (February 1978): 242–5.

Then came the moment when Foucault was appropriated by every man and his dog, the leftist backlash whereby he appeared as the thinker of technologies of power. Foucault became the thinker of reasons why workers would always be victims of technologies of power, why everyone would always be incarcerated, under tight surveillance. That started to some extent with the people at the CERFI (Centre d'études, de recherches et de formations institution-nelles,[22] 1967–87) who gathered around Guattari and were responsible for *Le Petit travailleur infatigable*, for instance, this idea of different forms of discipline. It was a reading that, even if it was linked to a discourse that more or less strove to be libertarian, was nonetheless completely suffocating as a discourse, giving the impression that we lived in an unbreathable world entirely governed by strategies of power. Those people took the panopticon literally; they thought that omnipotent surveillance networks had been put in place in the nineteenth century. They developed the idea that resistance is only ever resistance to an apparatus and that, on top of that, resistance is always included in advance. The two dominant aspects of Foucault's reception in the years around 1975 were, first, this whole elaboration of the disciplines and technologies of power, a whole discourse on the way in which individuals were entirely determined and tightly surveyed; and the second aspect was its appropriation as an overarching discourse on control by Glucksmann and what was then known as 'the new philosophy'.

So I then did the interview with Foucault that appeared in *Les Révoltes logiques*;[23] for me, it was a demand for clarification directed at Foucault, since he'd written an article praising to the skies Glucksmann's *Master Thinkers*, which came out in 1977. I put eight questions to him in writing and he replied in similar fashion. He answered four of them and left the other four blank. He must have seen that those four questions were a bit unorthodox, so he only answered the other four. The questions he left out more or less all had to do with 'the new philosophy' and asked him if – yes or no – those people were right to use his name. Not answering was a way of answering

---

[22] The CERFI (Centre for Study, Research and Institutional Education) was a militant extreme left collective that formed around the psychoanalyst Félix Guattari for the purposes of research in the arts and social sciences. *Translator's note.*

[23] 'Pouvoirs et stratégies', Michel Foucault interviewed by Jacques Rancière, in *Révoltes logiques*, 4 (winter 1977): 89–97; republished in Michel Foucault, *Dits et écrits III* (Paris: Gallimard, collection 'Bibliothèques des sciences humaines', 1994), pp. 418–28.

that indicated he had already moved on, and afterwards he found himself very much implicated in the whole Glucksmannian politico-fiction.

The last time I saw Foucault, that I really talked with him, was when I went to get his answers, and all he could talk to me about that morning was the 'Red Peril'. It was just after the pro-communist takeover in Ethiopia. His great concern, at the time, was the spread of communism in Africa. It was a somewhat disappointing moment. After that I wrote that essay with Danielle on the myth about intellectuals in which I tried to round out the angles as much as possible, but that was nonetheless the end of any relationship between Foucault and me.[24]

In that interview with Foucault you also express the fear that the thematics of the 'micro-physics of power' attests to a form of revival by philosophy of ordinary discourses and practices. You attack him for the fact that his philosophy takes back with one hand what it let go of with the other.

That's the formula I used to sum things up in 'La Pensée d'ailleurs'. Already in the interview with Deleuze in 1972, I'd really been struck by the two-sidedness of this discourse. On the one hand, Foucault insisted on the fact that power is here, there and everywhere, etc., that we need to get around questions about cause by designating targets, that power relationships are always localized. The problem is then to identify them, to call them by their name. And at the same time, there was this crazy outburst where he says that the great enigma today is power: who holds power, we don't know, etc. For me, that was quite an amazing back-flip. On the one hand, precisely designating power operations was a way of completely getting away from philosophical discourse on things like the desire for subservience that many people were concerned with at the time, from all those great discourses on freedom and subservience. And, on the other hand, all of a sudden, we see this strange assertion that power is the great enigma, and that we don't know where it is or what it consists of. We then see the re-creation of a privileged way of thinking that alone can broach what remains an enigma for the rest of the

---

[24] 'La légende des philosophes (les intellectuels et la traversée du gauchisme)', with Danielle Rancière, in *Révoltes logiques*, special issue, 'Les lauriers de mai ou les chemins du pouvoir (1968–1978)' (February 1978): 7–25. Reprinted in Jacques Rancière, *Les Scenes du peuple*, (Paris: Horlieu, 2003), pp. 285–310.

world. On the one hand, Foucault says that prisoners know very well where power lies. On the other, he says no one knows ... The consequence of that led to these completely abstract discourses on power and Glucksmann's notion of power as the power of a theory that preforms the lockdown of humanity.

Les Révoltes Logiques and the Fallout from May 68

Was Les Révoltes logiques *part of the process of distancing yourself from Foucault? How did the review get set up?*

It started off being based on my courses at Vincennes. I'd spent enough time explaining why Leninism was no good, working – second hand – on the USSR. The moment I launched myself into historical research work, I launched a course at Paris VIII on workers' words and practices; I can't quite remember what it was called. It didn't attract too many people; it wasn't really the issue people were interested in at the time. But it did interest Jean Borreil, who was doing a course in the room next to mine and came and joined me. Geneviève Fraisse came; she was interested because she was working on the history of feminism and she didn't have an academic base. Two or three other people including Alain Faure also came. After that, Jean Borreil invited a core of students he'd had in their *khâgne* year in Reims. That formed the first core of supporters, who called themselves the Centre de recherche sur les idéologies de révolte.[25] My idea, as with the *Cahiers marxistes-léninistes*, was just to put out a small bulletin that would publish research work. There again, things turned out differently. In fact, it turned into something else entirely, a journal that had quite an impact at a certain moment. The first issue came out in 1975 at a time when a whole series of leftist approaches were collapsing, and the concepts of discipline, the technology of power, popular culture, folk festivals and all the other forms of theory involved in the liquidation of the May 68 movement and of revolutionary movements in general, to call a spade a spade, were on the rise. In relation to that, a journal like *Les Révoltes logiques* looked like a new lease of life or a way out, with historical research that was at the same time linked to the big questions behind the militant movement of the 1970s. But it also had something about it that got away from Trotskyist, Maoist or

[25] The Centre for Research on the Ideologies of Revolt (CRIR) was set up at Paris VIII in late 1974. *Translator's note.*

Luxemburgist analyses or whatever else you can imagine. It had a certain success initially.

The first issue had a print run of two and a half thousand, and copies sold out very quickly. Later it took a dive, which was also linked to the fact that there was no structure to do a journal. It was kind of cobbled together, and it was slightly bizarre: not a real journal or a real militant group or a research laboratory, but a friendly cluster of people who got together. There were meetings at my place or someone else's place where one of us would give a talk on the research he or she was doing, which might then end up as an article in *Les Révoltes logiques*. That was hard to reconcile with the logic that gradually took over reviews and journals, which is that you have thematic issues and you commission articles as a function of the theme.

It was somewhat contradictory from the outset, since it wasn't the organ of a militant group wanting to illustrate and defend its political line, or the organ of a research group, since we were amateur researchers, and it wasn't a classic editorial review either. It came out at very irregular intervals, according to whether we had material or not, and according to whether there were people to work on it or not. And it also depended enormously on me. The year I was writing my thesis, there was only one issue the whole year.

What was the format of the articles published in Les Révoltes logiques? *You say you gave talks from time to time. Certain texts are linked to the zeitgeist; they're twists on the ideology of the day. Others are more historical and cover the history of the workers' movement. How were the synopses, main focuses of interest and kinds of investigations organized?*

On the one hand, we partly depended on the work particular people were doing, and so we had to build the issue around what was available. And there was an issue like the one on May 68 which is completely different since it was created all of a piece as an enquiry into what had happened to 1968 ten years on. That's not a typical issue. Practically all the other issues were done with whatever bits and pieces different people could bring along. I was working on the history of the working class. In the beginning Jean Borreil wanted to work on issues within independence movements in the south-west of France, Occitanie and the Langue d'oc, but he ended up doing something else. Geneviève Fraisse was working on feminism; Arlette Farge on her own subjects, at the boundary between feminist research and research around forms of popular sensibility. There was Patrice Vermeren's and Stéphane Douailler's group, who were working more on the history of philosophy as an institution, although that didn't stop them doing fairly hefty work on the issue of child labour, sort of incidentally. In a way, since they were professors in the écoles normales, where primary school teachers were trained, it was like an extension of their expertise. There were proposals that came from outside, which we accepted or we didn't accept; and sometimes these were from people who then joined the initial core group.

You've used the expression 'the decline of the left' several times, along with 'the left's change of course' and 'the collapse of the left' to describe the situation social criticism found itself in around 1975. What do you mean exactly?

There are several things. The evolution and decline of the Maoist movement is the first thing. A second thing is the overall dissipation of the autonomous militant dynamism sparked by 1968. The years 1968–70 were years in which the leftist movement didn't just mean the organizations. There was a global dynamic that was determined by the slogan of the day, 'This is just the beginning, let's carry on the struggle.' That was very powerful up until the years 1972–3. Around 1974–5 you could feel the backlash. Some organizations dissolved, like the Gauche prolétarienne, and some reasserted their permanence. A Trotskyist group by definition never dissolves. More than anything else, what you felt at that moment was the resurgence of the old parties – a resurgence that the return of Althusserism was part and parcel of. That was the moment when the dynamic known as the Union of the Left got under way, in all its recuperative power.

It was also the Deleuze-Guattari moment, the moment *Anti-Oedipus* appeared in 1972. The *Anti-Oedipus* effect was very strong at the time, with the break with the leftist militant model, identified as the model of the father. That was very strong in the leftist liquidation of leftism. Maybe it didn't function that way in the minds of the Guattarists who were the militant element, as Deleuze never had a profile as a political activist. It was the group around Guattari who had a militant practice, notably around the issue of the institution of psychiatry. But *Anti-Oedipus* was nonetheless overwhelmingly seen as the end of militant patriarchal archaism and as the liberation of desire and fun. It was a groundswell which you can't imagine now, but which had a very important role in the years 1972–4 in leftist student activist circles at university. The liquidating aspect was a lot stronger than the radicalizing aspect – at least, in people's perception. Anything went, like desire and so on. That was the moment when the retrospective view of 68 as the revolt of young people in support of free love was established. Because, for a lot of people, Guattari and Deleuze's 'desiring machine' meant free sex, endless fun and all the rest of it. It was a bit Jerry Rubin; or that's how it was overwhelmingly seen. That was a total misinterpretation of the significance of the notion, but it worked totally. It was also the time when people went off to the Ardèche; people had a great time, partied on, whatever. We experienced it on a smaller scale at Vincennes. I remember a discussion about some funds we'd been granted. There was a proposal to get a photocopier – that militant tool nonpareil – but somebody said that was old hat. A bar would be better. Lyotard said, 'Oh, yes! That's an idea.'

Afterwards there was also the madness over the machinery of power. On the one hand, the machinery of power; on the other, desiring machines. On that score, it's true there were two events that mobilized people again a bit: Lip, and then the Carnation Revolution in Portugal. You could say that it was this remobilization that kept *Les Révoltes logiques* going at the time because, in a way, *Les Révoltes logiques* was completely in step with Lip, with the idea of a type of speech and action, of working-class organization that, precisely, didn't separate the present struggle from organizing the future, or propaganda and militant action from appropriation of the means of production. The Lip moment was the moment when the Gauche prolétarienne was liquidated and an enterprise like *Les Révoltes logiques* was made possible. We felt like we finally had a grip on the autonomous working-class tradition that had wound its way through the workers' associations of the nineteenth century and revolutionary trade unionism. It was sort of leftism's second wind. At *Les Révoltes logiques*, this new lease of life was linked to a certain figure of the feminist movement. The latter had a very ambivalent impact at the time. In part its flourishing supported the theme of the liquidation of militancy, which was always male and patriarchal. But, at the same time, it was part of a remobilization over different objectives and different slogans – and different forms of struggle against different forms of oppression and domination shot to the fore. *Les Révoltes logiques* was an instrument that corresponded to that moment.

After that there was the final collapse: on the one hand, the whole 'new philosophy' wave, which followed on behind the Deleuzian wave; on the other, the rise of the PS (Parti socialiste). On the one hand, the liquidation of Marxism and, on the other, an imaginary neo-Marxism that was very strong. If you read the texts of Chevènement's supporters of the time, they were a lot further left than we were, in a way. They were committed Marxists. They were a lot more in the proletarian line than we were.

Cinema, Left-Wing Fiction and Popular Memory

In the same period, in 1976, you gave an interview on the 'brotherly image' to Cahiers du cinéma.[26] *Did the review contact you based on your essays in* Les Révoltes logiques, *or after* Althusser's Lesson? *They had met Foucault two years earlier, after having become aware of his memoir* I, Pierre Rivière, *which had got certain editors over the Maoist period. Did your encounter with this milieu also happen around a piece of work, or the attempt at defining a new figure of intellectuality – something that was very much in the air at the time?*

Their desire to meet me was linked to *Althusser's Lesson*, which they'd been struck by. *Les Révoltes logiques* hadn't yet come into existence when we hooked up. But they knew I was working on the history of the working class. So they invited me over through Dominique Villain, who was doing my course that year. Apparently there were two things that interested them: on the one hand, *Althusser's Lesson* and what you could take from it as a way of re-evaluating their dogmatic Marxist period and, secondly, the thematics of popular memory. They'd interviewed Foucault within the context of the critique of the retro wave. But there was a positive side to the critique of retro: the idea of popular memory. They wanted to talk about that. For the sake of protocol, as they had no idea about my personal relationship to cinema, they made me watch a certain number of left-leaning films like Straub's *Fortini Cani* and *History Lessons*, Kramer's *Milestones*, Godard's *Here and Elsewhere*, the film on the strike at the Darboy printers; that was the corpus. I think I was the one who broadened the commentary beyond the films they showed me – which were, to cut a long story short, more in the Brechtian tradition – by taking as a theme the kind of left-wing fiction that was pretty well illustrated at the time by films like Tavernier's *The Judge and the Assassin*, or films showing atypical workers like *Bof.* In the end, I didn't say much about the Straub films, which were their main positive reference; I talked a bit more about Godard. On the other hand, I started off with *Milestones* because, if you take a story like that about a left-wing American tribe, you could evoke a whole tradition of American cinema, with its basis in history and its classic storyline, as illustrated notably by the western, which is the story of the individual who ends up subscribing to a

---

[26] 'L'image fraternelle', interview with Jacques Rancière conducted by Serge Daney and Serge Toubiana in 1976, reprinted in *Et tant pis pour les gens fatigués* (Paris, Amsterdam, 2009), pp. 15–32.

collective symbolic system. It felt interesting to me to contrast this kind of genealogical fiction with French fiction and its relationship to a people who are always there already, presented to us in all their familiarity. It's in relation to that that I was brought round to developing this critique of left-wing fiction as being pro-family and to contrast a certain fiction bound up with the myth of identity to the 'sociological' fiction of identity, the fiction that is there so that social types can be recognized.

Was it a critique of identification of the Brechtian kind?

It was a bit different. You could call it Brechtian if you like. At that particular moment, I was also writing an essay on Brecht, which was reprinted a long time later in *The Politics of Literature*, but which dates from that period.[27] This critique of identity was also linked to the slightly uncomfortable situation whereby *Les Révoltes logiques* was theorized as a journal promoting popular memory. The concept of popular memory, which was very in vogue at the time, featured in the manifesto essay of *Les Révoltes logiques*, but I didn't write that and I wasn't at all comfortable with it. You can feel my distance in the *Cahiers du Cinéma* interview in relation to this notion of popular memory and the way it was hijacked by the famous left-wing fiction. It was sort of me who shifted the focus of the discussion in relation to their expectations by talking about the different types of fiction and about the difference in national representations between the French model and the American model. I used the iconography of the 1848 revolution to mark how left-wing fiction was based on forgetting the memory of the defeated and how, more broadly, the historic left was fuelled by the appropriation of those it had in any case brought down. For me, that was an important interview as it crystallized a certain number of themes. I think it might well be one of the first interventions that connected all those problematics of history and memory with what was put in place precisely as the constitution of a left-wing fiction, a doxa of the left, a new left ideology, all that ended up supporting Mitterrandism in seeking to appropriate working-class and popular memory as a whole.

To do that, I'd mobilized a memory of cinema which for me dated from twenty years previously. For cinema, it's the same as for the rest. There are things I got interested in at very different moments

---

[27] Jacques Rancière, 'The Gay Science of Bertolt Brecht', in *The Politics of Literature* (Cambridge, New York: Polity 2011), translated by Julie Rose, pp. 99–127.

of my life. I discovered cinema when I was in *khâgne*, as I had a neighbour who was a passionate movie-goer and he explained to me that the real cinema was not Antonioni, Bergman and all the culturally legitimate stuff. No. You had to go and see *Esther and the King* or *The Battle of Marathon* – that was the real cinema. That cinema was shown in Paris picture theatres like the Mac Mahon or film clubs like the Ciné qua non or the Nickleodéon. That was my initiation into cinema. Those were also the days of the New Wave and a more or less ambiguous relationship between the New Wave and the whole great Hollywood tradition. I got to know about cinema outside any initiation into art or art history, as a single whole that was polemical from the word go: the idea that the real cinema was Minnelli, Walsh or Antony Mann, and not the stuff considered fashionable by cultivated bourgeois. Afterwards, of course, I went to the Cinémathèque a lot, especially the one at Chaillot. They'd closed Ulm for renovations, but once they'd renovated it, they abandoned it for Chaillot. That was a pretty intense movie-buff period; I went to the movies a lot between 1960 and 1968. I soaked up all the great westerns, and the great musical comedies and films noirs, adding a few Europeans to the mix such as Rossellini after the shock of *Europe 51*, the New Wave film-makers and Mizoguchi. After 68, there was a period when I hardly ever went any more. The *Cahiers du Cinéma* proposal sparked a new kind of interest. Afterwards, every five or ten years, they'd approach me for a particular subject: visiting the people, school, history – up to the day when Antoine De Baecque asked me to do a regular column. There were the years when I wrote every two months. At that time I went to the movies a lot and I saw what was about to be released, which is not the case at all now.

It's always sort of the same thing, namely, that my different involvements in philosophy, film or a particular kind of art usually go through periods of intense commitment; it's not a continuous line at all. The things I've been interested in are things that have fuelled my discourse, the same way philosophy has. It's not like I decided one day that cinema and philosophy were two of the same kinds of thinking, but that's how territories and paths and investigations have been constructed for me.

Part Two

Lines

Heritage and Singularity

Before we step into your philosophical edifice, we'd like to ask you if you now see it as sitting within a tradition of the history of thought. Do you acknowledge any ancestors? Deleuze talked about a Spinoza-Nietzsche lineage; Foucault accepted his debt to Nietzsche and Heidegger. But you don't seem to claim a line of descent for yourself. Schiller returns, perhaps, Flaubert too, but that constitutes more of a broken line ...

I don't think my work can really be included in a specific tradition of thought. After all, my trajectory has been a little bit different from others. I spent a certain number of years saying goodbye to philosophy, and so I no longer had to worry about being in any philosophical tradition – I felt I was doing completely different work. That's one point. Another point is that at a given moment, certain individuals influenced me, people I can see myself as related to. I think there are really several strata; there are the philosophers I've known and who I can say influenced me at a certain moment, like Sartre when I was seventeen, Althusser when I was twenty-five, Foucault when I was thirty. I could do an inventory of what I owe to them: Sartre meant distance in relation to psychological and sociological analyses; Althusser meant a certain undermining of the idea of history, as well as adherence to a certain idea of the multifaceted nature of the times, and, in a sense, I feel like I've been more faithful to that idea than

Althusser was himself. Foucault meant an attitude that consisted in asking yourself not what you had to think, or what to base thinking in general on, but what made a particular thing thinkable, what made a particular utterance sayable. What I've retained of Foucault is the idea that what's interesting is the thinking at work within practices and institutions, the thinking that's part of the landscape of what is. And I've also kept a certain disjunction between what's known as theory and practice, the idea that things are not structured based on a theory which you then apply or knowledge about society which will then be transformed into action on that society – they're more like encounters between forms of discourse and practices that are developed within two different spaces. Those are philosophical influences you can spot.

Otherwise, in my method, there are things that stem more from literature: a certain attention to what we might call all the micro-events, a way of relating the issue of the event, of what happens, to a transformation in the landscape of the sensible. That's something I owe much more to Flaubert, Conrad or Virginia Woolf than to a philosopher like Deleuze. All the focus in my work on the way events are firstly transformations in what is perceived and in what is think-able – I get that from literature. But I also get that from the conjunction I've been able to establish between forms of literary narration and what I discovered by working in the workers' archive. There are a certain number of conjunctions specific to my work, such as having gone off to look at correspondence between workers with my head filled with the music of a phrase from Flaubert or Virginia Woolf, or certain expressions that might have come from Rilke, or then again, on the other hand, a certain number of philosophical formula-tions that might be in Plato. A whole knot of material has been elaborated in a relationship that's somewhat complex, completely specific and not shared, between philosophical utterances, literary utterances and the utterances I stumbled upon in the workers' archive. That is a second layer.

The third layer would be different philosophical and theoretical references that cropped up at one point. You mentioned Schiller and the moment when my reading of his *Letters upon the Aesthetic Education of Man* suddenly coincided with what I'd learnt from the workers' archive. That then allowed me to come up with the idea of a transformation in forms of sensible experience that was completely at odds with all the discourses on ideology and misunderstanding, reproduction and distinctiveness that ultimately capitalize on the vantage point of the inhabitants of the intelligible world over the unhappy prisoners of the 'cave' of the sensible. There's also the fact that at a given moment, I might have seen myself in a certain approach, might have decided that, after all, everything I was doing had something to do with criticism in the Kantian sense, the sense of 'how is this possible' – except that it's no longer 'how this is possible' from the vantage point of knowledge in general. It's now how is it that this was thinkable and how was this thinking about to be displaced, how was this mode of perception able to be displaced historically. There was also a moment when I saw myself in a certain line of descent from Hegel, in the sense in which Hegel is for me the classic example of a philosopher for whom the question of thought processes is not distinct from the question of their objects and results. However far I am from that speculative universe, there remains something fundamental for me, namely, that thought can't be separated from what it's working on, that thought is present in any given and in the transformation of its own given – and not in the fact of uttering theses about the world or about history in general; the fact that thought is transformed endlessly in tandem with its objects. I can see a sort of debt to Marx in the fact of always thinking from the standpoint of division, and feeling that a given, or an alleged given, is always based in reality on a division of givens.

But none of all that makes for a tradition. This broken line of connections marks more of a distance in relation to the idea that there's a school to which you belong, and masters who pass something on. That doesn't in any way mean I think of myself as someone who invented himself without having a master, not at all. Just the opposite: I think of myself as someone who's had twenty, thirty, a hundred masters, not just one. After all, that's the normal image of the transmission of thought: you have a master and then after that you become a master in turn. For me, the purpose of a master is to be the one who, all of a sudden, suggests an unusual subject, or a slightly mysterious landscape, or a question that hits us in the face and that we have to react to. Basically, anything that provokes us is a master, as is possibly anything that whispers answers to you in relation to the provocation. This twin function of provoking you and whispering the answers to you works through a host of texts that might go from children's prayers to Kant and Hegel, and it also works through all sorts of encounters offered by people as much as by texts. In the end, you could say that reading Gauny or Jacotot was more important to me than reading Heidegger or Lacan.

We weren't simply putting a question about debt in actual fact but also about originality in philosophy. In that sphere of activity what are the conditions for the new? It's a problem we'll come back to for

other spheres of practice. It remains the case that there are philoso-
phers who need to invent a tradition for themselves to give themselves
a boost, and also to give themselves stature. A person who claims
Plato as a master or as a cipher of his own thinking is bolstered by
several millenia. Doesn't every philosopher invent a tradition for
himself, no matter what the actual influences or debts he's incurred?

I don't need to invent a past tradition for myself, except possibly a
historico-political tradition, which would be one of emancipation.
And if I speak in terms of debt, that's also precisely because of the
fact that a singular history – new or not, that's not for me to say – is
made up for me of a whole host of encounters and provocations that
mean that all of a sudden something appears that didn't exist anywhere else before. That's sort of what I said once in a debate with
Badiou at the Collège de philosophie over *Disagreement*. Badiou had
attacked me for having pinched the ideas of the Organisation politique,[28] which he was a member of, for my own account. But I
stressed that the issue at the heart of the book was how to reconcile
Gauny with Jacotot, and that that particular question is one that I
can say I really am the only person in the world ever to have asked.
You could not reject my paternity of that kind of issue. In fact, the
questions I asked myself were linked to the peculiar circumstance of
having been for a very long time immersed in the workers' archive,
with possibly at the back of my mind a certain number of philosophical references or literary refrains to approach those questions with.
When I say 'refrain', it's not just a metaphor; it's tied to a whole
image of thought. In thought, there are also things such as that –
phrases that make you what you are and that you use to develop
something that you then put together with other phrases gleaned
from somewhere else. Little by little, based on these refrains that you
can't get out of your head, a certain form of intelligence builds,
whether in politics, literature, cinema or whatever.

Anti-Systematic Systematicity

For this interview, we'd like to pursue the idea of decompartmental-
izing your work, which is often divided into an aesthetic constituent
and a political constituent. You reject that division. Talking about
the approach you took in The Nights of Labour, *you claim, for*

[28] The Organisation politique was a radical left post-Leninist, post-Maoist
political organization created in 1985. *Translator's note.*

example, that it's more aesthetic than political.[29] *That book's exami-
nation of the labour movement in the years 1830–48 is actually
based on dual categories that derive from the exercise of faculties of
perception: the visibility or invisibility of individuals, an ability to
take the floor and speak or a presumed inability to use speech, the
indeterminate nature of action, or the opposite, anticipation of its
effects, etc. The unity that emerges in your work is no doubt open
and unstable. But it can also be identified by an unrelenting exact-
ingness of a topographical order, with a cluster of terms that are
connected in your writings to spaces, to what you call 'places',
'scenes', etc. Before going any further with this approach, we have
to ask you if you accept this counter-intuitive image of a system to
describe your work. And, if so, would you agree that this systematicity could be theorized through a fairly classic model of philosophy
as a tiered structure with an ontology, a morality, a politics, an
aesthetics and so on? Obviously, that's a provocative question since
you've just told us you didn't construct your philosophical project
in terms of these academic divisions, even though they existed at the
time you were studying philosophy.*

If we can talk of systematicity, it's in the sense in which there are
necessarily certain concerns that are constant in my approach, and
practices that are constant in my work, whether that work is on
politics, literature or cinema. On the other hand, I wouldn't talk
about systematicity in the sense of staggered layers built up, like the
Cartesian tree, with a primary philosophy and then a trunk, branches
and so on. I've never sought such a structure. I've never even sought
to make a theory of politics. I've been asked at various times to talk
politics, but it's never been my intention to make a theory of politics,
any more than to make a theory of art. What I've sought to do in a
fairly systematic way is to home in on a certain number of points
and places, starting from which things we could call politics or a
theory of politics, art or art theory might be distributed. I couldn't
start from some foundation and then deduce its various consequences
in the different sectors in which philosophy is supposed to be distributed, if only because philosophy is itself basically a sort of question: what makes a discourse philosophical or not philosophical? If
systematicity there is, it's also an anti-systematic systematicity, not
in the sense of a systematic search for chaos, but in the sense of a
search for forms of distribution that can make something like a

---

[29] 'From Politics to Aesthetics?' in *Aesthetics, Politics, Philosophy* (Edinburgh: Edinburgh University Press, 2005; edited by M. Robson), pp. 13–25.

system thinkable – and so for what necessarily precedes and conditions all attempts at a system.

What's at issue is not the idea of a system in itself but the idea of a philosophical system as a determination of the primary elements of things and of forms of knowledge. Behind this fascination with the idea of a philosophical system, there is the old Pythagorian dream of a world organized by the law of numbers. But, for me, the 'law of numbers' is firstly the legislation that distinguishes between ways of counting and making a number: democratic arithmetics or divine geometry in Plato. And it is precisely such a distinction that is in play when people define realms of competence that are called philosophy, politics, art, science, literature and so on. My approach consists in firstly theorizing the conditions that make these identifications and these carvings up of various territories possible. This doesn't mean starting out from an initial formula of rationality from which other formulae can be deduced as so many forms of transformation or specification. It means starting out from a certain number of scenes where what we can see at work and define and verify are the acts, dispositions and choices that allow distributions to be made and so enable thought activities, or speech performances, or manual performances to be named as philosophy, literature, or art, or else distinguished as philosophy or sophistry, popular art or high art, expression or reflection.

This division into territories isn't based on the nature of things or on the history of Being. There's nothing in the nature of things that establishes the existence of an area of Being called art. There are systems of reasons that either prohibit or allow our linking the exercise of a technical skill, used as a means to achieve a particular creation, with an activity that is an end in itself. There is no essential common reality that establishes the existence of politics; what there is, is a division of the common into two contradictory logics. What seems interesting to me is to look as closely as possible at the way in which divisions, and the assemblies of rationalities that structure those divisions, are carried out. The quest for a system presupposes its reversal, which is that we boil such assemblages down to a few simple elements. Based on which, the crux of any system is always the link-up. When you want everything to flow from the same organizing principle, either you're forced to stick to fairly empty generalities about the different domains, or there is a whole series of parallel or transversal logics that are actually there to stop up the holes. That's what I tried to point out in relation to Badiou, namely, that in order to deduce a theory of art from Badiou's system, you have to accept the postulates of modernism, but modernism is nothing more than a particular ideology of art in the twentieth century. You have to accept a whole series of adjustments between a general theory, with its concepts such as 'being', 'event', or 'subtraction', and accepted commonplaces about the art of the twentieth century or modernity. I've always proceeded the other way round, starting with scenes in which everything is verifiable, or where you can at least follow something organized, the organization of a political protest, for example, or the writing of a book, the organization of a certain art scene; or else I follow, as I did in *The Nights of Labour*, the trajectories through which the idea of a proletarian collective is formed. I start from that, from a set of scenes where I always insist on asking the same question about borders and distribution points, and I then define these as being what eventually allows us to investigate what things might mean – things such as theory, literature, politics, and aesthetics, for instance.

Speaking about Deleuze in The Flesh of Words, *you assert that a theory only gets interesting when it doesn't work.*[30] *In the 1960s, there was a whole philosophical tradition inspired by Bataille and Blanchot, in which the relationship between knowing and not-knowing became very important, the idea being that we had to reach the limit of knowledge for thinking to find a need to advance, a need to go further in its investigations. Has your own research developed in relation to those moments when thinking seizes up? Since, conversely, we get the feeling that your criticism of certain critical philosophies of the 1960s and 1970s is also a criticism of systems that are too well-oiled.*

I've got nothing against the fact that things are well-oiled. Let's just say that, for various reasons, I've acquired an ability to see, in would-be systematic thinking, the point where the machine seizes up, the point where you have to act as though the motor's turning over even when it isn't turning over, as if the material used was up to the job when it isn't. The problem has nothing to do with the resistance of the reality to the concept; it is that the heterogeneity of the forms of rationality at work in a particular practice won't let them be brought into unity. You then have to use the systems for intervening obliquely that I was talking about a moment ago.

---

[30] 'But, of course, the strength of any strong thought is also its ability to arrange its aporia itself, the point where it can no longer pass', in *The Flesh of Words: The Politics of Writing* (Stanford: Stanford University Press, 2004; translated by Charlotte Mandell), p. 164.

That said, the worst calamity for a theory is when nothing resists it. We have a good example of theories that nothing resists. Without wanting to be polemical, I think Jean Baudrillard will remain the classic case in point of a theory that nothing can resist; his is a dialectic that will always fall on its feet, always be able to absorb anything. It's clear, on the other hand, that there are systematic theories where you can nonetheless spot the point where it seizes up. One example occurs in Hegel at the points in his *Aesthetics* where he tries desperately to swing it so that everything hangs together – from any law of physics whatever to any work of art whatever – including the moment where he's talking about music and he says that to go from general principles to the concrete forms that embody them, you need technical knowledge he doesn't have – but that doesn't stop him making the connection.[31] There's the moment when Deleuze, among other things in *Essays Critical and Clinical*, tries to prove the absolutely material nature of literature by transforming a 'bass voice' mentioned *by* the text into a bass voice reverberating *in* the text.[32] For me to have anything to do with a theory, it must have points where it seizes up, where it measures itself against something it can't absorb. It's not irrelevant that one of the texts I've continued to construct my thinking around is Kant's *Critique of Judgment*, which has this incredible structure in which 'the analytics of the sublime' completely outflanks its own subject and is required to cover developments that have nothing to do with it, since Kant tackles the whole problematic of the Beaux-Arts which the two analytics have ruined in advance.

I'd say that in a way that's what's always made me keep at it, the fact that it didn't work. The most revealing thing on that score is my work on literature. For years, I had the idea that something was going on in the relationship of writing to literature that was fundamental to thinking about politics and subversion and liberation. I had the idea that something was going on and, at the same time, I was desperately looking for that something in a definition of the literary act or the literary object, a bit in the manner of Blanchot or someone, even if I've never had any particular affinities with Blanchot. I was looking to start out from the general concept of 'literarity' that I'd developed, and then move on to thinking about literature in general

[31] Georg Hegel, *Aesthetics: Lectures on Fine Art* (Oxford: Clarendon Press, 1975; 2 volumes, translated by T. M. Knox).
[32] Gilles Deleuze, *Essays Critical and Clinical* (London and New York: Verso, 1997; translated by Daniel W. Smith and Michael A. Greco), p. 108.

as an act that was in itself an act of subversion in relation to the order of things. For years I stumbled on. I kept trying different avenues till the moment when I was able to construct a historical concept out of the emergence of literature as a historic regime of the art of writing. Which at the same time didn't solve my initial problem since – that was just it – there was no essential literary act that could make the connection between what was implied in the concepts of writing and of literarity, and politics as subversion of the 'distribution of the sensible'. As much as I tried to make everything work, as much as I looked a bit desperately to the Fathers of the Church for a concept of writing that would allow me to make the connection between writing and politics, I just didn't manage to pull it off. The day I accepted that everything isn't connected – that there's a yawning gap between literarity, as a concept of the ability of anyone whatsoever to grab hold of words, and literature as an historic regime of the art of writing – I was able to make what literature might mean as a historic regime intelligible. And I could also think through the relationships between literature and democracy, while maintaining a yawning gap between the concept of literarity, as a concept of the speaking political being, and the existence of literature as this historic regime, with all the strategies that are woven together in it to harmonize or disharmonize words and things. I've always moved ahead with things that resisted me.

Similarly, I'd set out to do a sort of history of working-class thought and practice and I ran up against something absolutely heterogeneous to what I was hoping to see running through that history. I needed to take stock, that is, not only to deal with that and make compromises – which for me is what the authors of systems always do: it doesn't hang together particularly well but they manage to find a link – but to try and maintain both the overall inspiration and the different forms of intelligibility that could be constructed without that constituting a homogeneous system. You have to accept that things that refer to the same objective – political equality and aesthetic equality, for instance – don't fit. That's sort of why I set up this bipolarity between the politics of aesthetics and the aesthetics of politics, to say that we can construct a sort of place, a territory, on which the sensible forms that constitute politics and the forms of transformation of the sensible that constitute art can meet, but without our being able to define the relationship between the two as a systematic globality. But I should add that this approach, which leaves systems of reasons to their heterogeneity, has nothing to do with any drama about the absolute limit, the impossible, etc.

If we were to insist on the systematic nature of your work, we'd definitely hark back to what you call in several of your essays an 'aesthetic revolution', which is a term that allows us to link several swathes of your investigations.[33] It first involves an historical category that isn't necessarily tied in with the category of 'modernity' but nonetheless covers the past two centuries and functions as a force at work in what you later call the 'police' as well as, say, social issues. But it's a concept whose relevance is also almost ontological in the sense that an 'aesthetic revolution' could well be defined as the generic power of distributing or reconfiguring beings and actions.

There is a distinction to be made, all the same, between the two levels of generality. There is a general thread running through the idea of literarity, the way words take hold of bodies: that's a bit of a transhistoric thing – and I show in *The Name of History* and in *The Flesh of Words* that it can run equally through the monks of Egypt, or Don Quixote, or the French Revolution, or self-taught men, or the novel. There's this idea that these forces of transformation are at work deep within sensible experience and that they redistribute the relationship between capacities and incapacities: signs we decipher, landscapes that impress us, words that get us moving – towards solitude or coming together – truths we live in our flesh, suns we see rising over new eras ... In my work, that constitutes a sort of general backdrop.

And then there is what I've called more precisely an 'aesthetic revolution', the putting in place, which we can date historically, of a whole set of regimes of presentation and interpretation that comprise a pretty radical transformation in forms of intelligibility of what we call art. At the same time, they comprise a whole series of consequences in relation to the distribution of competences, but also in relation to ways of thinking what community consists of. The aesthetic revolution is both a set of very profound transformations in the modes of visibility, circulation, naming and intelligibiity of works of art, and in constituting or designating a new form of experience at the same time. This also takes into account a whole series of transformative effects that redefine lived worlds and, thereby, the distribution between what people are capable of and what they're not capable of, who is capable and who is not capable; and also the reformulation of a whole series of theories and utopias of community. At that point, we can effectively think of a revolution as being a

---

[33] 'From Politics to Aesthetics?', in *Aesthetics, Politics, Philosophy* (Edinburgh: Edinburgh University Press, 2005; edited by M. Robson), pp. 13–25.

transformation in the very distribution of the sensible world. At that point, too, the concept of an aesthetic revolution functions as a polemical concept in relation to the concept of modernity.

Privileging Space, Rethinking Time

In your work, the spatial dimension prevails to all appearances over the temporal dimension. Witness the recurrence of terms to do with space in your books – the place of breaking and entering, the place of those who have no part, scenes where the people are on stage – to say nothing of the operations associated with space: the 'distribution' of positions, 'displacement' of lines, 'crossing' or blurring of borders, 'off-centring' of a character, a film's storyline, etc. The study of a spatial configuration and the forces that occupy it, whether to do with real history or the study of a work of art, features in almost all your work.

Let's start simply with the role that the notion of space or metaphors of space might play in my work. That role is fundamentally polemical in relation to other already established uses of the metaphor of space in philosophy and, more globally, in the conception of thought, of knowledge, and in the relationship of knowledge to illusion. After all, what I've been able to elaborate around these questions of space is first and foremost a critique of the notion of ideology. Or, more precisely, it's a way of taking a step back since, as I've already explained, the notion of ideology in the Marxist corpus, and more especially in Althusser's hardened version, was an eminently topographical notion that defined an incapacity to understand linked to an incapacity to see, itself linked, in a very Platonic way, to the fact that we are in a space. There is this kind of circle, which I've often talked about, which says that people are dominated because they don't understand the laws of domination and can't understand those laws because they're in a place where they can't see them. My approach has been to take a step back. I've said: instead of talking in terms of correct or incorrect vision, let's talk in terms of place. Let's not say that people are there because they don't understand why they're there. Let's say: they're there simply because they're there. The fact of being there involves a certain degree of knowledge about what being there means. But being allocated a place like this has nothing to do with any illusory structure. There was this reflection on the spatial metaphor and this rejection of the optical metaphor that had been associated with it.

In relation to Kant, the relationship is in a sense analogical; it's definitely a question of a priori forms of experience but, of course, the space we're dealing with in these a priori forms of distribution of bodies in society and capacities attributed to those bodies is, from the outset, its own metaphor. Consequently, talking about space means talking about a place which might be completely material, but which at the same time symbolizes a disposition, a distribution, a whole set of relationships. That's the crucial element in the notion of space and it's associated with a double distance in relation to the issue of time. The issue of time is essential, we might come back to it – it's not for nothing that I named a book *The* Nights *of Labour.*

It's clear that what we might call a privileging of space is linked to two things. Firstly it's a matter of forgetting about issues of origins, of not thinking about the origins of thought or of knowledge or politics, but instead defining scenes – the notion of a scene is central and it also derives from a space–time relationship – based on which we can see things be distributed, the idea being that the origin is itself always a kind of scene. Rather than looking for some primal scene, we can find out what the essential elements are in various scenes that perform this distribution. That's the first point about the space–time issue.

The second point is that the classic role of time has been to act as a prohibition operator. I worked on Feuerbach for a long while and that's an expression you find in his work when he's doing his critique of Hegel as a philosopher of time, time being what excludes, whereas space is what introduces a coexistence. I didn't turn into a follower of Feuerbach for all that, I'm not trying to promote a philosophy of conviviality. What did get my interest every time – and particularly to the extent that all forms of prohibition, proscription or prescription always go through the idea that 'it's not yet time', 'it's no longer time' or 'it's never been time' – is that time always functions as an alibi for the prohibition. They say: it's no longer possible; it was for a while but not any more. Or: that could only take place in those times. I've tried to replace that with space in the sense that space is like a medium of distribution but also of coexistence.

In a way, this involves another theory of time – you have to go through a certain idea of topography, of the disposition and distribution of possibilities, to eventually rethink time as coexistence. What time classically denies is coexistence. Of course, space is supposed to be the form coexistence takes, and this means that in order to think of time as coexistence, you have to in a way turn it into a metaphor, often through space.

Yet time hasn't always been seen as the operator of a prohibition: it can also be loaded with a promise; it has even functioned more as a motor of endless promise.

Naturally, it's a bit complicated. I started out with two characteristic figures of prohibition: there is Plato's formula of the worker who is supposed to be in his place because the work won't wait. In other words, it's time that commands places and time itself is a principle of division: there are those who have time and those who don't. And then there are all those figures of prohibition linked to themes of the end – against which I went to war: the end of utopias, the end of history, of politics, of images. In discourse that deals with the end, time is invoked to say: it's not possible, it's no longer possible, and ultimately it was deluded to think it ever was possible. I thought of all these discourses on the end and what they allow us to see, namely, that the discourse of promise was always also a discourse of deferment of that promise.

And after that, of nostalgia, of loss and melancholy.

Of resentment, let's say. But resentment over false promises is the final form taken by a dialectic that's inherent in the promise itself. The time involved in the promise is generally also a time when the promise is deferred, or a time that says you musn't think it's going to happen just like that; it says it will only come to pass if you accept that it's not possible now. Without going back over the question of the relationship of the Church to the end of time, if you think of the whole issue of revolutionary promise in the days when it was systematized, put into theory, this was in the form of a promise for those who weren't in a hurry, for those who didn't believe that the future was already there. The idea of progress is also the idea that progress should be orderly, that it is first and foremost a way of making up for lost time; and to make up for lost time the forerunners have to move the stragglers forward, but not too fast. That's the demonstration I took from Jacotot. But it's also the whole experience of Marxism: the necessity of waiting, despite all the impatience, for the right conditions to be in place, thanks to the development of productive forces; but also the idea that that development itself spends its time creating new stragglers who will constitute brakes on progress, and on it goes. There is this dialectic of promise and the moment when finally what prevails is the idea that the promise itself was a lie.

But also, behind the dialectic of progress and delay, there is the opposition between those who live in the time of knowledge and action and those who live in the time they have to endure of survival and repetition. I may have exaggerated the role of time as prohibition to underscore the opposition between thinking that establishes this dividing line between the possible and the impossible, and thinking that focuses on the topography of possibilities. Obviously, it's not a matter of defining the general characteristics of time and space, but of defining ways of dividing the sensible. In the idea of 'the distribution of the sensible' there is precisely this link between the reality of lived space-time – for example, the working day – and the symbol of a condition. From that point of view, thinking about time is completely central to my work, but it is thinking about time as a division between antagonistic temporalities, before it turns into thinking about time as the time of promise or its deferment.

In sidestepping, as you do, any sociological or, indeed, Marxist notion of the 'distribution of places', a notion you're not happy with, something we might call an element of the ubiquitous crops up. If we follow the popular events and the courses taken by the proletarians you've studied, we're almost always getting through a barrier or crossing a border: always there and elsewhere. The theme of mental escape returns several times in The Nights of Labour, *and it's probably one of your first conceptualizations of the possibility of eluding a place in society that's allocated by others. In that book there is an attack on panoptical notions of power that insist heavily on this allocatory gesture of the panoptical apparatus and the visibility it creates. But you say that, in reality, there is always something that's not visible and that this something is also the most important thing: the possibility of escaping or of living in several places at once. Doesn't this capacity for ubiquity rest on or revive the question of the places each one of us occupies in society?*

In actual fact the quality of being 'ubiquitous' is much more peculiar to the scenario I'm attacking. After all, my work, especially *The Nights of Labour*, was constructed at the time, not from hegemony, but from the overwhelming importance a certain interpretation of Foucault's thinking had taken as being thinking about the discipline and technologies that put bodies in their place, with a whole theory about power as having all human beings in its sights and being capable not only of seeing them all at the same time, but of seeing to it that these beings internalize their submission. That's the panoptical apparatus as it was invoked in the mid-seventies: there is a central eye that sees you wherever you are. Not only does it keep you in your place, but it also chooses what you see and how you see it. That is, once again, the model in Althusser: the theory of the optical apparatus that produces not only optical illusions in the subjugated but also complete internalization of the arguments of the powers that be. I spent my time attacking that vision polemically, even if there was no direct polemic against Foucault.

On the one hand, I worked on other government archives – notably archives dealing with surveillance of theatres and cabarets – to show that those in power had little control over what they thought they were controlling. But I also showed, in the analysis of emancipation, that the problem wasn't how to escape from the clutches of a sort of octopus-like monster, but how to conceive of the possibility of leading lives other than the life you were in the process of leading. Hence the role given precisely to a different 'optics', a different type of relationship between place and vision: the insistence, especially in *The Nights of Labour*, on the possibility of moving your body and your eye: glancing out of the window and taking possession of the view, conducting an investigation like the building worker who has come to inspect, in his own way, the prison cell ... That's linked to the practice that changes timetables or their way of being internalized. Rather than being a preconceived idea about the ubiquitous, it's an assertion that every place can lend itself to a reconfiguring of places.

I've always tried to say that a human being who was supposedly stuck in one place was always in reality taking part in several worlds. And that was a polemical stance against this suffocating theory of different types of discipline, but also a more global theoretical position against all forms of theories of identity. I was trying to say that what defines the possibilities for individuals or groups is never the relationship between a specific culture, a specific identity and the forms of identification used by whatever power is at issue, but the fact that an identity is built on a multitude of identities linked to the multitude of places individuals can occupy, the multiplicity of their allegiances and of the kinds of experiences possible.

Excess or Event

Just as they reject any system, your written works resist any onto-logical style. We witness the dis-identification of human beings in them; we observe the insistence on 'mixed' entities inseparable from unprecedented capacities that can surge up anywhere and at any time; we contemplate unstable positions no matter how fixed places occupied in society become, and so on. A philosophy like yours shows indeterminate singularities, able to reconfigure themselves differently and to construct a scene that displaces the evidence of

*the senses. Your universe is clearly distinguished from Deleuze's
ontology which, you say, absolutizes the concept of difference to the
point of making it miss the myriad breaks or discrepancies it's meant
to account for. The ontology that we could nonetheless slate to you
is more an ontology of a surplus or excess in relation to the self –
terms which furthermore recur, along with their equivalents, in your
early works. '"The people"', you write for example, 'is the supplement that separates the population from itself, by suspending the
logics of legitimate domination.'*[34]

It all depends on what you mean by ontology. If you mean by ontology a theory of being as a being, or a theory of the being of being,
I've obviously never concerned myself with that, since I know nothing
about it and I have no means of knowing what being is as being.
Generally I only get interested in things I have the means of knowing
about, things I can make hypotheses about and then verify. If we go
back to the question of excess, I've never bothered doing a theory
about excess that would work as a theory about being as including
a supplement, a surplus, a plus, or any theory about infinity. I've
looked into a certain number of processes and ways of thinking
about those processes; and I've always tried to construct forms of
rationality applied to sets of cases that foreground something like
excess – excess not being an excess immanent to a being or in excess
of that being. When I've put excess into theory, it's always in relation
to two things. For instance, around the question of the names of
history, I spoke of an excess of words in relation to the bodies they
might designate, an excess by means of which bodies can appropriate
words to do things in excess of what is expected of them. In 'Ten
Theses on Politics', I built my reflection around the incomprehensible
seventh 'quality required to govern' that Plato sees as coming on top
of the normal criteria for testing the legitimacy of power.

In a way, excess is always linked to a duality, to a difference; it's
always a non-concordance. Excess is not an excessive, destructive
ontological power. There is excess to the extent that we can say there
are multiplicities, sets that don't correspond to each other. Between
the multiplicity of names and the multiplicity of bodies, there is no
concordance, and politics is possible because of this non-concordance,
just as literature is a way of dealing with this non-concordance.
That's sort of what I developed in *The Politics of Literature* around
disagreement and misunderstanding as different ways of dealing with

---

[34] *On the Shores of Politics* (London and New York: Verso, 1995; translated by Liz Heron), [translation modified].

the excess of words in relation to bodies and, by the same token, the excess through which bodies can appropriate words to make them mean something else and wrest them from their fate. Should that be called an ontology? I don't know.

In general, what I've come up with is more like a general poetics, a general theory about the multiple ways in which it's possible to make the gap work, this non-concordance between multiplicities. Similarly, I've always insisted on the fact that an ontology is always in a way a poem; it's never a discourse that tells the truth about difference, excess, or surplus, but a way of constructing something like a meta-phor or an allegory of this distribution. It's based on that that I've tried to say we can have an ontology of art or literature, but those are ontologies that are in some way constructed in practice. Literature constructs its own ontology and, consequently, you can perfectly well do an ontology of literary beings if you like, but always with the idea that an ontology is an occasional discourse. It's another way of weaving connections or of building bridges between various regimes.

Basically, the whole issue is whether you think you need to build a system of arguments that sets forth all the rationalities together. That doesn't seem to me to be necessary. Some people might need to construct an ontology, a great poem that will allow them to construct the relationship between different regimes of rationalities in order to make them homogeneous. Since I don't feel the need to homogenize, and since I think that after all we advance in our understanding of a system of rationality to the extent that we don't try at all costs to tie it to another system, I don't need to construct an ontology as such, even if I don't try to stop anyone else from constructing my ontology for me. I know someone who gave a very elaborate talk on the subject a long time ago. But he never came up with a written version.

Let's get back to the singularities and the moments that correspond to the scenes you study. You insist at several points on the fact that your attention turned to 'the multiplicity of micro-events' that trans-form the perception we may have of the coordinates, at once sensible and symbolic, in which our bodies move and our lives unfold. Yet we get the feeling that you use the term 'event' only pretty rarely. Would you say that, rather than the event concept, so popular with your generation of philosophers, you prefer the plasticity of a local description?

I'm not sure the event concept is interesting as an overall form of intelligibility. It tries to introduce a break in the causal chain, but it remains within the logic of a hierarchy. In the scientist logic, an event was the surface effect. In the philosophy of the event, on the contrary, it turns into a bolt from on high. The model for the event is the conversion: St Paul thrown from his horse. The event as a notion imposes a certain schema of identification; it constructs something like specialists, people who know how to identify what is an event and what is not. For me, the possibility that an action – walking in the street, looking out of the window, screening a film, people emerging on to the avenue, a show – might be an event is a possibility that can't be axiomatized based on an axiomatics of the event. I try to identify how a change is produced in a whole series of situations. Unlike theorists of the Other, of otherness, of the event, or of transcendence, I've always tried to theorize shifts whose power is uncertain in that they might cause significant transformations in the state of things, or not. There are small things you can pick up, in a little scene in an ordinary story like the ones I used in *The Nights of Labour*, where you can say that something is happening. But that 'something is happening' tells us nothing about power, about how that something is extended. You can always analyse a situation, small or major, in terms of an event. For me, that means localizing where the change is taking place. That small scene in Gauny's working day when he's looking out of the window can define an event. It can be nothing more than that, but in an event like people going out on to the street en masse, the event can consist of several things: in a transformation of the visibility of those people, or a transformation of the power they're opposed to. The event can consist of the assertion, 'we're not afraid', and from the moment you assert that you are not afraid, you are not afraid. A whole series of changes in relationships define a state. A state is defined by a whole identifying system: you are here, which means: look what we can see, what we can hear, what we're capable of. You have an event when there is a meaningful transformation of one of those elements. We might think about what could have happened with the 'Arab Spring'. In a way, that was an event that constituted a multitude who didn't know that they were a multitude.

Any state of affairs is always a landscape of possibility, and there exist changes in this landscape of possibility. Once again, these changes stem from the fact that this landscape is always itself composite. Consequently, the possibility that doesn't lie in people's physical strength may lie in their eyes; the possibility that doesn't lie in their eyes might be in their mind; the possibility that isn't in the workshop might be in the street. That's what interests me – the possibilities for reconfiguring a field of possibilities. Which sets my work apart from all the theories of the event that are actually theories about transcendence, or from theories like Foucault's which try to circumscribe, to systematize what it's possible to think or say or conceive (I'm thinking of the Foucault of *The Archaeology of Knowledge*). After all, what I've constructed has been both in reference to, and in reaction to, Foucault; I wanted to say that, in any given world of experience, there are several ways of systematizing this experience precisely because that world is made up of several worlds, of several lines of temporality, of several lines of possibilities. This also has consequences for the way we think about political rupture as well as artistic rupture.

That's an important bit of fine-tuning, since the entire vocabulary you use – 'rupture', 'breaking and entering', 'gap'– could lead a person to think that the scene of dissent refers back nevertheless to an irreducible event. It also poses the question of the place of thought in relation to events. We'd like to situate your thought by focusing on an expression that returns in different places, for example, in the title of an essay you wrote on Serge Daney: 'Celui qui vient après' ('The man who comes after').[35] *Foucault also thematized that notion, and so did Deleuze, and even Derrida. It's a philosophical trope from the post-68 period. In your work, how does this position of the philosopher operate in relation to the event? Isn't philosophy always in a perpetual state of deferment? Your position is, at the end of the day, that we can't say the event, we can't anticipate it.*

Coming after, in the essay on Serge Daney you cite, is the position of the critic. What interested me in relation to the position of the critic – well, in the days when such things as critics still existed; criticism hardly exists any more these days – is how the aesthetic regime corresponded to a transformation in the function of the critic. The critic is no longer a person who compares a work to a norm and who says if it's well done or not, and this also means he's no longer the representative of a preconstituted audience to whom the work of art is addressed and who says if the form of address is right or not. In an essay that remains just a conference paper, I studied this transformation of representative criticism into aesthetic criticism: the critic is the person who doesn't say either what the work of art should be or what the work of art is. The critic is the person who identifies what's happening.

But at the same time, identifying what's happening in a work of art, or in a situation – what does that mean? It means constructing

---

[35] 'Celui qui vient après – Les antinomies de la pensée critique', in *Trafic*, 37 (spring 2001): 142–50.

the sensible world to which the artwork belongs or which a political act makes possible. That's also what the logic of the supplement means. For instance, I've often insisted on the fact that cinema is an art of the visible that is largely invisible, that consists in what is said about it. The man who comes after is the man who makes a decision about what has happened. For me, that's not a decision of the kind that goes, 'right, we've been hit by an event', in which you organize a kind of process of developing whatever the event has made possible. No, the critic – or the philosopher, or some other name taken by the person who exercises this function of supplementing – is the person who says: here is the change that has occurred, and here is the sensible world, the sensorium this change belongs to. I'm not saying for a minute that it's necessarily the work of the philosopher; it's just the way I understand the fact of coming after. In a system of possibilities, you try to spot what has come along to displace that system and, by the same token, to construct the new order of the possible, or the new sensorium to which the work of art belongs – or the act, if we're thinking in political terms.

This might resemble other procedures, except that it's not about being wise like the bird of Minerva, and nor is it about being a sort of nomothete, a lawgiver of the event. That's just it, I'd say my work as I've been able to do it – this way of circulating between historic events, fictions, the history of the transformations of certain texts, and the history of literary and artistic events, or of little stories like the ones told in *The Nights of Labour* – my work has been a way of distributing the function of the person who comes after. We can define a kind of permanence in coming after, a constancy in coming after, which is the fact of constantly trying to mark possible worlds which are constructed right where they are, and which may well have been taken apart between each occurrence.

The Definition of a Scene

You said the philosophies of the event have created specialists in the identification of events. This question of identification could also be put to you apropos the 'scenes' we've been talking about from the moment we began this interview, and which are the raw material of your thinking. Since the term has cropped up several times without being defined, here are our blunt questions. How do we recognize a scene? How do we identify one? How do we describe, read or apprehend a scene and how do we identify what's happening in it?

Let's start with the meaning of the scene as the implementation of a method. The method I've followed in my work consists in choosing a singularity and then trying to reconstruct the conditions that make that singularity possible by exploring all the webs of meaning woven around it. This is the application of 'the Jacotot method': 'learn something and then relate all the rest back to it'; but it's a method I instinctively applied even before I read Jacotot. It's the method of 'the ignorant' in a way, the opposite of the method that first provides a set of general determinations that function as causes and then illustrates the effects of these causes through a certain number of concrete cases. In the scene, the conditions are immanent to their being executed. That also means that the scene, as I see it, is fundamentally anti-hierarchical. It's the 'object' that teaches us how to talk about it, how to deal with it.

That said, the scene is always constructed as much as it is identified. If I take the story that Gauny makes of the working day, I can identify elements of a scene there, not so much because of his way of describing a typical working day – a sort of microcosm – as the way in which the scansions of time are associated in his description with powers of subjugation or liberation. At that point, it looks, in a way, as if the scene contains another one. It can be linked to Plato and to the famous story of work that won't wait.

I identify a scene by the fact that it constructs a difference in a situation and, at the same time, creates a transverse homogeneity in relation to the hierarchy of discourses and historic contextualizations. That's how I find a potential scene in a letter Gauny sent to his friend, a Saint-Simonian 'priest', telling him: 'I won't be able to go and see you tomorrow because time does not belong to me, but if you're anywhere near the Stock Exchange at around two o'clock, we could see each other like two shades at the gates of Hell.' In those few miraculously preserved lines, I identify a possible scene because the factual description of a situation immediately turns into an emblematization of that situation, and so the scene then opens on to other scenes: there is both Dante, who is explicitly present, associated with the Stock Exchange just as he is associated with the factory in *Capital*, and then there's Plato, who is implicitly there for me. I have a scene about the distribution of human beings in terms of having or lacking time.

The scene is a theoretical entity peculiar to what I call a method of equality because it simultaneously destroys the hierarchies between the different levels of reality and discourses and the usual methods for judging whether a phenomenon is significant. The scene is the direct meeting of the most particular and the most universal. In that sense, it's the exact opposite of the statistical generality. Imagine a statistical enquiry into the awareness of time in workers of different ages and trades. What would disappear from an account like Gauny's of workers' experience of time would be the possibility of directly linking time, as lived experience, to time, as a symbolic structure in the experience of an individual whose business the universal is not supposed to be. That's the egalitarian challenge. Naturally the scene exists in this case if I make it exist through writing.

It's a different matter when the scene is already constructed. If we take the famous story of the secession on the Aventine Hill, I have a scene because this story has been written and rewritten several times. Livy tells the scene in the manner of a historian of antiquity, by transforming it into a fable, and that fable is immediately valid as a description and legitimization of a social hierarchy. Ballanche rewrites it in 1829 in a completely different manner – not by reversing the relationship between the terms, but by putting the fable at the centre of a whole drama built around the question 'do plebians speak or not?' That, for me, immediately has a double connection, firstly with Aristotle, with the opposition between *logos* and *phonè*, but also there's another, more immediate, connection, since the text was published in 1829 and, in 1830, the people of Paris came out on to the street around the issue of the freedom of the press. It's a question of intensity or of the maximum number of meanings that can be put in play, along with the multiplicity of scenes and discursive registers that can intervene in a scene. It's also a question of the capacity of a transversal that ensures that concrete history is both raw material for literary writing and raw material for moral philosophy, and that you can immediately bring together the discourse of the philosopher with the discourse of a person who, by definition, cannot be a philosopher – the worker.

I construct a scene as a small machine in which the maximum number of meanings can be condensed around the central issue, which is the issue of the distribution of the sensible world. From that basis I go on to construct the scene; I enshrine it as a scene as a function of its capacity to challenge all the concepts or discourses, all the fictions, that deal with the same questions, namely, what relationship there is between the fact of having time or not having time, and the fact of being able to think or not being able to think.

How is the scene different from the allegory?

The allegory is constructed to illustrate an idea, whereas the scene is first and foremost an encounter. I've encountered points that are like points of reality, which put in play a system of relationships that are also like an encounter, a clash between several registers of discourse. There is this kernel or core reality in an encounter, which I then redevelop in my fashion, and it's quite different from an allegory. In an allegory, there is an idea and there is its illustration. In a scene, the thought and the image can't be distinguished. If you think of the writing in *The Ignorant Schoolmaster*, with its systematic mix of voices, what makes for the strength of the essay, for me, is precisely that it's just about impossible to separate the story from the commentary, to separate what is presented there as the story of something real from my reflection on this reality or from a fiction that I might well have made up completely. What constitutes the scene, for me, is this intermeshing of the different levels of meaning and this transversal that runs between the different levels of discourse.

This theme of encounters, in particular missed encounters, has interested you ever since The Nights of Labour. *It seems to us in fact that a scene is also constituted by an encounter that has something unfinished, or incomplete, about it – it doesn't run its course.*

Yes, well, maybe they met that day; he simply said I don't have a lot of time. Of course, this empirical meeting between Gauny and his Saint-Simonian friend is to be placed within the broader issue of the missed meeting between workers and utopians. The fundamental issue is what we mean by a missed meeting. It's a meeting in which the meaning and the effect of the meeting are not necessarily what was anticipated. If we take *The Nights of Labour*, what we have is a series of missed meetings between utopians and workers, which is something we saw again in 1968 in the missed meetings between leftists and the workers they were trying to recruit. But, on the other hand, those are not missed meetings: they are meetings whose effect remains partly latent, the opening up of an effective space followed by the maintenance of what was latent, unfinished, in that meeting. The fact that the meeting has been both missed and not missed is also what allows us to have a relationship with the event, with history. Which is not just the history of resentment. If the meeting is successful, it ends in resentment. If it's missed, it ends in the disenchanted observation that it didn't take place; if the meeting is both missed and successful, it means its power persists.

We'd like to extend the question of the 'scene' as a category central to your philosophy as a function of another term that recurs throughout your work: discourse, or rather speech, the raw material of scene construction. It's the use of speech and all that you say in relation to the scene on the Aventine Hill about the transition from noise to speech. Let's now take the example of what happened in France in 2005 with the riots in the suburbs, as people were able to attack those eruptions as not having a discourse. They were almost universally disparaged, the claim being, to borrow your terminology, that people didn't get beyond mere 'noise', on the one hand, or that, on the other, this was the action of urban guerrillas. Listening to you and reading your texts, we might wonder if those particular events, like other events of the kind, should be considered scenes in which both narrative and words fail.

I think the power of the event is nevertheless completely bound up with the power of words capable of describing it. A political event is a change in the way a situation can be told and in the divvying up of capacities for telling it. Once again, the words used also indicate a future that's shared at the scene constructed. I think a wordless scene is a scene that doesn't construct a time or a space that can be shared, and I think that was the case in 2005. I was vehemently attacked because I said 'the rioters didn't speak'. Now, there are several ways of understanding the fact that 'they didn't speak'. The most current has it that they were illiterates and they only wanted to break things. The second tries to be positive; it says: in fact they did speak, in their mute language, which is, in itself, a protest against your language. That is the logic of the invisible committee. This would-be positive affirmation consists, for me, in saying: good for them if they don't speak the language of words – that way, we can interpret what they're saying without saying it. In actual fact, all the people who said, 'you're prejudiced, they spoke by not speaking, they spoke by breaking things, by burning things', could only say that because they already knew the meaning of what was happening. Personally, I've always fought against a certain fondness on the part of intellectuals for people who don't speak, since, that way, you can construct their discourse for them, you can say the speech they don't deliver, tell the meaning – which they themselves don't know – of what they're doing, and so on. From that point of view, I remain convinced that the power of a scene, meaning the power of a shift in sensible positions, is always linked to the fact that the noise turns into speech. Speech can sometimes be minimal, but I think it has to be there.

What struck me in 2005 was that the demonstrators both registered and rejected Sarkozy's words, the words of the politician, just because they were the mark of a stigmatization they were fighting against. They rejected what he said; they didn't try to take it up and positively assert that, OK, yes, *scum*, count us in, like in the song (by Alexis Bouvier, with music by Joseph Darcier): 'It's the rabble. Well, then! Count me in!' Lots of revolutionary movements in the past have started like that, with a capacity to turn round, sometimes in the form of a misunderstanding, the adjectives the people at the top have imposed on the people at the bottom. What struck me there, was the relationship that was maintained between people who speak and can use adjectives to describe, and people who were going off to demonstrate violently against the way people described them, without imagining that there might be something in the enemy's words that they could take up on their own behalf and everyone else's.

What kind of writing or what kind of description orders up a scene, and is it necessarily a narrative? It seems that, in your philosophy, there is this theme of the narrative that's connected to the motif of the scene. And, ultimately, a narrative is very simple – to make one, you only need two things: a subject and events. If you need a subject and events, that means there is probably something in your work like a theory of the subject that would be linked to the issue of speech and of names and of the place people are speaking from.

I think there are several ways of describing a scene. In one sense, a scene can't be narrated; it can itself, in a way, remain latent. If I take my example of the meeting at the Stock Exchange, in a way a fact is mentioned, but the overall scene of which this fact is in a way part, is something I keep to myself. The course of what is narrated is not the story of the scene – it's what allows me, personally, to coordinate the facts I put together. The scene can perfectly well remain latent as the principle of intelligibility behind the writing that is not itself written down as such. The scene can be narrated, it can be vocalized, at that moment; a narrator has to be invented for it, a mode of narration has to be invented.

These modes of narration can be different. The scene on the Aventine Hill is recounted differently in *The Ignorant Schoolmaster* and in *Disagreement*. In one case, what is brought to the fore is the way the senator makes himself able to speak to people who, for the people of his caste, do not speak. Jacotot always said that emancipation was not the method of the poor but everyone's method. What is described in *The Ignorant Schoolmaster* is thereby the way the person who is supposed to be educated finally attains another mode of speech. It's a question of the power you give yourself by assuming the other person can hear you. The thing is staged differently in *Disagreement*, where it's a question more specifically of the force with which those gathered on the Aventine Hill make themselves heard. You could say it's the same scene but, in one case, it's enlisted on the side of thinking about language and the power it induces, of thinking as belonging to all; in the other case, what is staged is the power of a political break-and-enter on the part of those who insist on being acknowledged as actors in a situation where they're not actors. In each case, the scene is a constitution of a subjective power: the power of an equal subject. Each time this power is constituted by the exercise of a dissensus: the interlocutor lends a capacity to speak to someone who couldn't be heard to speak, or else he himself asserts this capacity, which he is refused. The first scene is a scene of intellectual emancipation, in Jacotot's sense of the term: people adopt the presupposition of equality and they test it; the second is political: people test the equality that the other denies them. In both cases, the function of the subject is the function of an utterance that (re)constructs a distribution of the sensible. In a way, the modes of implying equality are at the heart of an experimental field characterized by a certain distribution of capacities.

Subjectivization in Words

Yet, in the scenes or narratives you've collected or constructed, there is something that emerges, which is that speech precedes the possibilities of subjectivization: it isn't subjects that are the origin of speech, but speech that constitutes subjects. It also seems to us that there are several types of speech. We don't know if it's the effect of the research itself or if there are actually several different concepts of speech, for you. In The Nights of Labour, *for example, 'mute speech' already appears; 'errant speech' crops up somewhere; 'working-class speech' hangs over or caps the whole thing off. Are there several kinds of speech that would correspond to several kinds of breaking and entering or of subjectivization?*

Subjectivization firstly occurs in the sense of taking the floor and speaking – that's the exercise of a capacity that was not acknowledged in the name of a subject who isn't one. The kind of breaking and entering in play here is a practical refutation of the hierarchical opposition between argued speech and the noisy voice. But this taking the floor and speaking is itself based on the fact that speech is available, in the form of the 'errant letter'; and seizing on words that are not addressed to you is already a form of burglary. That's the issue developed in *The Names of History*: there is this tension linked to the fact that the novelty of revolution is based on the appropriation of words that are old words, the words of the rhetorical tradition. It is by phrasing these time-honoured words that the proletariat takes the floor and speaks. Which leads to two reactions. There is an appreciation of living speech as opposed to the dead 'mute' language of the republican senators. And then there is the recourse to another type of mute speech: the *mise en scène* staged by the republican writer, Michelet, who eliminates mute 'rhetorical' words and replaces them with a mute form of speech that really speaks, the speech of things themselves that silences the speakers because it speaks better than they do, more authentically.

A sort of confiscation of speech?

It's not exactly confiscation of speech, it's the establishment of a new hierarchy, which says that true speech is speech that doesn't speak, it's speech that is written down wherever no one speaks – on things, on the ground. People have gone on and on about the rhetorical speech of the republican orators as being the mark, or imprint, of death on the living. Think of Marx and his assessment of the French Revolution as a restaging of an imaginary antiquity. Well, what matters is that the political transition from mutism to speech is made using words that aren't yours, that already exist, the subversive act being appropriation of those words.

In *The Nights of Labour* I show a form of appropriation, the appropriation of a kind of speech that is not public speech or poetic speech or novelistic speech. It's a speech regime that is a regime of dis-identification. That's different from the rhetorical appropriation of words by which politics traditionally declares itself. In this case, you borrow a form of speech that creates an impact, since it's speech that derives from an experience that is not yours, or speech to which you have no access. At the same time, we also find the same counter-strategies: people have said that the poetry they were reading and doing themselves was already outdated, old-fashioned poetry and they have compared this borrowed speech with the authentic voice of the people. That's already the argument of kitsch. But, here too, what counts is the appropriation of speech that allows you to tell your personal experience differently, to subjectify daily experience and phrase it in a language that is no longer the language of everyday life or of work.

So, there are several levels, several forms of appropriation of the 'errant letter': you take up the rhetorical speech involved in the assertion of a collectivity, or else poetic speech through which experience can be re-described. And in both cases there is an appreciation of the mute speech that takes up and annihilates these forms of bur-glary. It's a tension between several modes of speech.

Faculties or Possibilities

Where you talk about everyone's 'competencies' or 'capacities', phi-losophy usually thinks in terms of 'faculties'. How could we describe this use of the faculties – of seeing, hearing, thinking, etc. – that you mobilize in your topographical descriptions of scenes staging the people, and beyond, in the politics of art and literature? Another problem here, also linked to Kant: you don't refer to the analytics of the sublime in his third Critique *which has inspired numerous thinkers in the field of aesthetics up to our own day. You prefer the analytics of the beautiful in the reading Schiller proposed in his* Letters Upon the Aesthetic Education of Man.[36] *There is a concep-tual nexus there that we feel is extremely interesting: theorizing rupture in the distribution of places and parts, without falling back on the paradigm of the clash that's supposed to have produced it.*

I've never asked myself about a theory of faculties. Among the think-ers of the late twentieth century, there is someone who did, the only one who did, really, and that's Deleuze, who tried to hitch his think-ing to Kant and the whole problematic of the transcendental. I think that was a choice of intellectual approach for Deleuze, taking this reference system borrowed from Kant, but that it wasn't absolutely necessary. It was a convenient way of conceptualizing it and putting it. But I must admit, the theory of faculties is something my genera-tion as a whole found itself a bit removed from. The question of faculties was turned into a question about regimes of thinkability. That was the structuralist effect: people no longer worry about how a faculty called 'understanding' should accord with a faculty called 'imagination'. They no longer worry much about the relationship between the intelligible and the sensible. They worry about the way the perceived can be constructed as producing a certain form of intelligibility. They're interested in the way sets of facts are handed

[36] 'The "free agreement" between understanding and the imagination [which Kantian aesthetic judgement consists in] is already in itself a disa-greement or dissensus. It is not necessary to go looking in the sublime experience of size, power or fear to discern a disagreement between thought and the sensible or to ground modern art's radicality in the play of attrac-tion and repulsion,' in *Aesthetics and Its Discontents* (Cambridge: Polity, 2009; translated by Steven Corcoran), p. 97.

down to us as facts, and regimes of interpretation are able to subsume those facts. There is this radical shift from faculties to structures, in relation to which Deleuze is something of a survivor. In Deleuze, there's this incredible anchoring in French university philosophy which is pretty amazing for those of us who went to the École normale in the years 1960–62 – the moment when we felt liberated from all those histories, including phenomenology, when we got interested in problems to do with the presentation and interpretation of the facts instead and stopped worrying about the question of how a conscience was going to cope in the face of a world.

I, myself, have never thought in terms of faculties, but in terms of possibilities, the way things are perceived in this or that way by people situated in this or that position. My whole thing has been constructed around all the topics concerning illusion and ignorance, whether in Althusser, Bourdieu or others. I have no reason for talking in terms of faculties. I have reasons for talking in terms of the carving up of the perceptible and the thinkable, and in terms of regimes of concordance and non-concordance between what is perceptible for people situated here or there, and also about the way their own discourses or their own demonstrations are visible or invisible, are either speech or noise. It's in relation to that that I got interested in the Kant-Schiller duo in terms of a redistribution of the possibilities of experience, inasmuch as those possibilities are immediately hierarchical categories, distributions of places that people are able to occupy within hierarchical systems.

Consequently, I've never started with the question of how understanding and imagination can agree according to some regime of normalcy or excess; I've started specifically from the question of the overall reconfiguration of a host of phenomena that elude the hierarchical distribution of different forms of life. What interested me in the Kant-Schiller case was the fact that aesthetic suspension is first and foremost suspension of any hierarchical regime. We're no longer dealing either with the understanding that determines sensibility, or with the anarchic revolt of sensation against understanding. This is immediately translatable into political terms. We are dealing with the manifestation of a difference in the sensible which is not resorbable either as the excess of a faculty or as the disarrangement of faculties among themselves.

That's what interested me and it's the reason I reread Kant via Schiller, after stumbling on the *Letters Upon the Aesthetic Education of Man* in a second-hand bookshop. Once again, chance plays a big role in my itinerary, along with autodidacticism in practice and not just celebrated in theory. From then on, what's been central for me is the category of play in Kant and Schiller insofar as it infers the existence of a category of sensible experience that's not subject to any hierarchical distribution but, on the contrary, refers to a capacity of humanity, a perspective of humanity that's no longer divided. I then decided that what causes dissensus is the analytics of the beautiful, it's the theory of free play in Schiller, the concept of an aesthetic experience as a suspensive experience in relation to the normal – that is, hierarchical – ways in which sensible experience is organized. What was central for me was a deliberate condensation of Kant and Schiller, Gauny's looking out of the window, Baudelaire's essay on (songwriter) Pierre Dupont and the workers who know how to 'enjoy the beauty of palaces and parks', all these forms of reconfiguring experience, of what a human being who's supposed to be from the wrong side of the fence is capable of perceiving and feeling and speaking in the language he's supposed to be able to use. In a way, the dissensual is located there first of all. In a sense, it is indeed the analytics of the beautiful – the aesthetic education of man, the idea of an aesthetic community – that has been in operation in all the aesthetic utopias that have worked, especially at the start of the twentieth century. That is my fundamental point.

In relation to that, the aesthetics of the sublime is part of what we could call the reinterpretation of the 'aesthetic revolution' within late modernism. After all, if you take Lyotard's analyses of the sublime, they already presuppose the Adorno-Greenberg moment – the moment when people liquidated all those stories about an aesthetic community, all those hopes of constructing a community as a matter of perceptible links between movements and ways of seeing, a bit in the style of Dziga Vertov. But it was also the moment when people liquidated all the forms of unbridled aesthetic appropriation that fuelled the emancipation of the working class or democracy, in the broad sense of the term. If we think of the Clement Greenberg moment, of his famous essay in the *Partisan Review*, that was after all a way of saying that the whole catastrophe came from the poor, from the fact that the poor wanted a culture.

Are you thinking of 'The Avant-garde and Kitsch' (1939)?

Yes, 'Avant-garde and Kitsch'. That essay, after all, promoted the idea that the catastrophe in art and, implicitly, the catastrophe of totalitarianism linked to it, stemmed from the fact that that particular culture was created for the poor and that, little by little, high culture was contaminated, perverted by this appropriation of the aesthetic experience on the part of the poor. There was this very strong moment of double liquidation. For Adorno, it's more complicated, but 'Avant-garde and Kitsch' is the first of the major manifestos that rang in the whole of the end of the twentieth century by saying that we'd been had by the poor and that's why nothing worked any more. That's a whole reinterpretation of the art revolution, of its either more-or-less clear or completely confused relationship with the political and social revolution. It was after all the springboard.

After that, the idea was established that the real aesthetic was the aesthetic of the sublime, which is in a way an aesthetic you can be sure the poor can never steal from us, to cut a long story short once again. I think there is a very strong line of descent from the 'Avant-Garde and Kitsch' moment – what we might call the whole elaboration by the Frankfurt School of the misdeeds of popular culture, and the defence of high art as the only art that was still a refuge of subversion – to the aesthetics of the sublime. You can see perfectly well how that eventually leads, via the idea that the only truly subversive art is an art that makes a total break with all the forms in which ordinary people can appropriate art and culture for themselves, to a redefinition of modernity in art as the shock of the sublime.

Finally, what's significant in Lyotard is that his declaration that the sublime is the principle of modern art remains a matter of speculation. If you remember how Lyotard proceeds, that declaration comes after a fairly flat discourse which is quite close to Bourdieu-style sociology and which says that, for the mixed public of the end of the eighteenth century – which takes Greenberg's argument back quite a long way – there could no longer be any norm of artistic taste. As a result, he says, the analytics of the beautiful is a huge joke that tries to put order where there can't be any anymore because anyone at all can have access to art. The sublime remains the refuge of art, the sole category that distinguishes it as art, but, in a way, no work of art or artistic break ever actually illustrates this in Lyotard's essays. No interpretation of what might have happened in the history of art between the end of the eighteenth century and the beginning of the twentieth ever actually illustrates this kind of effectiveness of the sublime as the law of art. It's really a delayed reinterpretation of the history of the 'aesthetic revolution' and of the aesthetic utopia. Of course, there is a background to this, which is all the work Lyotard did in *Discourse, Figure* and his vast knowledge of art, but, nevertheless, the declaration of a radical heterogeneity doesn't even try to base itself on any history or counter-history of modernity. It seems like a re-elaboration of the already established vision of retrospective modernism. Kant is called upon by Lyotard to provide a philosophical basis for what, in Greenberg or in the Frankfurt School, is still interpreted in terms of Marxist history. The sublime provides a formula for a radical gap that invalidates the whole aesthetic tradition based on the analytics of the beautiful.

Behind the issue of faculties, there is the postulate that the new can only arise in the form of a radical excess, of a going further, which is common to both Deleuze and Lyotard, even if they draw opposite conclusions from it. As for me, I've always tried to theorize otherness (*altérité*) as becoming other (*altération*) and a faculty as a capacity defined within a polemical distribution of possibilities.

Aesthetic Revolution, Democratic Revolution?

We've talked about what you call an 'aesthetic revolution'. Is there an exact similarity or simply a historic conjunction between this aesthetic revolution and something that isn't a category in your work but which other political theorists call a democratic revolution, in the sense of the political and social revolution that followed on from the French Revolution? Are they the same phenomenon or two distinct, if parallel, lines?

Let's say to start with that the notion of an 'aesthetic revolution' is a complex one. It doesn't have something specific to all political revolutions that can truly be identified as such, namely that, at a certain moment, the people are down in the streets and power is overthrown. With the 'aesthetic revolution', we're dealing more with a huge transformation in forms of experience that, at the same time, doesn't have anything like an epiphany as a trigger event. And the notion of a democratic revolution is itself stretched between two ideas: the political revolution brought about in the name of people power of some kind, and the much broader notion of a transformation of forms of life implying the weakening of forms of the hierarchical organization of different lived realities. Starting from that, the 'aesthetic revolution' takes on a whole host of meanings that have different connections to a 'democratic revolution' of variable extension.

There are the new modes of perception, of the perceptibility of things, which we call art and the aesthetic experience, and which may define specific institutions but also promote different ways of life, great utopias of social transformation, lots of different things. The aesthetic revolution can provide a basis for dreams of a Hölderlin-style 'aesthetic Church' or the project of a revolution in sensible forms opposed to the machinery of state, as in the Hölderlin-inspired fragment *The Oldest Systematic Program of German Idealism*, published in 1797. It can be the basis for the idea behind the Soviet revolution as the constitution of a new sensorium, as we see in a number of Soviet artists. But it can also designate the attainment of autonomy on the part of an aesthetic sphere that was itself to become part of the overall management of society. It also designates a whole series of forms of transformation of lived realities: these 'non-political revolts' against the forms of suffocation of capacities imposed by the distribution of forms of life that Charlotte Brontë evokes in *Jane Eyre*; but also all the diffuse forms of appropriation of modes of aesthetic perception by the little people, simple people, or people without a history. All these transformations of lived realities are accompanied by transformations in interpretative modes.

That's at the heart of the nineteenth-century novel: not only the elimination of the hierarchy in subjects, but also the relationship with the new capacities on the part of the individuals who make up the people. Yet it's also at the heart of transformations in painting, if you think of all the connections between the new forms of painting and the new leisure time people enjoyed at the end of the nineteenth century, but also of all the connections between the transformations in painting and the transformations in all the forms of distribution, posters, newspapers, etc. That makes a whole set of links between transformations in art and transformations in the hierarchy of life forms. Does that define an age? The notion has two drawbacks: one is the danger of identifying the differences in regimes with some kind of evolution in history. The other is that the notion of a 'democratic age' imposes a vision of democracy as a state of society, the famous 'equality of conditions' invoked to cover up the violence of inequality and the struggle for equality.

Philosophical Writing and Ordinary Discourses

In Disagreement, *there is a passage where you vehemently attack analytical philosophy and the project that consists in purging the language of philosophy, and avoiding possible misunderstanding of words, or at least avoiding any multiplicity of meanings.*[37] *Your*

---

[37] 'Ancient received wisdom, very much in vogue again these days, deplores the way people fail to understand each other properly because of the ambiguity of the words exchanged, and requires us always, at all times, or at least wherever truth, justice, and good are at stake, to try and give each word a well-defined meaning, one that distinguishes it from all other words, discarding words that do not designate any defined property or that inevitably lead to homonymic confusion,' *Disagreement: Politics and Philosophy* (Minneapolis, University of Minnesota Press, 1999; translated by Julie Rose), p. x.

*philosophy isn't able to rely on the idea of philosophical language
as an exteriority. Even more than other writers and thinkers, you
are faced with the question of the difference between orders of discourse. Do you see any difference between the language you use and
ordinary language? How do you solve the problem of the specific or
specialized nature of the philosophical lexicon, knowing that, if we
follow you to the logical conclusion, there must be some level of
blurring between the latter and other lexicons? It's a matter of
method and of the constraints imposed on writing.*

It's not a question of language but of style. The language we speak,
that philosophers speak, may have a certain number of specific
words, but it remains everybody's language and it uses the same
forms of liaison, syntax and predication. When we talk about language, what we actually mean is a form of writing or a form of
utterance. I have no idea what philosophical language should be in
general. We can see that philosophical language covers an absolutely
vast spectrum and, after all, we still have the example of Plato before
us, and the speed with which it's possible to go from common language, and its objects, its ordinary preoccupations, its ways of
expressing itself or questioning and answering, to the bottomless pits
opened up by words that are, furthermore, the most ordinary language has to offer, those that only function insofar as they keep a
low profile, like the verb 'to be'. Plato draws dizzying formations
from them, such as *to ontos on* ('that which really is'), in *The Sophist*.
After all, the thing that gives a language its force is this racing full
speed ahead from the most trivial thing to the most enigmatic. There
are ways of racing ahead that can be very different: there's that transition from the most insensible to the most sensible and from the
most prosaic to the most abstruse in Plato; there's the way Flaubert,
in the middle of a passage with a stylistically homogeneous texture,
suddenly and without our realizing it, takes someone else's thoughts
into his own text. There's a whole host of ways of doing it. Every
piece of writing that's worth its salt is writing that's able to cross the
widest spaces without saying it's crossing them. For me, this has
always been the problem of not declaring transitions, of not saying,
'until now I've been recounting something and now I'm going to
explain the meaning of what I've recounted', or 'we have been in the
realm of empirical example and now we're going to reflect on what
this empirical example gives us', or 'we have been using ordinary
everyday words and now we're moving on to philosophical words'.
    My principle has generally been to introduce myself into other
people's discourses; I don't use philosophical concepts in general, I

only use them where they define something like Kant's language, Plato's language, Hegel's language – insofar as they, too, are event-related configurations. Starting with that, I then try as much as possible to construct a level playing field where you can go from what seems to be narrative to what seems to be commentary, or from words that are the words of philosophers to words everyone uses. I've made a lot of use of the moments when philosophers turn themselves into narrators, when they themselves provide this intermediary between the different forms of discourse. Of course, some of these forms of narration can be more lavish than others. There are the myths in Plato, there are the descriptions in Hegel's *Aesthetics*. In Kant, I had to content myself with the minimal narrative element constituted by his discussion about the way of describing a palace in the second paragraph of the *Critique of Judgement*. That was enough to establish a link with the carpenter's window in Gauny or the evocations of parks and palaces in Pierre Dupont's *Le Chant des ouvriers (Workers' Song)* and the commentary that Baudelaire does of it.

The important thing is always to be able to construct a certain form of homogeneity between the sequences, so that if there's been a shift, it is specifically a shift in thinking and not simply a transition from one lexicon to another or from one kind of concern to another. I've always tried to define common objects. If you take my work on literature, I try to define what might be concerns common to Hegel and Flaubert or, if you like, Hegel and Balzac, to take a marked gap, because Flaubert has some idea what Hegel is getting at, which doesn't seem to be the case with Balzac. And yet Balzac, by re-mythologizing the setting of bourgeois daily life, does actually seem to bring a contradiction to the Hegelian description of a world made prosaic. What is important is to manage to define common objects of thought, and then to describe these objects of thought in a way that shows how they're shared between people who are supposed to be specialists in several domains of thought or several forms of discourse and writing.

But you have been led, either through commissions, or your teaching, or a liking for polemics, to do more demonstrative books. How do you link narrative, narration, this idea of crossing the greatest possible spaces without saying so, of not declaring transitions, with the simultaneous requirement for rhetoric and demonstration that is also one of the modalities of thinking?

For me, in spite of everything, thinking is tied to this capacity to dismantle boundaries that essentially happens through the labour of writing. Writing, in this sense, is theoretical labour since it's a matter of finding the form, and the modes of utterance and of making connections that can perform such a decompartmentaliza- tion and set up a scene of shared thinking. The demonstrative books certainly correspond better to what usually goes by the name of thinking. But for me they are more rhetorical books – that is, books done to bring the labour of displacement back to what's generally seen as the terrain of theory. There is a sort of reversal; my sup- posedly more poetic, more descriptive books are for me the true theory books, whereas other texts that adopt the demonstrative mode do so because they're responding to specific demands (for example, giving a paper at a conference on the question, 'What is Politics?') and also because they were delivered originally in English and conform to that model, both due to the context and to my diminished capacity to play around with heterogeneous registers of discourse in a foreign language.

In a way, I always suffer from adopting what seems to people to be the normal way of thinking and which for me is a way of com- municating the results of thinking, a way of confronting a certain number of established positions. The labour of thinking doesn't involve demonstration as much as shifting the markers demonstra- tions operate through. In the middle of *Disagreement*, there's an issue of the difference that insinuates itself between one kind of hearing and another, one kind of understanding and another. And, for this reason, that demonstrative book had to be constructed around a certain number of speech scenes, whether those speech scenes be the fable of the Aventine Hill, the tailors' manifesto or, in a more direct mode, the argument of the Holocaust-denier Rassinier the scandalous nature of which, I try to show, has to do with the fact that it turns a logic of suspicion largely shared by scrupulous historians and realist politicians back against the reality of history. At that moment, heterogeneous speech scenes are woven together. And it's this interweaving that allows me to define a theoretical sto- ryline. So, in the last part of *Disagreement*, there is an interweaving between things that in principle don't meet up: the discourse of con- sensus, the Holocaust-denying argument, the history of mentalities, the humanitarian scene.

Otherwise, besides these writing strategies, there are moments when you can do something like statements of accounts. For two or three years, I did theses; I couldn't have done so before that and I couldn't do it now. Like the eleven theses on politics that became ten. That was something I was able to do at a given moment, but at the same time those theses are still constructed around a series of scenes. It occurs to me sporadically that I can transform thinking in scenes into thinking in theses, but that's not the most important aspect of thinking for me.

That approach is basically in line with a whole tradition of thinkers who have provided a critique of commentary in general – thinkers such as Blanchot, Foucault or Deleuze, in their different ways. Those are people who have rejected the doubling of a pre-existing work by commentary. We could extend that reflection to philosophical language and epistemology based on a question that follows on from our discussion of style and narrative, narration. Can we speak of such entities as 'concepts' in your work? At the end of the day, we get the feeling that concepts are incidental to the way your thinking operates. Since the start of this interview, we've been using a number of what we think of as your concepts, recurring terms that can be attributed to your work or are attributed to you anyway by commentators and are accepted in discussion as crucial to your œuvre. This is the case with 'scene', 'speech', 'disagreement' … We could easily draw up a list, so much so that the question arises: what is the status of these words?

I don't really know, basically, what people mean by 'concept'. The word can mean several things. Take a simple case to start with. In *Disagreement*, 'archipolitics', 'parapolitics' and 'metapolitics' can be called concepts in the sense that, starting with a number of distinct features, those terms define three types of philosophical operations in politics which may serve to classify the many forms of what we call political philosophy and reduce them to a few fundamental models. 'Disagreement' already presents a more complicated case: it's not so much a concept of 'politics' as of the kind of rationality that politics belongs to – more precisely, the kind of negativity that's in play. At the same time, it's a notion that maintains a very particular relationship with language. For me, it expresses in the most precise way possible the polemical knot between the different senses of the word 'to understand' (see, comprehend, agree) that sums up the sensible and conflictual dimension of the political community – as it was already formulated in Aristotle's *The Politics*. But in most languages that formula is untranslatable. And, to communicate in English, I had to replace it with a Latin word, even though it doesn't belong to the Latin tongue: *dissensus* – a word that sheds the power of being understood proper to living languages in favour of the possibility of a functional definition.

A 'scene' can be said to be a concept since it designates an essential operation in my work, one which can be linked to a central notion that defines the object of my work – the notion of a 'distribution of the sensible'. But what exactly do we mean by that as a concept? We could say that 'distribution of the sensible' is a performative notion since it allows us to analyse what makes a situation or an action political, or what makes for the scope of a literary text. You could say that *The Nights of Labour* is an illustration of the concept. But I didn't have the slightest clue about the concept when I wrote that book. I just constructed the kind of discursive storyline that my subject seemed to me to dictate and it was only fifteen or twenty years later that I used the phrase to formalize the terrain I was striving to steer historic narration, philosophical argument and literary performance on to. You could also say that it's just a name that sums up the way I approach and interpret situations and texts and notions. It's a notion that says what I'm doing, what kind of universe structures what I'm doing, what kind of rationality it involves. The 'concept', then, designates a displacement operator, the opening up of a field of thought. In that sense, I prefer to think in terms of the process of conceptualization, the theoretical storyline or the construction of a conceptual landscape. That's also why I said that concepts aren't the 'tools' mentioned in the Deleuze–Foucault interview we talked about earlier, but more the markers of lines that join separate points and constitute a territory at the same time. What could be called my concepts – and this is certainly true for many other people – are different modalities of the same basic operation. I don't think concepts are like notions that fit together to constitute a system. They are nouns that designate a mode of approach, a method, and that outline a terrain of thought and suggest ways of orienting ourselves on that terrain. Notions such as 'distribution of the sensible' are notions that suggest ways of making the world intelligible but which, at the same time, merely describe what I'm doing. So, that's what a concept might be for me.

By entering into the style or language of philosophy, we're also dealing with philosophy as a profession. We'd like to go back to that because this issue of a profession, of competence, runs through a good part of your work. To begin with, though, if we see The Nights of Labour *as an important beginning, the status of profession seems ambiguous. On the one hand, a person is never just his or her job – we are always more than our jobs. On the other hand, you stick to describing people by trade fairly insistently in that book since such descriptions operated in the period studied. It corresponds to the language of the day, and it also says something about the style of the personalities involved when you describe them as being cobblers or tailors by trade. Do you think there is such a thing as a profession of philosophy? What does it differentiate or delineate as a kind of practice?*

The notion of a profession is ambiguous. There is a profession listed in the institution, and I've exercised that profession, or trade, even though no one really knows what it consists of or what it's for. This also means that I've benefited from the fact that, in all the confusion of a certain time, you could make the most of the fact that no one really knew what it consisted of any more. It also means that my work as a researcher is work that has largely been disconnected from my job as a philosophy teacher. I've hardly taught anything of what's in *The Nights of Labour* or what's in *The Ignorant Schoolmaster*. There is a research process that ended in my texts and in the notions I've formed, and that process may have informed, one way or another, the manner in which I've been able to perform a role as a teacher of philosophy, whereby I've tried to get my students to read Plato, Aristotle and Hegel. I've got people to read all the texts that everyone else gets people to read, maybe with my own concerns, as I've spent my time rereading those texts and relearning them; then, on top of that, I've told my students a bit about the research I was in the process of doing. But I've never taught my students a philosophy that could have been called *my* philosophy.

My work in philosophy has been largely unteachable, a way of moving between texts of philosophy, the workers' archive and literary texts, and then drawing conclusions from all that. This presupposes a solitary process where you make your own time and where you're completely independent of any effects produced or any effects that are supposed to be produced. So, in a way, it's an amateur approach, one which also addresses amateurs, readers of books for instance, rather than students involved in what's known as education. The factory you're talking about doesn't define a profession or a trade; it defines a practice, one that not only questions allocations of professions but also the relationship between the expert and the amateur.

Philosophy in Effects

Let's look more closely at the question of the effects of philosophy as a discourse. You've rejected identifying concepts with tools, the idea, inspired by Foucault and Deleuze, of philosophy as a 'toolbox'. Concepts and philosophical discourses, you say, do not act. At best, they offer 'a reading of the terrain', 'lines between this or that point',

*a 'territory' – in other words, they describe, they trace or draw
(cartography again). If the image of the toolbox makes you uncomfortable, isn't that because it implies anticipating the effects of a
concept on reality, when, as with any work or discourse, we can't
predict a thing, according to you, about its possible uses? The idea
of an effect nevertheless appears to always subtend a conceptual
construct, even when the choice is taken not to name that effect.*

There are two things in the question of effects. There is the effect
immanent to the work itself, as it is carried out in its specific forms.
And there is the effect we anticipate on the person who is the
addressee of the work. That particular kind of anticipation itself
presupposes a certain idea about the addressee's capacity. And that's
where you find the tradition I've never stopped fighting: the tradition
that holds that there's a certain kind of link between thought and
politics, the idea of the work of thought as being demystification. It's
that schema that thinks people are living in ignorance, that they have
to be taken out of their ignorance and shown what they don't see, a
whole logic in which action depends on an awareness that people
can be given about things they can't see.

In relation to that, I've striven for two things. The first has been
to focus on my work without worrying about what the reader would
make of it and especially without assuming he's incapable. The
second, which is linked to the first in a way, has been to take a further
step back and ask myself more precisely about these schemas themselves, about all the great explanatory schemas, the ones that explain
why people are victims of illusion or what modernity consists in.
Before saying whether people are labouring under some illusion or
not, you need to know what you mean by 'illusion', what kind of
relationship you're constructing in talking about an illusion. Before
knowing whether Mallarmé, Schönberg, Mondrian or Malevitch
really took the revolution to the world of art, what is the revolution
in the art world? What's representational, non-representational, figurative, non-figurative? What's abstraction?

What I've tried to do is a bit the archaeology or genealogy of these
explanatory systems themselves, behind all the theories about coming
to consciousness, class consciousness, ideology and its demystification. I've tried to work out what the *mise en scène* was, the kind of
distribution of the sensible that was behind the construction of all
these theories of mystification and demystification. Or else I've tried
to see what the mutation in the regimes of interpretation of experience was in all these discourses on the revolution in art, the move
from representation to non-representation or to the unrepresentable.

Step by step, I've been led to reconstruct a whole landscape of what we call modernity and it corresponds very little to the accepted landscape; it corresponds to it even less since the accepted landscape is largely a reconstructed and retrospective landscape. The major modes of intelligibility of art and of politics today are products of resentment. On the one hand, the reasons why the revolution will occur have become the reasons why it's impossible to believe in revolution; on the other hand, the discourses on modernity and, consequently, the discourses on postmodernity, are the discourses of people who wanted to draw a line under what was once the dream or project of an art that was in step with modernity. I was led to react to the politics of these discourses before going on to confirm their falseness through work on genealogy.

At the same time, denouncing other people is of no interest to me. What I'm interested in is getting what is said in the name of emancipation, in the name of aesthetics or literature, to be intelligible. That's necessarily polemical but, basically, it's not the polemical aspect that interests me. What interests me, whether I'm working on the way Vertov makes a film or on the emancipation of the working class, is to try to enter into the tenor of an experience, into the way in which a certain kind of perception is conceptualized and produces effects for itself. In a way, the work I try to do is about constituting a certain number of forms and objects and regimes of thought. There's also the fact that this can be useful to other people in rethinking their own work, which is something people do very little of when it comes to politics, but are happier to do when it comes to literature or art or aesthetics. Maybe it's not worth the trouble going back over the reasons for this here. The essential point, to return to your initial question, is to separate two things: the effect of displacement as it is effectively produced in the books I write and insofar as I can control it, and the way others might perceive it and take this or that lesson or encouragement from it.

The Rest is up to You

Let's keep going down this path. On the Shores of Politics *ends in theses, such as the ones postulated in their day by Marx or Benjamin. If we go further back in the history of philosophy, there is Spinoza, at the end of* Ethics IV, *the bit on human servitude, inserting an appendix with chapters that aren't theses exactly but that serve as a means of memorizing all that has been posited previously with a view to a future use or application. Based on these examples, we wonder what the status of certain theses in your philosophy is.*

Should they, too, be memorized or applied? We'd also like to compare this idea of a thesis with the term 'principle' which recurs in your texts, notably around the 'principle of equality'.

Let's start with the theses. Once or twice in my life I happen to have called texts 'theses'. There are the theses on politics. Around the same time, I'd published, in the form of a satirical article, rules for the development of racism in France.[38] A bit after that – but it was never published – I wrote eight theses on modernity in art for a conference. What's the purpose of theses? Firstly, there's something like the irruption of a sudden personal acceleration – I think, I don't really know – which means that at a certain moment, a number of things you've been circling around come together, and you stumble upon them, so to speak, in the form of a set of potential utterances. But a thesis isn't a memory-jogger or some academic formulation removed from the results of work. The theses sum up things taken from what I've managed to write over a whole period of research, but they're also part of a specific polemical approach, and they're also designed to throw a cat amongst the pigeons. The theses on politics were put together for a conference in Italy, but they're also an extension of the events of 1995: the autumn strikes and the great apotheosis of the whole intellectual movement of 'a return to politics', which ended in the most abject support for the government offensive against pensioners. Through the intermediary of the CFDT[39] and left-wing intellectuals, Arendt's thinking about political purity became the government's thinking. So my theses were also a way of marking the end of a certain journey, of saying: all your carry-on about the return of politics, the purity of politics, politics as opposed to welfare, the beatification of the Hannah Arendt–Léo Strauss couple – look what it means in the end. It was a way of saying something like 'we need to have done with all that'. In a sense, it wasn't my way at all because my way has always been quite the opposite, it's been indirect, never direct or blatant. But also, on politics, my strategy has always been to say, 'This is what I've got to say, full stop. This is what there is to say about politics and there's nothing more to say.' Except that people always want you to reconsider the full stop ...

---

[38] 'Sept règles pour aider à la diffusion des idées racistes en France', in *Le Monde* (21 March 1997), reprinted in *Moments politiques* (Paris: Lux/La Fabrique, 2009), pp. 71–5. *Translator's note.*
[39] The *Confédération française démocratique du travail* is a major French trade union.

The theses on politics aren't utterances of principle; in this case they sum up polemically what we might see as the principles of intelligibility of politics: which doesn't mean principles of politics, in the sense in which the axiom of equality is a principle of politics. The theses on politics are not a development of the egalitarian axiom; I don't know if the word 'equality' even appears. The theses on politics are a kind of journey through the intelligibility of politics, a polemical journey designed to split supposedly basic notions in two based on the utterances of political philosophy themselves. They were written under the effects of reading Hannah Arendt's little posthumous text, *What is Politics?*, which had just been translated into French. They are in a way a comment on a reading and not the product of a desire to explain what politics is from its principle to its consequences. Basically, it's not an exposé that goes from principles to consequences; it's a decisive operation that tries to race across the field as quickly as possible so as to totally reconfigure its intelligibility. In practice, the theses are governed by an accelerative function. At a given moment, there's the feeling that you can go through everything again, from the little passage in Homer where the word *demos* appears right up to contemporary discourse on the return of politics, to say: 'Look. This is how the whole intelligibility of politics can be thought of based on a radical division of what the principles of politics are assumed to be'.

By clarifying the forms of utterance your philosophy takes, we were also wondering how certain of your utterances and principles, certain of your theses – the term doesn't matter here – might be extended by you or by others into practical maxims. The theses on politics don't look like practical maxims, of course. But it seemed to us that the question of constructing a set of practical maxims was, on the one hand, a legitimate political endeavour and, on the other, an open question in your work as a whole. That's something you both resist and call for at the same time.

The issue of practical maxims is complicated. A maxim is not exactly an utterance destined to be applied in some form. My work rests on personal maxims that can take the form of thetic utterances, but you could extend what I say about politics and apply it to them – that is, that the fundamental problem is the opposition between two worlds. Everything I've produced as theory has always also been orientated by the theory that there is a gap between a body of thought and the idea that there are practices, forms of application, that could be deduced from that thought. In a sense, I could adopt the maxim I attributed to Mizoguchi at the end of the essay that was used as a preface in *The Intervals of Cinema*.[40] Mizoguchi's film, which deals with injustice, slavery and liberation, the collective and the individual, seems to say to the viewer: 'This is what I can do with the appearances available to me, the rest is up to you.' I think that that 'the rest is up to you' is an essential maxim in my work. That's just it – the description of a lived reality, a world, doesn't imply any consequences about what has to be done. All it implies is the question of what you would prefer to do based on the description offered.

A maxim is aimed at defining an attitude. The overall sense of what I've done is that there is no necessity and no knowledge of any necessity that justifies action. What is given as the law of the world is a law that results from a certain number of relationships, of forms of domination, and of choices. The twin maxim would be: firstly, 'the way things are is not necessary'; we could replace the description of the world in terms of possibilities. Secondly, this description doesn't say what needs to be done; it just tells you: based on this, it's up to you to work out what you want. Behind this repositioning of the relationship between knowledge and action, there is, of course, the maxim that sustains research itself – the maxim of equality that functions basically the same way as Kant's maxims, as a form of universalizing the very conditions of a practice. What am I doing as a researcher? I'm betting on equality. And that means a lot of things at once. I'm betting I'm not searching for something that's unknowable, that I'm not faced with the unknowable, the incomprehensible, the sublime, etc. When I'm going to talk about art, politics, emancipation, literature, I force myself to go and look at configurations whose forms of articulation can be studied; that requires work, it presupposes going to work every day, we've already talked about that. I've imposed on myself as a practical rule to work every day, to go to the library, learn something, write, and so on. For me, that's an egalitarian maxim. To caricature it a bit, the inegalitarian maxim says that it's a bit of a bore to have to go out, that it'd be better to stay at home and look at the papers or watch telly to see just how stupid people are, and tell yourself: I must be really intelligent since everyone else is so stupid. The choice of maxim is also this: are you

---

[40] 'The same cinema that says "Tomorrow belongs to us" in the name of the rebels, also flags the fact that it can offer no tomorrows other than its own. That is what Mizoguchi shows us.' (In *Sansho the Bailiff* (1954), in *The Intervals of Cinema* (London: Verso, 2014; translated by John Howe), [translation modified].)

intelligent because everyone else is stupid, or are you intelligent because they are intelligent? That's a Kant-style maxim: am I betting that the capacity to think I'm granting myself is everyone's capacity to think, or is my thinking to be distinguished by the fact that everyone else is a moron? It's also for that reason that I've placed a lot of importance on the question of fatigue, that is, essentially, on laziness. You go to work every day like everyone else because you think that thinking belongs to everyone, because you think that the world is not some great unknown – that there's a whole chunk of the world you live in that you can know about, that it's possible to understand a bit how it was formed, if you take the trouble. That whole set of attitudes is opposed to the attitude of the intellectual who knows why others are morons, which is roughly the standard definition of an intellectual.

There is a maxim that is an initial choice and that produces a kind of analysis that in the end says: 'this is what you can say about the way what we call politics, literature, etc, functions'. After that, the question is what kind of maxim the reader would like to apply. For politics, this means: if there is no world revolution, it's not because the moment isn't ripe; it's because the issue is what those who want change actually want, what those who want an end to injustice actually want. It's a question of what potential worlds you see as being possible, of the capacity you grant yourself to change the world in a way that's in keeping with what you see as being desirable. Basically, there is at the outset an egalitarian maxim that has a certain number of consequences and they are all there at the outset, including in the frustrating form that means that, when people ask you what needs to be done, you answer that it's up to them to work out what they want to do.

The Laughter in a Thought

This way of bringing the polemical dimension of situations to light can also be seen in your handling of humour, a factor too often underestimated on the part of commentators. We could connect this laughter to a philosophical notion of humour in thought as being linked to its conflictual dimension. Is that something you hold to?

Yes, it's obviously a dimension that's there and it's in keeping with other things I said earlier about the fact of eliminating the gap between different levels of discourse. If what I'm writing is polemical, I try to incorporate the position I'm being polemical about without resorting to denunciation as a form, but, at the same time, you have to mark the difference. The question of humour is a question about the minimum difference that creates a levelling and makes sense. In principle, there is humour when we describe something that's not natural as if it were natural. We know these questions about what's natural or not natural have a long history; we might think of Brecht. It's always a matter of bringing out the fact that something doesn't add up, without saying: this is good, this is bad, this is true, this is false. We're back to the question of effects. Humour requires a listener, a reader, a viewer, whose support depends on not being spoonfed. I try to construct a discourse made up of minimal differences in level because, beyond that, any difference in level is an effect of control and points to what the real discourse is as opposed to the false discourse, the illusion, the misleading discourse. It's also a way of undermining the position of the scholar. I might well have been marked in my youth by Sartre and his criticism of the spirit of seriousness; unfortunately, Sartre's style doesn't escape the spirit of seriousness all that much. I think there's something that is part of the somewhat probabilist nature of the discourse you're maintaining. The trick is to produce a discourse that is not unconcerned with the idea of a kind of truth but that, at the same time, doesn't tell the truth.

I think there's a whole system of minimal differences in level, of a not too great distance in relation to what you are saying, that's part of the pleasure you can have writing, because writing has to produce a minimum of pleasure. That's not always the case when you're responding to a commission. What makes talking about a text interesting is the possibility of finding an internal gap. After that, there's still the question of how you deal with that internal gap. You either stumble on it like an idiot and say 'so that's what's behind this', 'that's why it's contradictory or ridiculous'. Or you adopt a strategy of suggestion, which is not the same thing as suspicion. We're back to a problematics of Mallarméen poetics: suggesting instead of naming, suggesting instead of putting down, calling for the reader or listener to get to work, in a way, making them laugh. But there's laughter and then there's laughter. There's the sniggering of resentment. And there's the laughter of those who have been able to come through a certain historic experience and to learn to measure what words mean, but without resentment.

Part Three

Threshholds

Demystification or Deconstruction

Your approach can be interpreted as starting off in the 1970s with a 'critique of criticism', a critique of forms of uncovering or demystification that give the theorist an overriding position and guarantee him power over his subject as well as over his readers. Several commentators, however, like to classify you as being part of what the Anglo-Americans and Germans call critical theory. It's true that you regularly go in for virulent demolition of the positions of certain philosophers and intellectuals on a case-by-case basis in your work, dismantling false problems of democracy, for example, and numerous other issues.[41] How does such a dismantling differ from a – sophisticated or euphemistic – form of demystification? The fact is that you, too, reveal something that is not necessarily visible or perceptible before reading you. There's an expression for what we're supposed to be unpacking that recurs fairly frequently in your work in this context: 'consensus' or 'the platitudes of consensus'. Even if the way you operate isn't identical to the 'revelation' practised historically by the Marxism you criticize in The Philosopher and His Poor, *how does this not put you in an overriding position vis-à-vis your reader?*

---

[41] *Hatred of Democracy* (London: Verso, 2005, 2009, 2014; translated by Steve Corcoran).

We'll try and start with the role of consensus as a notion. What does the notion of consensus mean? It designates a stable organization of the relationship between sense and sense, between 'sense' as a perceptible given, and 'sense' as its intelligible meaning – in other words, between what is given and what is thinkable, a kind of organization of the possible. The issue is not to show what it's hiding, but to disconnect the elements that make up that arrangement. If we take *Chronicles of Consensual Times*, I tried at different times to pinpoint a certain number of instances where we can say that consensus is being expressed, and instances where consensus runs up against a contradiction, an impossibility, derision, or open warfare. If we take the first text that opens *Chronicles of Consensual Times*, which was about the 1995 strikes – 'The Head and the Stomach' – for me, it sort of wrong-foots the logic of demystification, which says 'you think that's what's happening, but in reality this is what's happening behind that'. This critic tells people they're morons because they believe something is happening without realizing that nothing is happening, or that it's happening somewhere else. That's how stuff à la Baudrillard still works: you think there was a war, but I can tell you there was no war. It's the logic still used by a man who once translated *Capital*, who was once a Marxist scholar and who, at a certain point, morphed into a postmodern demystifier, running on empty a mechanism for uncovering the true, hidden side of things, even if this hidden side no longer has any substance. So, what did I try to do in that essay on the 1995 strikes? Precisely to put the order of consensus on display as the order in which there is a great mind who knows and people who don't know. That's the way Juppé constructed the scene: you're good, you're decent, you work, you have a whole heap of worries, you're anxious about the future and you've gone out on to the street, but I'll explain to you why we can't do what we're doing any other way. Consensus is really the linking of two things: the *mise en scène* that shows that there is a necessity, that this is the way things are; and, secondly, the idea that there are people capable of understanding why things are like they are, and others who aren't capable of understanding this.

What do I do in relation to all that? I intervene in relation to the scene, where some bloke says he's going to explain, and I bring out what disturbs that scene, the fact that people reply that it's not worth the trouble of explaining because they've understood perfectly, but obviously what they've understood is not the same thing. I intervene at the point where some entity has already performed a critique of consensus and shown that what is in play is not understanding or not-understanding, but two separate sensible worlds clashing. At that moment, there is something like a dismantling of the official scene constructed by those who think and know. Against those who know the hidden side of things, the truth of things, I pit a scene where there is no truth of things, only two worlds colliding and which we can already make out in the collision itself. It's only an initial response, but at that moment my critique is much more a deconstruction of mastery, whereas the usual demystification is a logic of mastery.

If we take all the texts I've written about racism, the point is to look differently at what's going on in there. I don't hold a Marxist line that says that racism is a superficial symptom covering something more profound. I tackle the thing differently. There is an official – consensual – explanation of racism: poor little whites, overtaken by progress, have it in for immigrants. All I say is that we need to look a bit at the legislation, at laws, decrees and government measures. You are going to see a clear figure of racism emerge from all that, one that completely undercuts the ludicrous discourse that people who think they're on the left, on the extreme left, radicals, etc., repeat ad infinitim about racism as a kind of popular rage. I try to deconstruct the Brice Hortefeux-Marx-Gustave Le Bon[42] alliance that binds 'left-wing' thinking to state racism. We still think of certain measures our governments take as being a concession to popular racist sentiments as defined by crowd psychology, but racism isn't a matter of crowd psychology. We can make that claim perfectly simply. It's not a matter of demystification.

Of course, you could say there is an established, official truth and that that's not how it is. As soon as you say that that's not it, you are effectively practising a kind of critical deconstruction, but this deconstruction always tries to relate the world, which is supposed to be unequivocal, to be a world of necessity, back to something equivocal, involving confrontation and choice. By the same token, you thereby relate the world back to forms of intelligence that are no longer manifestations of the intelligence of those who know, who see behind or

---

[42] Brice Hortefeux was the inaugural minister in the Ministry of Immigration, Integration, National Identity and Co-Development created by Nicholas Sarkozy in 2007. He launched a whole raft of tough new policies, notably promoting *immigration choisie* (controlled and selective) over *immigration subie* (uncontrolled and undesirable). Gustave Le Bon was a scientist and the author of the seminal work on crowd psychology, *Psychology of Crowds*. Published in Paris in 1895, it has never been out of print and is considered a work of reference on the irrationality and loss of individuality of people in a crowd. *Translator's note.*

see further than other people. Which also means that I don't delude
myself about the scope of this kind of criticism or operation. I try to
destabilize a dominant intellectual opinion that believes itself to be
left-wing when it's completely reactionary. This only produces limited
effects. Once again, you need to understand that I'm not someone
who intervenes on the public stage in a spontaneous, deliberate way.

*When you talk about the strikes of 1995 or in a text like 'Philosophy
in the Bathroom', you nonetheless show something that wasn't
visible, you uncover.*[43] *What do you call that kind of manœuvre if
not demystification?*

I think you can think of it in terms of dissensus, meaning that a way
of organizing the visible is disturbed, or a way of organizing the
relationship between the perceptible and the thinkable, the perceptible and the sayable. It's a matter of producing a shift in visibility, but
at the same time it has to be a shift that anyone at all can see – well,
a shift that doesn't presuppose any particular position. I have no
particular reason to have any specific insight into the immigration
issue, or into the issue of the Romany in France, or social struggles.
But I may have a particular way of seeing what's causing the explanatory machinery to seize up, or maybe of scrambling the puzzle and
putting the pieces back together differently. That may well be a poetic
operation, working in the gap between it and an academic operation.
It's a matter of undoing the relationship between a poetic operation
– making visible what was not visible – and an academic operation
which claims to reveal the invisible that was hidden by the visible.
Analysing things in terms of the way the sensible is parcelled out
means saying that the sensible and the intelligible aren't just given,
but that there's always a connection between the sensible and its
meaning, which can be transformed by considering each piece of the
puzzle separately and reorganizing them – and doing so, without
changing level.

---

[43] For an example of this approach: '[This "philosophy of life"] agrees perfectly with the multitude of recommendations that we are constantly fed by
doctors, psychologists, hygienists, nutritionists and others in hundreds of
magazines and special programmes, teaching us how to take care of our self
and how to live life harmoniously in the everyday. The question that thus
re-emerges is the following: is there really any need of philosophy if all it does
is repeat the media refrain of the everyday care of the self?' ('Philosophy in
the Bathroom', in *Chronicles of Consensual Times* (London: Bloomsbury
Continuum, 2010), pp. 78–81; translated by Steve Corcoran, p. 80.)

Consensus and Stupidity

The dismantling you're talking about can sometimes be a violent intervention, where you're clearly infuriated by certain manifestations of what we might call a form of 'idiocy' that Flaubert perceived and exposed perhaps more in his correspondence than in his novels. Do you subscribe to Nietzsche's often-quoted definition of 'philosophizing' as 'damaging stupidity'? What position would you adopt in relation to that requirement? The problem of stupidity is how to damage it without necessarily falling into a condescending stance in relation to its concrete manifestations; that's doubtless the touchstone of any philosophy that takes stupidity as its subject. When Nietzsche makes that claim, or when Flaubert gets carried away in his correspondence, it's not against stupid people in particular, it's against a state of thinking or of the thinkable in a given era, what people see or don't see. It's almost a metaphysical problem. Do you think of yourself as belonging to this line of thinkers?

If we're talking about damaging stupidity, we have to start with the fact that stupidity is not the property of stupid people alone. What I would identify the concept of stupidity with is the concept of consensus – meaning, the regulated state of relationships between the perceptible and the thinkable, bearing in mind that we have to think of stupidity in relation to intelligence. Stupidity is something that's constantly constructed by people who go to a lot of trouble just to wind up saying all the stupid things we hear every day, from the basic forms you get on the box to the interventions of eminent thinkers in the 'op-ed' pages of journals for intellectuals. We can clearly see that a whole lot of effort, and intelligence, go into it. That's a very strong Jacotist theme: stupidity is produced by the labour of intelligence. As much intelligence is exerted in saying idiotic things, even if not in the same way, as it is in saying reasonable things. Damaging stupidity means damaging a consensus, damaging the effort, the labour, that screens out the whole world of the perceptible and the thinkable. It also means, for me, that the character who is supposed to damage stupidity has no identity. I think a lot of official philosophers don't damage stupidity in the slightest.

But we also need to see that stupidity is split in two. You alluded to Flaubert. In Flaubert, there are two kinds of stupidity: the stupidity of consensus, of the standardized discourse, the discourse of the local councillor at the agricultural fair in *Madame Bovary*, the clichés about the evolution of society, about the social classes, the virtues of working and of progress, etc. That is institutionalized, established stupidity. And then there is another kind of stupidity, which consists in undoing this whole fabric of relationships between sense and sense – between sense, as the perceptible, and sense, as its intelligible meaning. When Flaubert says that masterpieces are stupid, he defines a different kind of stupidity, which is the fact of being put forward, just like that, without meaning anything. This can end in a radical decision: since the meaning is stupid, you destroy all that produces a meaning. Consequently, you will put stupidity in art, namely, the decision not to produce meaning, interpretation, any effect of interpretation, against stupidity in the sense of a consensus.

The work I'm able to set myself stands between these two kinds of stupidity, between stupidity in the sense of a consensus, and stupidity in the sense of a radical desertion, the choice of non-sense, of saying nothing, of speaking without passing on any message, without interpreting anything, without choosing. I think that, between consensual stupidity and stupidity as speech inhabited by a radical mutism, we can define another operation that tries to realign the relationship of the perceptible to its meaning. This also means that we may well need stupidity in the art of literature if we're going to deconstruct consensual stupidity. It's in this sense that I say we're also dealing with a poetic operation. You have to always keep this perspective of the other kind of stupidity if you want to deconstruct the consensual stupidity. Once again, these are operations which, for me, are always unpredictable and which, because of that, don't define any specific competence. We can simply say that that's the way I've personally used a qualification as a philosopher that not everyone has acknowledged, a qualification that consists in messing up existing orderings of meaning.

Warding Off Mastery

In the 1970s, you attacked Althusser and the Althusserians for having constructed a theory that described and analysed social and political struggles as they should have been, rather than as they were. Since Disagreement, *doesn't your demanding notion of what defines politics in relation to what you call 'the police' risk falling under the fire of a similar attack? By defining what derives from politics and what escapes it in such a rigorous and restrictive manner, aren't you defining a norm of politicization against which effective struggles and the people participating in those struggles (in particular those who have read you) tend to be measured? On the positive side, this remark calls up two other questions. First, how do you relate to current struggles and to existing forms of social conflictuality? There are, it seems, two options provided for by your political thinking. Is it a matter of localizing centres that are more inclined than others to favour an advance in what you call 'the cause of equality'? Or is it a matter of identifying 'scenes' where established distributions and redistributions of places are turned on their heads? Does this amount to the same thing? Second, since you have been so attentive to the rhetorical and political effects of the theories of your contemporaries (with Althusser or Bourdieu, for instance), how do you theorize the effects of your own thinking – on activists, on the one hand, and within art and cinema, on the other? So, the first question is, how can we get interested in all that escapes your relatively restrictive definition of politics? Second question, how do you think through the effects of your own thinking and your own rhetoric?*

First of all, I didn't exactly attack Althusser for that … I didn't attack him for defining a form of politics as it ought to be and losing interest in politics as it was. I attacked him more for sub-scribing to politics as it was, reserving a particular form of politics for himself, the class struggle in theory. I criticized him for endors-ing this division between the practical conduct of the class struggle, subject to the monopoly of the PCF, the Parti Communiste, and the class struggle in theory, entrusted to intellectuals. In other words, and to cut a long story short, I criticized him for a certain arrangement along the lines of: 'I'll let you lead the proletariat, and you'll let me do theory.'

OK, but the dichotomy between struggles as we dream of them and struggles as they are is nonetheless very common in critical opera-tions. It has led many revolutionaries and theorists to deplore the fact that history was not up to the hopes that had been built up.

Once again, I'd say that the measure of how high hopes are is defined by historical movements. There are a certain number of movements that have defined hopes of liberation, emancipation, people power, communism. For me, the issue is not to look at any one political situ-ation and identify whether it's up to it or not. The issue is whether we can see some heterogeneity in these situations. The operator 'politics-police' is not something I hold to essentially. I've always said the opposition is blurred all the time, that it's never clear-cut, but it does nonetheless cover a certain number of divides. In a given strug-gle, is there simply a realignment of parts, or does a new entity turn

up and exceed the realignment of parts? Is this or that specific
outcome being sought, or is it about asserting a competence, shared
by all, through people who *are* up to it? I think we can define such
a gap in any and every situation.

Take the relationship between the 1995 strikes and the 2010
strikes. In the 1995 strikes, there was the possibility that a certain
space in a given conflict could be identified with a popular public
space – which is what happened when all of a sudden everybody began
to march, and the people who were on foot because of the strike went
and demonstrated with the people who'd forced them to go on foot.
There is a reorganizaion of a political space at play here, based on a
specific conflict that takes on a concrete figure. If we compare that
with the way the strikes of autumn 2010 concentrated, at a certain
point, on the issue of the refineries, we can see that, in this case, we're
dealing with a strategic model. An available pressure force is brought
to bear on the adversary, but this comes down to saying goodbye to
forms of action based on the assertion of a competence shared by all,
or of forms of union between the people on strike and the people
known as 'users'. In any situation there exist internal criteria of dif-
ferentiation: who is leading the movement, what is the movement
about, what model of confrontation with the enemy predominates? I
think that, within any struggle, there are alternatives that present
themselves and are translated by the results into the capacity for
expansion and for mobilization that a conflict creates.

I've never got directly involved in saying that this movement is
good or not for whatever reason. On the other hand, I've tried to
answer those who were busy explaining why it wasn't good. In 1995,
when the intellectuals mounted a great offensive against the strikers,
I tried to unpack the argument of a whole swathe of the intellectual
left who were denouncing, in the name of Marx as well as Hannah
Arendt, this retrograde movement of workers clinging to their archaic
privileges. By the way, *Le Monde* didn't publish my article. Once
again, I try always to think of the alternatives that are immanent in
situations and movements.

*You give a lot of thought to the speaking positions of authors you
criticize. Does the history of the reception of your works allow you
to reflect on these questions in relation to your own work?*

Let's say firstly, to go back a bit, that I haven't particularly attacked
the writers I've criticized for not worrying about the effects of their
discourse. I've attacked them especially for speaking from within a
predetermined staging of causes and effects. In Althusser, it's a
formula of the kind that goes: 'if we tell that to the proletarians,

we'll deceive them and disarm them'; in Bourdieu, it's: 'aesthetic disinterestedness is a trick designed to delude the petits bourgeois, who don't know what determinations guide them, and to humiliate the proletarians, whose tastes are always "self-interested"'. With that, of course, they determine the effect of their own discourse at the heart of the staging of effects: if you denounce the production of the effect of illusion, you range yourself on the side of those who produce lucidity. I locate myself from the outset outside this whole *mise en scène.*

But there remains the other problem, which is the problem of the effects of the mode of utterance, effects like the production of disciples who are going to repeat what you say. After all, my dominant mode of writing is one in which the method is so wrapped up in the description, in the subject, that it's pretty hard to work out which major concepts or analytical grids can readily be applied. There is something there that's linked to my own way of thinking and writing which means that it's harder to use what I write as a corpus that can be recited or as a transposable method of analysis. I have a mode of intervening that's hard to systematize. What people can hang on to is more a certain catch phrase that can turn into a sort of *shibboleth*, such as 'distribution of the sensible'. It's perfectly clear that 'distribution of the sensible' is in circulation all around the world, well, not everywhere, but at least in the world of exhibition curators – with relatively uncontrollable effects, if we isolate one notion to get it to cover everything. I haven't worried particularly about being useful or detrimental to exhibition curators, even if they've been very useful to me in distributing my writing. I've always tried not to set up disciples, not to create a school. Anyway, even if I'd tried, it wouldn't have worked, because the conditions for that to really work have never come together. I've always tried to speak to anyone at all, students, readers. I speak to readers; I never talk to a fixed audience, I stopped having a public platform the day I quit teaching. I didn't keep up a seminar to gather a core of disciples around me, or something in that line. Basically, I speak to the people who are sitting in front of me or who are about to read me in a way that isn't prescribed by the mode of writing, by a *mise en scène* of effects. I have the profound conviction that the mastery of effects is an illusion I can't share. I think that what I've said produces effects I can control, can verify; and then there are the uncontrollable effects. I'm not going to worry about whether this particular artist, who sends me a DVD of a video claiming it's my thinking, actually respects that thinking. I'd say there's a side to this where people do what they like with what you give them; that's the first thing.

But I have a certain number of objectives all the same, and one is to deconstruct positions, to muck up a certain consensus; on that score, I can track various effects that are relatively controllable. For instance, the penetration of the idea of the equality of intelligence, the idea of equality as a starting point, all that could be called the Jacotist side of my thinking and what that produces as an effect – that's something I can more or less verify. It has effects in the area of political activism as much as in the area of theoretical discourse or art practice. I think I've produced the effects I wanted in the sense of saying to people that they weren't obliged to think like this or like that. A moment ago, I seemed to be treating the effects I've had in the art scene a bit too casually, but I actually think I've helped a heap of people see that they weren't obliged to desperately theorize what they were doing according to models taken from Benjamin or Derrida or someone. Similarly, I think that, in the political arena, I've helped people see that the signifier 'democracy' might have other virtues, other meanings than the meaning normally accepted in so-called radical circles, namely that it is simply the system, the ideology or discourse that covers the domination of the bourgeoisie and of capital.

There is an overall effect in relation to critical discourse, in relation to positions of mastery, which happens both because I try to make it happen and because my mode of writing stops people from transforming it into another sort of mastery. I can tell this by the sorts of books people read or might use. When people only read *Disagreement*, it makes me anxious, because they're looking for a theory of politics they can apply. Once they start reading *Short Voyages to the Land of the People* or *The Nights of Labour*, that means there's been a change of position apropos the quest for a solid theory of politics and things are moving forward. From that point of view, I'm glad my most translated book is *The Ignorant School-master*, an apparently unlikely and untimely book, that, to start with, in France, made people wonder why I'd written it, what the point of it was. Whether it's translated into Japanese or Korean, or now in Arabic, in a heap of other languages, it means that in spite of everything the effects I was hoping for have actually been produced.

Locating the Unconscious

Since it's a question of rejecting positions of mastery for oneself, let's talk about the category of the unconscious which isn't entirely absent from your work. One book actually uses the category in its title, based on a paper you gave to psychoanalysts, though you were quick to say that you were proposing an indirect reading of Freud: what interests you is the marshalling of art material in the elaboration of Freudianism.[44] *That's not enough to exhaust the subject. Does what's sometimes called the hypothesis of the unconscious seem interesting to you or simply valid, verified, verifiable? Connections can be made, in any case, between parts of your thinking and the psychoanalytical tradition, in particular its Lacanian development. We're thinking of your treatment of the relationship to knowledge. There is a particular comment you make in this vein on the position of the psychoanalyst, which is thinkable in your terms as a form of 'ignorant mastery'. For Lacan, in fact, the analyst knows nothing, he is just 'assumed to know' by the analysand. The analyst–analysand relationship thereby represents a kind of transaction or connection that perhaps isn't all that different from the one Jacotot can be used to set up.*

Psychoanalysis, Lacanism – I got to know a bit about all that in the context of the 1960s: the Althusser-Lacan context, the structuralist context, which is to say that psychoanalysis was in those days a theory of determination by the structure, by the narrow strait of the Signifier. At the time, then, it was in no way a theory of the ignorant schoolmaster, but much more a theory that referred back regardless to pretty overwhelming knowledge of the fact that people are ignorant but don't know they're ignorant. The psychoanalysis I first became familiar with was a psychoanalysis of ignorance that was in step with the theory of ideology. The second thing to say is that I've always been interested more in what suddenly emerges than in the substrata it emerges from, and so, in what makes a sensible landscape move, not in what's behind it. I've been interested in what produces a change in the way you look at things, not in what needs to be interpreted. I've always paid attention to shifts and not to interpretations. Which means that what's kept me busy is not the dream as a tapestry to be interpreted, but daydreaming as a moment of interruption of a certain course of sensible experience. In a sense, if I say

---

[44] 'I am not concerned with the way in which the literary and artistic figures he chose fit into the analytic romance of the Founder. What interests me is the question of what these figures serve to prove and what structures allow them to produce this proof. What these figures serve to prove at the most general level is that there is meaning in what seems not to have any meaning, something enigmatic in what seems self-evident, a spark of thought in what appears to be an anodyne detail.' (*The Aesthetic Unconscious*, Cambridge, UK, and New York, USA: Polity Press, 2009; translated by Debra Keates and James Swensen), p. 3.

I was firstly interested in emergence and daydreaming rather than in the substratum or in the dream and what it reveals, then I guess you could say that I was more interested in the conscious than in the unconscious.

Being interested in what's produced in the field of the perceptible and the thinkable may well also mean deciding not to be interested in the reasons why you're interested in it. Of course, as I was saying a moment ago, in my way of being interested in stories from letters exchanged between workers, or in tales of day trips to the country, or descriptions of the landscape you can see from the workshop window, or missed meetings outside the Stock Exchange or at the gates of Hell between a worker and a bourgeois apostle, there is certainly a whole set of unknown reasons worth analysing. But, in a way, I'm not interested in analysing them. I sort of adopted the attitude expressed in his day by Rilke, when he said, 'if I have myself analysed, I won't write any more'. What's important in what you don't know about yourself is also what that can produce in perception, what that can produce in thought. These kinds of slightly strange encounters that I set up between little narratives and a worker's papers, Plato, literature, this little machine that I've built as an effect of what I don't know about myself – that seems to me to be more interesting than the fact of knowing. In a way, for me, there is consent to not-knowing and to what this not-knowing produces as an effect of knowing, rather than an interest in a whole dimension of elucidation. I've always thought in terms of production and not of revelation; that's a fairly important point that distinguishes me from those of my generation who've been in analysis and have become Lacanian analysts. That's one point.

The other side of the question, of course, which only occurred to me later, is that one possible position of the analyst can be compared to the position of the ignorant schoolmaster. It's quite clear that *The Ignorant Schoolmaster* was first read and appreciated by certain analysts and psychiatrists, by people belonging to that world and not at all by teachers – we've already talked about that. There's a feeling of kinship that I didn't yet have when I wrote *The Ignorant Schoolmaster*, for the reasons I said, meaning that I first experienced Lacanism as a theory of knowledge about what people didn't know, a form of mastery that wasn't ignorant at all. Basically, this involves the issue of the gap between psychoanalysis as an overall system of interpretation of the world and what can play out in the analytical session, in this relationship of one individual to another in the analytical experience. There, we can say that something happens between the analyst and the analysand that might be related to what Jacotot says about the dissociation between the effect of mastery and the effect of knowledge. That's what explains the interest of certain analysts in *The Ignorant Schoolmaster* and their lack of interest in *The Aesthetic Unconscious*. I wrote the latter for psychoanalysts, but no psychoanalyst to my knowledge has ever commented on it. Which means what for me? Which means there is a dissociation to be made between what happens in the act of analysis and the way the theory of analysis itself works as an overall interpretation.

But even if there is this very important dimension of ignorant mastery in certain kinds of practice of analysis, it remains the case that what comes down to a global interpretative discourse is nevertheless something that derives more, for me, from mind-numbing theory than from liberating thought. Individually, the psychoanalyst can function as an ignorant schoolmaster, but when he starts to become a sort of analyst of society, he immediately turns into the guy who, after all, knows all about ignorance, and what people imagine themselves to be, what society is, etc. I recently reread the chapter in Book XVII of Lacan's *Seminar* on 'the four discourses'.[45] and I said to myself: 'It's fairly extraordinary that this story of the "four discourses" was put together in 1969, and that it starts with the idea that knowledge is the part of the slave but then ultimately ends in capitalist discourse; there's something very powerful in there after all.' With that, I type 'the four discourses' on Google and I see a commentary that takes us back to an analysis of consumer society, and I note that this pretty incredible essay serves to fuel a pretty banal line that a lot of psychoanalysts actually take on the theme: capitalism equals democracy equals consumerism, and there you have it.

Equals loss of the symbolic order.

Yes, precisely. There is that duality. There is this coming together that is amazing and that I personally had forgotten about because, after 1969, I stopped going to Lacan's seminar. When I read that volume of the *Seminar*, after having written *The Ignorant Schoolmaster*, I underlined all those passages and I rediscovered them recently. I see that the things I was dealing with – regarding Aristotle, the slave, the slave's knowledge and the issue of whether slaves speak or not – the Lacan of 1969 was already dealing with them in a way. At the time, I didn't know that, I didn't take any notice; I got to that point on my own. I don't know if Lacan would have taken me

---

[45] Seminar, Book XVII, *L'envers de la psychanalyse* (Paris: Seuil, 1998).

forward at the time; maybe not because that wasn't what I was looking for at that particular moment. I think you need to find your own way to get to the same point. 'He said all that in 1969. Why have I worn myself out?' But at the same time if I hadn't worn myself out, what was said in 1969 wouldn't mean anything to me. There is this aspect of kinship which is very strong. Once analysts turn into interpreters of society, they put all that at the service of a discourse that matches up to a somewhat tired post-Marxism on the illusions of democratic individualism and a vision of the old Pascalian sage, who says that men will always live in illusion while believing they can extricate themselves from illusion, and so on.

You've just contrasted a concern for what emerges that's geared to daydreaming with a concern for substrata geared to the unconscious. This means that, for you, the unconscious is not located in the background or in the subterranean geological layer governing the upper or phenomenal layers. Contrary to the psychoanalytic tradition, you're interested in the perceptible, not in what causes it. But there are many psychoanalysts and theorists who hold that the unconscious is always in the perceptible already, that it's only active and detectable in what we perceive rather than behind the scenes of real life. Freudian slips are emergences: what we perceive can slip and these slips are precisely what interests you, aren't they? You seem to be employing a notion of the unconscious that implies a dualist metaphysics.

That's possible. Basically, the question is what you do with the 'un', with the negative prefix. In actual fact, I can well see that we're not obliged to relate the theory of the unconscious back to a sort of theory of layers, etc. But, even so, the issue is sort of about the new, the issue of what happens when the un-known, the un-familiar, is at work in transformations of what is perceptible and what is knowable. Do we pay attention to the transformation of the perceptible and the thinkable, or do we ultimately pay attention to the fact that the transforming operation is itself an operation that doesn't entirely know what it's doing? In a way, that really is what interests me, and it very quickly involves these differences of opinion at the level of the morality of the use of the unconscious. We're either interested in what people do or else in the fact that they know not what they do.

Proletarians Then and Now

So we can compare your work with other closely related inquiries, as we've just done with a section of psychoanalysis, let's go back to

The Nights of Labour. *Several of your readers look to that book as providing the keys to reading the historic situation of socialism or of the class struggle after the nineteenth century. Have you yourself followed through by looking into, say, how workers' nights or spare time are organized at a later date? Are there researchers around today who are doing this work, taking inspiration from you? The current risk in your work may well be nostalgia. When you're asked, for example, what the 'principle of equality' is, you often answer by referring to your work on the 1830s. Aren't you hanging on to the past there in a way that puts* The Nights of Labour *to the test?*

There are several ways of answering. Let's say firstly that *The Nights of Labour* is a work that was transformed in the writing. In the beginning, I embarked on a great historic project that was supposed to go at least as far as the birth of the French Communist Party with the transformations in working-class thinking. All of a sudden, it turned into something else, namely, an historically situated sequence. And what mattered then was that this sequence was the production of a figure of working-class man and of the emancipation of the working class that was completely outside traditional forms and, by the same token, outside normal use of the past, where the past explains the present or is a reference point that allows you to measure any transformations. In *The Nights of Labour*, the past doesn't pass, in a way, although that doesn't mean it's always present. This past doesn't pass in the sense of a relationship of the past to the present, a way of using the past that doesn't serve to understand the present, as they say, but rather to destabilize it, to take away some of its obviousness.

My problem has never really been to see if we could look at the past as a means of understanding the present. No. The present has been more like a sensible universe constructed starting with a moment in the past that called a whole series of things into question – things that touched as much on the theory of historic causality as on the theory of emancipation or social transformation. Basically, I think that it makes no sense knowing if you can do it again today, partly because the historic conditions are different, and because you can't throw yourself into the issue of autodidacticism in 1830 in the same way, and because the relationship between social affirmation and the transgression of a certain distribution of intellect can't function the same way. I think that was an historic moment that I loosened up and got to float. By the same token, it dismantles a whole established order, a whole hierarchy of the sensible and of thought. I don't think anyone's trying to do the same thing now; maybe there are people who thought they could do it, that they could try it out with people living in poverty, intellectuals living in poverty, whatever. It's not a matter of nostalgia for the past; it's a matter of changing the relationship of the present to the past. That's what I was trying to say by 'a past that doesn't pass'– meaning, a past that puts a kind of radical requirement at the centre of the present. There is this quest for a complete revolution in the sensible world that I'd like to maintain as a perspective of the present without trying to see if that's how it works with people living precariously.

And this chimes in with what I was trying to say earlier. When I was working on *The Nights of Labour*, people told me that wasn't it: my workers were artisans, not real workers, which means the organized working class, factories, the working masses, trade unionism. Well, we now see that history has gradually swung round a bit closer to my artisans than to the factory model. We are today finding ourselves faced with all these forms of a return to a kind of artisanal labour – working from home, small businesses, family labour, child labour. At the very heart of capitalism today we are tending to revert to forms that look like the ones I evoked. The uses of time in today's capitalism also tend to be closer to the same alternation between work and unemployment, and to the same part-time work and all forms of mixing temporal regimes and activities and, by the same token, conditions. But I'm not trying to say that what I said is up to the minute. I'm just trying to say that in any event we've got over the idea that the past has well and truly passed, since we are now beyond the Ford system of mass production. We can see that this insistence on 'post-Fordism' seeks to hide the fact that we are not simply ahead of Fordism today – we're also behind it.

To conclude, *The Nights of Labour* was translated into Hindu two years ago. I was invited to talk about it in Delhi, where I was asked to debate with a group of individuals who were also working in factories during the day and who got together at night. It was a group a bit like the worker-writers I'd talked about; they've put together a collective anthology around the diary that one of their uncles keeps, a daily diary that says 'one day I did this and another day I did that', and then 'everything else is ordinary'. There is a kind of use of writing as a measure of the relationship of the ordinary to the extraordinary, within a division of time between work and writing that echoes *The Nights of Labour*. The art collective that initiated the translation of *The Nights of Labour* and that introduced me to these people made a film out of the work involved called *Strikes at Time*, which was shown at the 'Paris–Delhi–Bombay' exhibition. The film is constructed around this division of time and it ends with a bit of a quote from one of Gauny's letters that I'd published: 'I no longer have faith in time'. There's this relationship between time as a vector of historic faith and time as the operator of a division. In a way, I was also talking about 'strikes at time'. The presence of the past in the present is not just a sort of perspective; it can also be actualized in countries that are both third-world countries and advanced capitalist countries at the same time, that integrate all the pre-capitalist and proto-capitalist forms of labour.

It remains the case that the main proletarian characters in The Nights of Labour *are exceptional figures in the working-class world and the trades of the period. Some sociologists attack you for not questioning the fact that you entered that world via the working-class aristocracy and magnified exceptional figures who aren't representative of the working-class world of the day. As a result, you don't query the universalization operation, of which these figures were possibly the mould, in the rest of your work. What do you think of this criticism? Does it undermine the empirical basis most central to your philosophical edifice?*

There are several questions in that question. There is first the question of what we're talking about. Of course I'm talking about exceptions. If we're talking about what happens when, all of a sudden, significant collectives emerge, such as 'proletarian', 'worker', 'workers' movement', 'emancipation', or 'world of workers', we are necessarily talking about an exception. The norm is that people stay in their place and things carry on the same as always forever. But everything that stands out in the history of humanity works on the principle that something is happening, that people are starting to talk. I start out with those that do the talking. If we talk about 'working-class speech', we're talking about the people speaking. That feels like a truism. And yet, it's the opposite of a certain scientific method that holds that, when we talk about popular speech, we're talking about those who don't speak. It's the same old Aristotelian principle, namely, that you have to do democracy with the people who don't go to the Assembly, because those people at least won't be there, getting in your way. The historians have adopted that for themselves: essentially you have to get people who don't talk to talk. It's a strategy used every bit as much by political leaders as by historians or sociologists to say that the speech that counts is the speech of people who don't speak. I started out with the fact that if something happens, it's an exception, and we should look at the exception. If we're talking about speech, we're talking about people who speak, which also means that their speech is taken as speech; it's not just a matter of expressing a way of being, it's a specific production: 'my' workers make literature, good or bad, and philosophy, profound or superficial – that's not the problem. What matters is whether these are language creations of the same nature as the rest. They speak as an exception, as an act of breaking and entering.

So we then have to talk about the conditions for such an act of breaking and entering, for the way it happened, through experiences we can seize on and particularize. Of course, this shatters a number of schemas according to which what people say is merely the expression of what is happening underneath or elsewhere. As a result, people are going to interpret this in completely fantastical terms, of the kind that go: 'Ah, yes, but these aren't workers like other workers, this is working-class aristocracy!' With that, they wheel in quite mad ideas about the degree of qualification that such-and-such a trade represents. They say to you: 'This movement, they're tailors, and tailors are working-class aristocracy.' No, tailors were poor blokes; it was the kind of trade people who had no qualifications went into. People think it all goes together: complexity of the work, remuneration, cultural baggage. That's a mad idea – you have to remember that the slaves of antiquity often knew more than their masters, and that consequently the level of knowledge and the level of skill are things that are absolutely not a sign of elevated social status.

To get back to what I did, I started out with speech that expresses a radical change in direction, with people extricating themselves from the sensible universe they are supposed to live in, because if the word 'worker' defines a sort of subjective symbolic position and not just a social condition, it necessarily follows that a break has been brought about by operations that mean a signifier such as 'proletarian' is no longer going to mean a poor bloke, but is going to signify a position in relation to the symbolic order that structures a society. For me, this kind of operation has been the mould for thinking about the event as a relationship between two possible worlds.

Just as I've performed a division in the figure of the worker, the labourer, I've formed the notion that such a division is what ensures that there is politics. The conditions that are alleged to define someone as being a political subject are in reality split in two by a dividing line. I've also been able to posit that we have art from the moment a certain kind of division between liberal arts and mechanical arts no longer exists, which also means that we have art from the moment we can no longer distinguish art from non-art, can no longer distinguish between what belongs to art from what doesn't belong to art. I've performed these operations and they involve taking exceptions that produce radical change, a new signifier, a new configuration of experience.

With a society, we can always show sections, provide statistics and so on, but if we consider the very idea of society as a constructed signifier, we get interested in the people whose speech constructs the signifiers 'society', 'social', 'socialism', and so on. For me, that has been a mould, a personal operation of thought that has forced me to bring together different forms and levels of discourse that are supposed to be entirely heterogeneous. It's not as though you've got the empirical world on one side and theory on the other. There's a way of perceiving an experience that allows us to construct ways of making the experience intelligible along with what creates a break in that experience. Once again, this also means constructing a certain mode of thought, of writing, in which transformations in thinking are always transformations in the thinkable. In a way, what happens at the level of the experiences I describe is also what happens at the level of my writing. You don't set out from a starting point where it's a matter of saying what politics is – you delve into a world of meaningful structures and you try to see a certain dividing line emerge, based on which you might then be able to map out the political landscape.

Equality/Inequalities

You assert several times that inequality is 'unthinkable' except on the basis of what you call 'the equality of intelligence'.[46] In fact, you show that inequalities are experienced by, and are familar to, those who condemn them in theory every bit as much as those who experience them directly, and that there is no political interest in explaining things that people already know. But you also say that inequality is 'only possible' on the basis of 'the equality of intelligence'. This last phrase strikes us as a lot harder to grasp.

The expression 'inequality is only possible on the basis of equality' is certainly ambiguous. In fact, inequality can only function through

[46] 'The equality of intelligence is the common bond of humanity, the necessary and sufficient condition for a society of men to exist. [...] It is true that we don't know that men are equal. We are saying that they *might* be. This is our opinion, and we are trying, along with those who think as we do, to verify it. But we know that this *might* is the very thing that makes a society of humans possible.' (In *The Ignorant Schoolmaster: Five Lessons on Intellectual Emancipation* (Stanford: Stanford University Press, 1991; translated and introduced by Kristin Ross), p. 73.)

equality, but that doesn't mean that equality is the basis of inequality in general. Inequality is perfectly capable of taking care of itself, without needing anyone to give it a basis. And equality does not produce domination following the old familiar logic – namely, that equality leads to despotism. That old chestnut! No, it means that whatever the case you have to have a whole series of egalitarian relationships for inequality to function; people have to do what they're asked to do, and to do that, they have to understand what they're being asked to do and to understand it's in their interests to agree to it. This doesn't just function with the submission of the unequal – all inequality functions with the cooperation of the unequal. It's a bit like what was for me at the heart of the problematic of intellectual emancipation, of egalitarian emancipation: there are moments when you can radically turn round the relationship between equality and inequality present in any situation in favour of equality. I think we really need to reformulate the expression. It's not that equality is the basis of inequality, but that inequality can't function on its own.

Equality is nevertheless defined against a backdrop of inequalities that change over the course of history. You talked a moment ago about the fact that the stakes of autodidacticism are not the same now as they might have been in 1830. Implicitly, by saying that, you assert that the question of the division into manual and intellectual might not have the same weight as it once had and that the materials themselves for constructing inequalities are not the same at different periods in history. The problem of equality is consequently posed against a backdrop of a historicity of inequalities. We can't completely ignore that even when the aim is to postulate equality before all else. How is the cause of equality fundamentally related to the study of inequalities?

Obviously, I've got nothing against the study of inequalities and the forms they've been transformed into historically. But the essential point in the historicity of forms of inequality is that they lend themselves more or less to the construction of scenes of equality. That for me is the fundamental point: the affirmative nature of equality and the construction of a scene whereby equality is confirmed. That's something that for me establishes a radical break with those who say that first you have to study the specific historical form of inequality, and so understand the logic of the system, before you can develop strategies that are a match for it. What remains absolutely true is that the construction of scenes of equality is dependent on what existing forms of inequality bring to it. You can clearly see that what makes the present situation so painful for the cause of equality is not, as some say, that everyone is so happy and overwhelmed with consumer goods that they no longer have any incentive or energy for revolt. What is today in the process of disappearing is the existence of places where equality and inequality meet. That's been something very powerful about working-class space, about the power dynamic that could be organized in that space. It has also been very powerful at other times in relation to the education system. Well, today we see that there's been a dispersal of spaces where domination can be staged, which means that the opportunity for staging any coming together tends to be more and more limited.

In a way, the whole class struggle, as it's been conducted by the dominant class, is a struggle that seeks to systematically evacuate all the places where people meet. The fact that commercial firms build in foreign countries, in places where there is no social life, and the fact that a mass of so-called political, state or government decisions are made in non-spaces like the institutions of Europe, to say nothing of all the places where the great economic and state powers meet – all this means that, ultimately, there are no more places where people not only physically meet up but also where skills are pitted against each other. What could once have happened in a strike involving occupation or in negotiations in an industrial dispute? It wasn't just a matter of the power dynamic in a particular place; it also meant opposing one competence to another. It's clear that even this meeting of competences or minds is no longer relevant when the places where the intelligence at work in capital could confront the intelligence at work in labour are now being deserted. This is also what's in play in the whole dismantling of public-service systems and social institutions. In all these domains, the tendency to privatize public utilities or to bring social security provisions under state control also means a continuing loss of the domains where the powers that be could confront each other.

And this has favoured three different types of conflict: the entirely localized conflict, like the one involving the RESF (Réseau Education Sans Frontières),[47] an organization that looks after the defence of the *sans-papiers*, illegal immigrants, around the issue of schooling; the different forms of symbolic demonstration of the Seattle or Geneva

[47] The Education Without Borders Network is a militant association whose main aim is to prevent the removal of children of undocumented immigrants from school in France. *Translator's note.*

kind, which produce those moments when the official world and a counter-world clash for a week; or the current forms, such as occupying different spaces, places where people power and state power potentially meet, but also places where the intelligence and courage of the people can still show themselves. We necessarily have to take into account the question of the place that the current distribution of inequalities gives to conflict and thereby to the assertion of an egalitarian capacity. Differentiating between inequalities always more or less tends to prevent any capacity for equality from asserting itself as such.

That leads to another question. On several occasions you've expressed your irritation with theories that see power everywhere, an explosion in forms of power, as in the traditions inspired by Foucault. By distancing yourself from this metaphysics of power which was very big in the 1970s and which can take various forms, you can be attacked today for having neglected power struggles in your work, or at least for having downplayed them. To simplify, let's say that your postulate of 'the competence of anyone at all' is endowed with an intrinsic force in any place and at any time, and that this capacity isn't affected by any power dynamic. The assertion of equality, in your work, always has an already autonomous capacity to reconfigure places and subjects that's independent of the power relationships that pre-exist it.

In *Disagreement*, I said the 'police' in a way provide politics with its spaces and subjects. The configuration of the police order defines the possibilities of politics. The police order is primarily an order that tries fairly systematically to prevent such encounters. There are several ways of doing this, one being to fire on the crowd and the other being to leave public space as the only place where collective power is allowed to be visible ...

The Ordering of the Common

We've flagged the fact that to postulate equality means asserting the 'competence of anyone at all'. Through that, you see competence or capacities in an absolute way rather than in a gradual or relational way. It seems to us that this way of thinking is quite distinct from another concept of emancipation that also developed in the 1970s, within the tradition we might call Spinozistic, and which constructs the concept of 'competence' differently. Within this framework, the business of emancipation doesn't consist in recognizing the absolute competence of each and every person but rather different, specific, competences. The stakes of political thought then come down to seeing what these different aptitudes consist of, to the ordering of capacities for action, and the form this ordering takes. It's a matter of thinking of the common in an architectural way as an ordering of differentiated powers. How do you position yourself in relation to this kind of approach? By seeing competence in absolute terms don't you rule out any theory about the accumulation of power? In the name of an in-principle equality, aren't you forced to set aside the individual and collective issue of the growth of each person's potential?

Let's start with the notion of the competence of anyone at all. It doesn't mean that anybody is competent to do anything, or is simply competent in general. The competence of anyone at all covers two ideas that are closely related and yet distinct. The first is the idea of the conditions for politics: for there to be politics and not just power, you have to have a competence to rule, that is to say a non-specific competence that doesn't belong to a specific subject. There is politics, in this sense, when anyone at all has some kind of power. The second idea is the idea of the equality of intelligence, which I took from Jacotot. This doesn't mean that everyone is equally competent in all things; it means that although it is distributed differently, intelligence is the same for everyone. We can always encounter or construct situations where we can verify the equality of intelligence.

What really matters to me is to not define competence in the traditional way. At the heart of the idea of competence there is, after all, the whole notion that competence is the other side of the coin to incompetence. To put it in a nutshell, if we are competent, that means all the others are incompetent, especially when it comes to political competence, such as the powers that be think of it, which is as the incompetence of the greatest number. Saying you are amazingly competent at doing practical things means you are totally incompetent when it comes to theory or politics, and so you have no business taking an interest in them. I've shifted the relationship by insisting on the fact that any competence is always double: it is both a skill, a kind of know-how, a specific ability, and always the presupposition of a relationship between competence and incompetence at the same time. That's the fundamental thing. Behind any specific competence that's put to work in a practice, there is always a presupposition, a choice, as to the relationship between competence and incompetence.

I don't have anything against the idea of an assemblage of differentiated competences, but I have a lot against the idea that a scene of the common can be constituted by bringing these competences together. I'm thinking of the thesis on the 'specific intellectual' formulated in the Deleuze–Foucault interview of 1972, which we've already talked about several times, and which was very much Foucault's idea, even if the theoretical underpinnings were more Deleuze's. Foucault thought that, in place of the old subject of politics as defined in terms of classes, workers, the people, we would have specific competences. You gather lawyers, doctors, prisoners, prison guards, supervisors and social workers together, around prison, each one bringing their specific knowledge. Think of all the developments that have occurred elsewhere based on the theme of knowledge sharing. But even if that's all well and good, it has never defined a political scene. I think the idea of a new politics delivered by 'specific intellectuals' was doomed from the start. After all, to cut a long story short, the 'specific intellectuals' Foucault addressed turned into intellectuals typical of the CFDT (the Confédération française démocratique du travail), which led to what we saw in 1995. That doesn't mean they were any stupider or nastier than the rest of them, but there is always a moment after all when so-called 'specific' intellectuals find themselves in a situation where they decide that it's either the government or the strikers who have the political intelligence.

Heterogeneous competences are being put to work all the time in the constitution of a political scene of the common – that's perfectly true. But I don't believe that such a scene is constituted by an organized combination of competences. Political and social movements have always been made up largely of people who may well have been doctors, lawyers, teachers or social workers, and who were more or less faced with concrete situations and invested their knowledge in the form of concrete motivations, but this combination has not in itself defined a new scene of the common.

We weren't thinking of the rise of 'specific intellectuals'. We had in mind Deleuze and Guattari's discourse on 'the collective assemblages of utterance' and the critical thinking that has, in France, since the 1970s, been tied up with various forms of the common and of collectives as places promoting the practical politics of emancipation in action. That's a theory that is most likely historically linked to the idea that the challenge for collectives is first and foremost to allow individuals to achieve things they weren't capable of before being propelled into the collective assemblage, to do more than they

were doing on their own or in groups of compulsory, inherited,
allegiances, like the family or militant circles or professional circles.
We get the impression that your reasoning covers a given jurisdic-
tion, as if the possibility of realizing one's desires or of following an
inclination was ultimately secondary for you when it comes to defin-
ing emancipation or politics. It's a paradox.

No, people can think of the accumulation of competences in terms of
a collective assemblage of utterance but, basically, I don't really know
what is meant by 'the collective assemblage of utterance'. There is a
whole host of forms that have been part of past labour movements,
past political and revolutionary movements, that we could consider
specific assemblages of utterance. We've constantly seen that a militant practice was a practice that not only produced an accumulation
of knowledge and skills but also an intensification of desire. In a sense,
I could say that that's what I've always said, though in a different way
– meaning that the great emancipation movements have been movements promoting the accumulation of competences in the present,
perhaps every bit as much and even more than movements intended
to pave the way for a different future. In a sense, that's what *The
Nights of Labour* is all about. There are people who make themselves
capable of what they weren't capable of, who achieve a breach in the
wall of the possible. By regrouping according to various modalities,
they accumulate this competence and start living in a more intense
way, which brings all kinds of enrichment. Maybe there's no need to
think of a new kind of militant or intellectual; it's something that has
been fundamental to any egalitarian emancipation movement.

It's understood that an egalitarian movement is not a movement
of people who are constantly preoccupied with the feat of achieving
equality. An egalitarian movement is a movement of people who
place in common their desire to live a different life – to put it in the
most classic terms. I've always said that equality was a dynamic and
not an end. You don't come together to achieve equality; you achieve
a certain kind of equality by coming together.

But talking about an assemblage or an association, to go back to
the socialist lexicon of the nineteenth century, also means focusing
on what used to be called in the Marxist or libertarian universe
of the 1960s and 1970s the 'organization issue', the constitution of
rules for operating collectively that allowed the accumulation of
skills. You say, for your part, that emancipation takes place as soon
as there is a commmon stage, that basically it's not necessary to
think about these rules of common life. The history of the rules of
common life or the history of commons *provide other archives for*

*thinking through the extremely diverse modalities of what you call
the 'distribution of the sensible'. This last point leads us furthermore
to a different kind of friction with what is now claimed of Deleuze
and especially of Foucault around work on oneself, on one's relationship to oneself, on 'techniques of the self'. You spoke about the
'method of equality' as a collective method that can also be put to
work in educational relationships. But can we also think of the
'method of equality' as a certain way of relating to oneself, to one's
own desires, to the conception one has of one's abilities? Isn't there
also an individual and subjective moment in the 'method of
equality'?*

In a sense, I started out from there, from Gauny's monastic economy,
that is, from the emancipated worker as a worker who makes himself
a rule of life out of doing his budget. Every item in the budget of the
'coenobite', the community-based monk, is thought of in terms of
the accumulation of freedom it can produce. Gauny says there's no
need to spend money on the ironing because at the end of
the day an unironed shirt is part of the free man; in itself it points
to a rebuff, a rebellion. The rebel doesn't need an ironed shirt.
On the other hand, Gauny gives a lot of importance to shoes because
the rebel worker has to do a lot of walking. He calculates absolutely
everything with a view to working out how any expenditure of
money translates into a gain in freedom. That was something
that was fundamental, that you always find a bit of, wherever
people who don't have a lot to spend ask themselves about their
budget. In the diary of the Indian worker I referred to earlier, we see
how much is spent on a certain item mentioned. This also indicates
what is dear to you. It's one of the rules of life that has always been
important. We know to what extent the anarchist labour movement
was associated with a whole host of naturalist and gymnastic movements. I think there's a whole tradition of working on yourself as an
integral part of the labour of emancipation, which I've tried to
present in relation to all its collective dimensions.

In a way, the weakness of my work isn't so much having sacrificed
individual subjectivization to collective subjectivization, but the
opposite – having thought of emancipation based on forms of self-
transformation that I stumbled upon in my work on the archives.
But working on yourself is fundamental to any approach to equality.
That said, you need to see what you mean by working on yourself.
I'm not a big fan of all these themes of taking care of yourself, things
like that don't interest me enormously; it's more what kind of body
you build for yourself, what kind of attitude, what kind of daily life.

Why does the thematics of 'taking care of yourself' as a condition of emancipation or as the primary element in politics worry you? Is it because of the individualism it implies?

To say it 'worries' me ... is saying a lot. It's the reflexivity I don't like, if you think of 'care of the self' in the sense of constructing a self in which you then gaze at yourself. In the Indian texts I referred to, there's a whole discussion about needing to move on from the question of the 'who' to the question of the 'where'. The important thing is to construct the space where you are rather than constructing who you are. Personally, I've always thought – it's my old Sartrean roots – that you are first and foremost what you *do*. You give yourself things to do, rather than defining the kind of self you want to adopt.

Dis-identification and Subjectivization

Actually you've insisted ever since The Nights of Labour *on 'dis-identification' as the fundamental criterion for getting your political bearings. Isn't there the risk of a contradiction between this requirement of dis-identification as a condition of political subjectivization and a parallel requirement, in your work, of the 'symbolization' of the common: the necessity, for politics to take place, of constituting a space of equivalences between local situations that can be experienced or thought of as heterogeneous.[48] You sometimes give the impression of deploring a symbolization that's impossible. In a way, then, you echo a discourse of lament by implying that there is no strong collective symbolization anywhere today, whereas up to the end of the 1970s there was. Whether or not you really adhere to this lament is certainly an important question, but the more interesting point remains this tension between the requirement of 'dis-identification', on the one hand, and the requirement of symbolization, on the other. Both of those requirements run through your thinking about the conditions for politics. It's a sort of dual movement in your work.*

---

[48] 'I have insisted on the fact that what has been called the "labour" movement was first a movement of subjectivization, a labour of symbolization: it requires people who belong to a more or less narrowly defined social group to be up to intervening in the question of symbolic divisions of society.' (In 'Xenophobia and Politics', an interview with Yves Sintomer, reprinted in *Et tant pis pour les gens fatigués*, op. cit. p. 201.)

Let's say first off that the two terms are not opposed. Political subjectivization is a symbolic operation to do with an established identity. So it is once again a form of symbolization. Symbolization is
constructed based on a certain social substance, which it then works
on from the inside. If you think of what used to be called the labour
movement or proletariat, you can easily see that we have a single
noun for two things: first, the existence of a mass of people belonging
to the same social background which is already included in a symbolization of the collective order; second, dis-identification, which
transforms the very sense of that symbolization, making it no longer
the designation of a collective identity, but the designation of a collective capacity to construct a new common. There has always been
a sort of objective contradiction here: there can be no dis-identification
without an identity, and there is no going over to the other side
without the possibility of symbolizing a certain number of common
features based on a group of people sharing the same community
life. There is a possibility of working to resymbolize being together
based on community life. Community life means people share the
same background in life, a sensible world, a time and a place, a
speech world.

Obviously, there has always been tension between the demonstration of the militant subject and the existence of a community life,
which it's a matter of transforming but which is also an element that
allows people to form a community and to be able to gather together
and say 'that's enough', to occupy the streets and the factories and
bestow a kind of collective material power on themselves. Subjectivization, for me, is the symbolic operation that separates a community
from its identity. Once again, that community has to exist for it to
be divided. We could compare this with three other ways of thinking
about subjectivization today. One way downplays subjectivization
because it considers the subjective community as being produced by
the subjectivization process itself. That's what I'd call the vitalist
vision represented by Toni Negri. Another way, conversely, thinks of
symbolization as a summoning power, carried by the noun – meaning,
in the final analysis, by the idea behind the noun. That's the sense
of the revaluing of the noun 'worker' once advocated by Alain Badiou
and of the revaluing of the noun 'communist' today. Lastly, there's
a way of thinking that sees the community not as a division but as
a coming together. That's the idea of hegemony that's been resur-
rected by Ernesto Laclau and Chantal Mouffe. Those are so many
different ways of dealing with the tension between a group and its
name. But subjectivizations take place all the same on the basis of
the alliance of people who have a common relationship to certain

situations, whether these people be Tunisians deprived of the power and the means to work, or workers in the grip of a system of exploitation, or peasants in the grip of a system of expropriation, or whatever.

Politics and Institutions

We recall that you defined politics in Disagreement *as 'the institution of a part of those who have no part'. The domain of politics is, then, one of those where you finally had a way of doing a philosophy that was probably more traditional than what relates to aesthetic issues. Why traditional? Because you accept the principle of the definition of an essence that has structured a large part of political theory. Why have you agreed to play the game, right when your thinking was leading you to invent a different way of articulating political issues? The second question bears on the word 'institution'. You say that politics is 'the institution of a part of those who have no part'. You've been questioned a lot on this 'part of those who have no part', but less about the term 'institution'. Can we think of politics without an institution? Isn't there a theory specific to the institution – we're thinking of the various institutional analyses and certain social and political theories – that could constitute a development of your work? More broadly, can we conceive of emancipation without institutions, or what would the institutions promoting emancipation look like?*

Let's start with one thing. Nowhere in *Disagreement* is it said that politics is the institution of a part of those who have no part. I do say that there is politics wherever there is such an institution. That's important: there is no definition of politics in there; what there is in there is a sort of narration of 'when there is politics', of 'where we can say there is politics'. Once again, *Disagreement* presents itself as a criticism of political philosophy, which means very precisely a critique of a definition of politics based on a definition of the human being, of community, of the human bond, etc. Even in *Disagreement*, which is a book that meets the demands of what is considered theory to the hilt, even there the question of 'what' is referred back to the question of the conditions in which you can say that there is something like politics. What is important is that these conditions are conditions of a division. What *Disagreement* states is that politics only occurs through a division of what is given as the essence of politics. Aristotle defines politics based on the human capacity for language. Well, you will only get politics by dividing this capacity, by bringing out a gap, a division, within this definition. Similarly, if we start with Plato, we find that politics only occurs once you look into the rest, into the last term on the list, into what doesn't enter into the credentials to rule.

This is important and it's linked to what I was saying a moment ago, which is that, when it comes to politics, I've spent my time saying: this is what in my opinion we can say about politics if we really want to talk about politics other than in the terms of political philosophy, other than in the terms of a simple definition of what politics is based on, some political property. *Disagreement* says that there is no property that ensures that there is politics; there is politics through division of the property that is supposed to ensure that there is politics. I think that's fundamental, which means, in a sense, that I'm playing the game set up by people who want a definition of politics – but that I'm doing so by disrupting the rules because I say: what you call politics is something that ends in a contradiction; what you proclaim as the return of politics is in fact its elimination. Consequently, your definition of the particularity of politics just goes round in circles, which forces us to think of politics instead as what comes along and disrupts whatever presents itself as the normal form of human alliance and the governing of mankind. There is this essential side to my definition of politics. What is thereby defined is a tension between two logics. That's the first point.

The second point is that, when it comes to the institution of a part of those who have no part, it's clear that 'institution' in this sense means an emergence, a form of declaration, a demonstration of a part of those who have no part. It is an institution in the sense of: I declare, I demonstrate; something appears in a public space and constructs a specific public space by so appearing. Which also means questioning what we call the institutionalization of the institution, with all the objections that endlessly return, such as 'spontaneity isn't the only thing, you also have to have organization' – all the things we are familiar with and which are both absolutely irrefutable and totally uninteresting. Once again, as far as organization goes, it exists always and everywhere. No need to wear yourself out shouting about it from the rooftops. The only question is: what is being organized? Why? And, so, how? All I've said is that if we have to have political institutions, they should be political institutions only to the extent that the politics involved is specific and genuinely anarchic, as opposed to all that brings natural or social forms of authority to a conclusion in forms of government. Yes, we can say that politics needs to be given its own institutions: parties, schools, newspapers, universities, cooperatives. But we also need to bear in mind that for this to make any sense, these have to be political institutions. And we need to bear in mind that politics never exists in a pure form. If politics means that there exists something like the power of the people, which is the power of anyone at all, if this power has any specificity, there have to be institutions without our necessarily expecting them to represent politics in all its purity; but in any case they have to be different in their mode of existence, their finality and their structure, from state institutions.

Obviously, what we call political parties are state institutions, and what we may have seen elsewhere as revolutionary parties were institutions based on compromise between the party as a state institution that potentially enabled them to have seats – if not in parliament, then at least in the European Parliament or in the regions – and the party as an embryonic form of a different state. If the term 'political party' has any meaning, it has to be as a form of assembly, a mode of utterance that's specific. Its forms of utterance, of declaration, of action have to have a form of temporality and a kind of objective that are different from those defined by the calendars of the state or the media. A political institution in this sense is an institution that has as its goal an increase in the power of anyone at all. Obviously, there's little chance, little reason, for it to be guided by the hope of having a junior minister's office in a left-wing government. There are institutions that have that as their goal. In the system we're familiar with, there are people who are candidates not, of course, with a view to becoming president, but to perhaps being able to pick up a few seats as deputies or Members of Parliament, and being given a junior minister's office in higher education, for want of scoring the education ministry. Those are undoubtedly respectable goals in themselves. I'm just saying that a genuinely political institution does not have that as a goal; its goal is to develop the power anyone at all has in relation to all that is negotiated within this system as participation in state power. I am not against institutions per se, but I am against the 'spontaneity vs organization' claptrap. I am against all that comes along and redirects the idea of an institution based on liberty and equality towards the idea of an institution within the state power game as it is defined.

The Place of the Social

In your notion of historic change, one element is oddly absent: society, social classes, the composition of social classes. To explain history through the social or with the social, though, is one of the current modalities of analysis of history, in particular in the traditions of thought from which you derive. This absence speaks volumes and incites us to ask you what weight you give what is generally called 'the social' in your work. Is it non-existent in the sense that the social is an invention of what you call 'the police',[49] *a sort of fiction of a relationship that is for you always discordant, different or non-existent? A second aspect of the question: we could say that ever since* The Nights of Labour, *you've put the power of the imagination in the place occupied by the social in other people's work. In this, you've followed Schiller's line in his* Letters Upon the Aesthetic Education of Man *and forged the idea that the power of reconfiguring through the imagination is the principal motor of historic transformations in politics as much as in art. How exactly do you position this power of the imagination vis-à-vis the weight of the social so often mobilized to theorize history?*

I've always objected to resorting to the social as an explanation in the sense of an explanation from the base up, from what is below, this graduated thinking in which changes in society explain changes in politics and in ideology, this whole system of explanation that looks for the reasons for change in the transformations in the composition of society, or the way of organizing change. I don't think your generation has any idea of the weight this discourse had at a certain time, since it was supposedly inspired by Marxism and was meant to provide the answers about which class or sub-class, which class element in terms of its composition as a class, which class position or class attitude, might prove to be an ally of the proletariat in the revolutionary struggle. It was very powerful, rooted as it was in academic culture. That's what I was referring to earlier apropos the causes of revolutions which always had to be economic crises. There is a very powerful tradition according to which what appears on the scene must be explained by something behind the scenes, resulting in those incredible discourses you got in France in the 1970s about which fraction or sub-fraction of which kind of bourgeoisie could be the proletarians's ally. You have to bear that extraordinarily powerful tradition in mind. You also have to bear in mind something that's less of a

---

[49] 'Politics is generally seen as the set of procedures whereby the aggregation and consent of collectivities is achieved, the organization of powers, the distribution of places and roles, and the systems for legitimizing this distribution. I propose to give this system of distribution and legitimization another name. I propose to call it *the police.*' (*Disagreement,* Politics and Philosophy (Minneapolis, University of Minnesota Press, 1999; translated by Julie Rose), p. 28.)

caricature, but that nevertheless remains for me a fundamental point of divergence, namely, the quest for the right figure of the proletariat. People say: the old-style proletariat is finished, but there are new figures that play the same role: in the Italian operaist tradition,[50] you thereby get the metropolitan worker, the precarious worker, the cognitarian worker, whatever, which will finally be the right figure.

I'm not about to say that the work of the imagination takes precedence over all else and that the social is nothing. But we need to rethink the social not in terms of a compact stratification, but more in terms of scenes and conflictual places. What is the social for me? It's the place where a conflict between competences is always in operation. The social is the place where the following question operates: is the fact that the workers want to make more money a private matter, or not? It is the place where we pose the question of whether this or that disadvantage or hardship people are experiencing is a purely personal, private affair, or a public issue that calls for collective action. The social is the place where the issue of a division takes shape. That's what I tried to say in my 'Ten Theses on Politics'.[51] It's not like there's politics, as the place of collective action, in one corner, and the social, as an obscure sphere of interests in the manner of Arendt, in the other. No, the social is the very place where we pose the question of what is social and what is political, what is private, of the order of the individual, of ordinary obscure life, and what is of the order of the public stage, and thereby also of a public competence. I said it in *Disagreement*, the social is several things at once, it is the metapolitical body that explains politics, and it can also be the object of a utopia, or of philosophies of the compactness of the social body, of the social bond. But the social is also the place of constant conflict, the place where the political can always surge up again, in the work of reconfiguring the givens which we might call the work of the imagination.

The imagination is not a particular faculty. It can be found at work everywhere; it is potentially present in every one of the conflicts we call social as a *mise en scène* of the question, 'is this private or

[50] Operaismo, or Workerism, was an Italian theoretical and political movement of the 1960s and 1970s that sought to restore the centrality of the working class in opposition to movements then seen as excessively 'ideological'. Tony Negri was one of its leading lights, and the terms 'precarious worker' and 'cognitarian worker' are his. *Translator's note.*

[51] *Aux abords du politique*, pp. 223–54. (This essay is not included in *On the Shores of Politics* (London and New York: Verso, 1995; translated by Liz Heron). *Translator's note.*)

not, does this simply involve a reassembling of parts or the emergence of a part of those who have no part, of a genuinely political dimension?' That goes back to the question of the present, of what emerges in the present. A social conflict is, or is not, the place where a political subject emerges. We need to get away from the idea of the social in terms of composition.

At the same time, it's clear that the class struggle – let's call it that, keep it simple – also produces radical transformations in social composition that are also operators of politicization or de-politicization. If you take de-industrialization, some people think that's the effect of technological transformations, that there are no workers anywhere any more and that everything everywhere is done by robots. That may well not be the case now: with films coming out of Bombay and similar places, we can see that we're living more in an age of the sweatshop system, of piece-work done at home, than in an age where robots do everything. But what is certain in any event is that we can no longer identify 'the part of those who have no part' with a class of people coming out of car factories or steelworks en masse. But this isn't just the consequence of a re-composition of classes produced by an automatic re-composition produced by technology. The big factories, and the mines, still exist – elsewhere. The de-industrialization of the industrialized countries is not just a technical necessity. It's a manœuvre in the class struggle led by the dominant class. There's a very strong link between the forms of economic and political domination and what can be constituted as an identifiable figure of 'the part of those who have no part'. The effect of this is what we're seeing now, what we've had in all the recent movements: demonstrations in the street of something like the people in general, the people of no particular identity, simply a crowd of people who aren't afraid to go down into the street. In Tahrir Square or in La Puerta del Sol people simply come together. You can always explain, and it's probably true, that in the demonstrations of the Indignant,[52] there's a certain kind of social persona: IT specialists, since there are so many of them around some of them are inevitably there; graduates who can't find jobs that fit their degrees; actors and performers between jobs. It's perfectly clear that the destruction of the economic industrial fabric and the inflation of a precarious 'intellectual' sector produce forms of shattered identity. But that's just it – those identities are not going to be put back together again in the unitarian form of:

[52] The Indignant – *Indignados* in Spanish – is the name adopted by the peaceful protest movement that sprang up in Madrid's main square, La Puerta del Sol, in May 2011. *Translator's note.*

'we are cognitarian workers, we are the new force'. For the moment, they can only be put back together again in the form of people w ho are out on the streets, the 'indignant': the noun is the absence of a name, the absence of an identity sufficient to put a name to a subject corresponding to a social group that's even a tiny bit substantial.

Newness and Historicity

We'd now like to discuss your notion of history based on the problem of the new. Your thinking could be seen as preserving a structuralist predilection for long-term changes, the postulate of relative excep-tionality in transformations in politics and moments of transition between what you call 'regimes of art'. Let's locate ourselves pre-cisely at that particular point of your work where you evoke, in The Distribution of the Sensible, *in* Aesthetics and Its Discontents *or in* Aisthesis, *changes in these 'regimes of identification of art'.*[53] *How do you envisage these metamorphoses in 'regime' and the forces that cause them? Based on that example, can you tell us how you think of the new and how we can recognize it?*

Let's start with the regimes. I've always insisted on the fact that they have a historicity and yet, at the same time, they don't define a breakdown of humanity into ages. The three regimes of art are not three ages of humanity. We can historicize them, since we can't find anything in Greek theatre, for instance, that corresponds to what I call an aesthetic logic. We can also say that there exist modes of perception and conceptualization of aesthetic experience that are genuinely modern. But this historicity can't be defined in the form of a radical break. I've insisted in particular on the fact that, for me,

---

[53] By 'regime of identification of the arts', we need to understand how 'we perceive very diverse things, whether in their techniques of production or their destination, as all belonging to art. This is not a matter of the "recep-tion" of works of art, Rather, it concerns the sensible fabric of experience within which they are produced. These are entirely material conditions – performance and exhibition spaces, forms of evaluation and reproduction – but also modes of perception and regimes of emotion, categories that identify them, thought patterns that categorize and interpret them. These conditions make it possible for words, shapes, movements and rhythms to be felt and thought as art.' (*Aisthesis: Scenes From the Aesthetic Regime of Art* (London: Verso, 2013; translated by Zakir Paul), p. x.)

the 'aesthetic regime' is an inclusive regime to the extent that it functions overwhelmingly by recycling and reinterpretation, which means
that works of art that derive from other regimes take their place in
a new regime by being modified, altered. We can also say at the same
time that a regime is not historic in itself, that regimes can coexist,
and that, at the same time, there is a historical dimension to their
emergence.

I've also stressed the fact that the 'aesthetic regime' is an unstable
regime. On the one hand, it's stable to the extent that it can accommodate anything but, at the same time, it's unstable to the extent
that it has suppressed any specific norm that would allow us to say
'this is art, this is not art'. It defines a sort of substance peculiar to
an aesthetic sphere and, at the same time, it doesn't define any rules
that would allow us to distinguish what comes within the purview
of art and what does not. The substance of the aesthetic sphere is,
then, threatened on both sides from the outset, caught as it is between
the norm of representation and the temptation of ethics. This sort of
divided loyalty comes into play in some way the very moment the
new is heralded. Think of all that's already in play in the critique of
the 'representative regime' in Rousseau and in the critique Schiller
makes of that critique. If we were to sum up, Rousseau shows in a
precisely dated essay, the *Letter to D'Alembert*, that the 'representative regime' is contradictory: it claims to have an effect of moralizing
from the outside while producing an effect of pleasure it defined as
intrinsic. It claims to define a pleasure and an extrinsic lesson at the
same time. It is, in a sense, the first appearance of the new. All of a
sudden, someone says 'the emperor has no clothes', the regime is
contradictory. But what he proposes as a remedy is a strictly ethical
definition of the collective festival that is supposed to replace
representation.

Then Schiller comes along and replies that we certainly can't
expect theatre to teach young girls how to protect their virtue, or to
teach us anything remotely to do with moral behaviour. On the other
hand, we can expect a specific form of refinement in sensibility which
consists precisely in the capacity of no longer being forced to define
a choice between pleasure and morality, no longer being forced to
expect a specific tendency produced by representation. Schiller
thereby defines a transformation in the very mode of sensibility in
place of the effects, more or less contradictory, of sensible pleasure
and intellectual or moral education. But by the same token, he once
again defines an unstable boundary between the aesthetic sphere
and the ethical sphere, since this transformation in the very mode
of sensibility is itself theorized as an element of the possible

transformation of humanity, as the promise of a form of community that politics can't achieve. The definition of an aesthetic specificity is from the outset on the cusp of a radical shift to a new form of 'ethical regime'. And we will then see the return at different high points in the aesthetic regime of the declaration of a form of disappearance of art into life that seems to be a constituent form, a *telos*, immanent to the 'aesthetic regime' itself.

So, we can point to the moments, the events, that caused a scandal and produced a break with a certain consensus. That said, the shift from the domination of the 'representative regime' to the domination of the 'aesthetic regime' is a process that was spread over a hundred years at least and that essentially functions in retrospective mode. I tried to say that in my books on literature. You can pinpoint the moments when the word 'literature' changed meaning, even without this change in meaning ever being thematized. If we follow La Harpe's *Course in Literature* between the years 1780 and the early 1800s, we can say that the meaning of the word changed between the beginning and the end of the *Course*. But nothing of that change was conceptualized or even mentioned. And if we take an institutional landmark, we realize that it was only in the 1850s that the heading 'Literature' replaced the heading 'Belles Lettres' in the library catalogue.

The possibility of objectively spotting the new exists inasmuch as a dominant regime defines criteria of acceptability on the basis of a recognized normativeness. If there are constituent poetic arts, if there are academic rules of painting, if there are institutions that embody normativeness in painting, like the salons of the nineteenth century, then we can say: this is not acceptable to the Salon, to the Academy. This is therefore going to be produced elsewhere, in independent bodies; a *Salon des refusés* will be created, followed by a *Salon des indépendants*, which will flag the fact that something is being produced that no longer corresponds to what the still dominant academic logic calls painting. So there is a novelty that it's a matter of identifying, and not just taste: what the Impressionist School produced en masse as painting, has the appearance, the texture, of what was previously considered by the whole pictorial tradition as preparatory sketches, rough drafts. In France up until 1914, the salon as an institution is a landmark that allows us to say that something is unacceptable and so, to spot the difference of the new.

On the other hand, a perfect 'aesthetic regime' is a regime in which there is no such normativeness at all. If you compare the scandals produced by Jeff Koons or Murakami at the Palace of Versailles to the scandals of the nineteenth-century salons, there is something fundamentally different. People can no longer say that a thing is unacceptable because it doesn't conform to the recognized criteria of art; they simply say that a thing doesn't have its place here. And the people who say that will be royalists or reactionary Catholics. There is a moment when the new – whether it's extolled or rejected – can no longer be defined with reference to some objective criterion. It can then only be along the lines of an individual event like a work of art, a book or a film, which makes it very hard to say that you're about to define a new regime. Basically, despite the dominant belief, it's pretty rare now to see the new making waves as the new.

In politics, there are forms of novelty, as far as events go, that force things to speed up, impose a new temporality. In art, the new is often a matter of a retrospective declaration. Who at the time saw a historic break in Duchamp's *Fountain*, right when Stieglitz was trying to introduce the United States to Rodin, Cézanne and Picasso? It is not the same new that is going to be identified and analysed thirty or forty years on, even when we're dealing with an artwork that more or less created a scandal.

You've insisted on the fact that moments of rupture in history can't be identified neatly, that there are symptoms like what you've just described with the 'Rousseau symptom'. Well, you've described this Rousseau symptom by saying that the Geneva philosopher was at the time expressing the 'contradictions' in the previous regime of art, that is, in the prior historic configuration. Are you putting forward a more general idea of historic change here – as being accommodated above all by the contradictions immanent to a 'regime'?

We need to look at what the word 'contradiction' means. What is declared to be contradictory by Rousseau is a logic of compromise that was put in place in the seventeenth century between a certain kind of politico-social requirement and an ethico-religious requirement. On the one hand, there was the constitution, in seventeenth-century France, of a certain legitimacy of the spectacle, contemporaneous with the freezing of the language. This legitimacy of the spectacle was constituted by a tight relationship between a normativeness from on high and the education of a public that was to define itself in the subjective terms of taste and pleasure. There was this constitution of a twin legitimacy that we could call political and aesthetic, linked to the establishment of a certain kind of royal power, which coincided with all we know from elsewhere about the domestication of the aristocracy, and in particular the domestication of taste, the legalization of taste.

And then, on the other hand, there was the compromise between the specific demands of this legitimacy and moral norms hostile to the theatre, dictated by the Church. What Rousseau condemns is this compromise whereby the theatre, as a politico-aesthetic form of legitimacy linked to the monarchy, had to justify itself at the same time in relation to an ethical norm overwhelmingly annexed by the Church. Rousseau, perhaps as a citizen of Geneva, a region where there was precisely no theatre and so no compromise, put his foot down and said: this little game you've concocted, you inconsistent Catholics, doesn't work. But exposing the contradiction in the logic of representation in this way was just one element in all the transformations that were happening in society, in public opinion, and the workings of royal power over the course of the eighteenth century. But it was a symptomatic element that created waves.

Things happened at a much more global level at the end of the eighteenth century, with the establishment of museums and the way pictorial works and sculptures were uncoupled from their time-honoured function. That began before the French Revolution. The taste legalized by the French royal family gets de-legalized. But this process is of course speeded up by the Revolution and especially by the pillaging of artworks carried out by the revolutionary armies. All of a sudden all pictorial artworks from all over the place were brought to Paris, differences in genre became blurred and the whole legitimacy of pictorial taste as regulated by the Academy of Painting was completely undermined by the mix. The question of the relationship between this great wave and the educative function of the arts was then posed again on a grand scale. Take the debates that took place when all the chests of what had been looted over the border in Italy and Spain and the Netherlands by the revolutionary armies turned up at the Louvre. The curators said to themselves: this is amazing, all these treasures of the legacy of liberty that once belonged to kings now belong to the republican nation. They opened the chests and they saw portraits of sovereigns, more or less indecent mythological scenes, and tons of religious paintings, and they asked themselves: where is the liberty in all that? What are we going to be able to do with it for the betterment of the republican people? It is the treasure of the legacy of human liberty, but there's nothing but stories of kings, courtiers, priests, naked women, courtesans, debauchery. The solution they hit on was to say that it was not the contents of the paintings that would instruct the people, but the way they were exhibited, their spatial disposition. We have clearly reached a point where the circumstance of war means that pictorial legality no longer functions, with the paradoxical result that by wanting to educate the

republican people with all these looted artworks, they were necessarily led to erase the very contents of the paintings and to give a
new power to the exhibition space itself.

In a way, the famous disinterested gaze is also the result of an
internal contradiction of a different kind. No longer do you have a
guy who says the system isn't working any more; you get people
tasked with re-exhibiting, giving a new legitimacy to artworks
through their very visibility. Not being able to do this, they invent
the museum of the future where people will no longer know what's
what, whether what's happening on the canvas is moral or not, or
what lesson it might provide. This is not simply an intellectual affair;
it takes on a quite considerable material aspect. These are things of
which it's not enough to say, as I mentioned earlier with Lyotard,
that at the time of the salons taste was changing, that legitimacy no
longer existed. Something much bigger was at work, namely, the fact
that it was now the people who were supposed to be the subject of
art. The question is what mode of existence you give the people, now
they are the subject of art, through what you exhibit and introduce
them to. How are you going to present a legacy to the people now
they are the subject? There you have an example of an active
contradiction.

But that's just it: a system's contradictions don't shatter that
system. A system rests on contradictions. What this produces historically is adjustments. In this instance, not a new kind of painting, but
a new way of looking at painting linked to a new mode of putting
it on show. From one adjustment to another, you slowly get a
revolution.

Should we think of change differently, depending on whether it's
political or aesthetic in nature? Should we picture different kinds of
historicity or modes of historicity according to the kinds of human
activity?

I was trying to show there that one of the elements in the historic
overturning of a 'regime' of art is linked to a specifically political
acceleration that has military consequences. But I should insist on the
fact that this didn't change all that much in pictorial practice itself,
and that it was only to do so very slowly in interpretation. There's a
moment when things change radically because the people became the
subject of art, and this had already begun before the Revolution, with
all the problems of the eighteenth century. It was the Greek people
who wrote the *Odyssey* and not Homer, says Vico; poetry is the
expression of the people. With Winckelmann, it was Greek liberty
that was embodied in the statues and not the skill of the sculptors any

more. There again, we have a whole series of elements and accelerators that produce certain effects that aren't immediately theorized, thematized or transformed into a new form of visibility. In the realm of art, regimes of perception are slow to change. This brings us back to the question of different regimes of historicity.

I think we need to reverse the usual hierarchy of temporalities a bit. It is accepted, and this is the consensual view of things, that politics is a long-haul business, since it's considered part of the exercise of the virtues of science, prudence and foresight, which are the privilege of people who know, who possess these virtues. People think that art, on the other hand, is the realm where things happen fast, as it's supposed to be the realm of boldness, imagination and spontaneity. This is the normal consensual view that pits the rulers, who carry their gaze into the distance, against these public entertainers or these wildly enthusiastic spirits and lunatics, who live in the realm of rapid emergence, or risk, although such risk isn't all that serious anyway, since it's not really going to change the world. Well, we need to completely reverse that view.

How do we know that politics exists? We know it exists insofar as it is the power of an entity known as the people, because there are moments of dizzying acceleration when all of a sudden nothing is what it was. There is the constitution of a political scene where we see a whole semi-instantaneous transformation of the visible, the thinkable, of the whole universe of the possible. Something unthinkable in June 1789, namely that an Assembly, a parliament, should judge a king and condemn him to death, is thinkable three and a half years later. If we think of what happened in 1968, we see that politics shows us moments where the whole normal order of the visible, the sayable, the thinkable, finds itself turned on its head.

That is not how it works in the world of art. A painting will be rethought two hundred years later, people will say at the start of the nineteenth century: this is extraordinary, Frans Hals, this use of brushstrokes is completely modern, Titian's use of colour. The new is thereby caught up in the logics of retrospection and interpretation. There is a certain idea of the people going full speed ahead in politics between 1789 and 1794, and then you see the time it takes when it comes to art. Take the way people became distanced from the academic tradition in the nineteenth century. That distance was first created by the fact that artists stopped studying exclusively at the Academy and took to the museums, saw that that wasn't how the great painters of the past painted; and then a whole series of distances is thereby created, linked to the fact that people were going to compare what Velasquez, Hals, Rembrandt and Titian were able to do with what was taught at the Academy. Of course, there are moments when you can identify accelerated changes. If you take Kandinsky's series of *Compositions*, you can see exactly how he goes from a figurative art that refers back to certain kinds of popular Russian folk imagery to something we could describe as a purely abstract assemblage of colours. We can spot these transformations, but they're not what constitutes the regime change. They are produced within a regime of perception in which, before Kandinsky went from coloured scenes inspired by popular Russian illustrations to something purely abstract, there was all that work of looking and all the work of critics who reviewed and thought differently about the figurative artworks of the past only to isolate the abstract pictorial components.

Even if 'regimes of art' can't be confused with eras in history, we might once again stress the fact that the changes in those 'regimes' have been few in number over history. Similarly, people have often interpreted you to be saying in your philosophy that politics is pretty rare. How do we analyse the present when we adopt this view of history? What can we do with the present and in the present if we know how rare change is? What should we look for? These are both problems of theoretical method and of practical orientation in history.

We're back to this sorry business of rarity. I've been accused of saying that when it was actually a thesis of Badiou's, and then all the old Marxists, who like to pit spontaneity against organization, leaped on it – that old spontaneity vs organization thing just keeps coming back. At the end of the day, I'm not happy with the wording. Politics exists as a function of moments that are exceptional. That doesn't mean that politics started on the 27th of July 1830 and ended on the 29th. But let's say that there's a whole dynamic of republican hope, of social emancipation, etc., that we can relate to the effect produced by an extremely short and exceptional run. Politics exists since there are moments when what shouldn't happen happens. All of a sudden, the normal powers are delegitimized, what happens in the street is no longer what normally happens in a street, people no longer look at the organs of power in the usual way or at those around them in the street. That's what's important first and foremost for me, namely that there are moments when politics, as a conflict between two sensible regimes, shows itself in a violent manner in a change in all the modes of visibility and in all the kinds of relationships that existed till then. It's something that happens in a more or less lasting way; it's what we experienced in 1968. After the event, you can say it was a momentary fit of madness that immediately petered out. It doesn't matter. There are moments when no existing hierarchy seems legitimate any more. The fact that three weeks or two months later, they are re-established, triumphant, is one thing, but it doesn't stop the fact that there was a powerful political moment when people suddenly told themselves there was no reason why all activities, whether managing common affairs, or running a firm, or the public service, should function according to this division, this hierarchical order. At certain moments, an entity known as 'the people' appears, as a subject of power that is no longer the usual one – people voting every five years to elect their leader. There is a sensible form of existence of that entity. Politics exists, and we know this because periodically it reappears.

At any time in the present, the issue is to try and home in on this mode of reappearance. The constitution of an unprecedented spectacle, an unprecedented occupation of places, is for me more important than knowing the right slogans and ideas that cause people to come together in the street. If we take the expressions touted by the Indignant of Madrid as an example, we could say: it wasn't very powerful, they just wanted leaders who were less corrupt and more respectful of the people who elected them, it was no big deal. But at the same time, for me, it was more important than the iron bar put on the TGV line.[54] Why? Because an entity calling itself 'the people' appeared and said: 'After all, it's up to us to think and decide.' That is the central issue, which we find even in forms that are a bit foreign for us, like the Icelanders communicating by email in order to change their Constitution themselves. As people said at the time, you could say that was reformist, but the idea that people write their Constitution themselves seems to me to have something more important going for it than great radical speeches as we get to hear them in political forums in countries like ours.

The essential element in each present time is to know what, in that present, manages to revive the idea of a common capacity in the form of practical action. All of a sudden, people move into a space and say they won't budge. This can have quite different outcomes; obviously, when it happens in Tunisia or Egypt, and there are weapons pointed at you, it takes forms that are different from in Madrid or even Tel-Aviv or Santiago. People go down on to the street and say

---

[54] In 2004, an iron bar was placed on a TGV line in France in a bid to derail the train. This act of sabotage was attributed to the French direct-action group known as the 'Comité invisible' and its leaders were arrested. *Translator's note.*

they are the people, and they demonstrate this by being where they're not supposed to be and forming a collective people completely different from the collective people that the people in power control.

Let's get back to what you call the 'aesthetic regime of the arts'. One could get the feeling that for you it's a matter of the latest 'art regime'. Does history stop there? You've said in any event that this is a regime we can describe as unstable because it blurs the distinctions between art and non-art. Current art is thereby characterized by a tendency to indistinctness that has a positive side, but which is also one of the reasons art can lose any critical impact, as you show in Aesthetics and Its Discontents.[55] *Indistinctness in the creation of contemporary art thus has two faces. Which poses the following question: under what conditions can indistinctness change signs in contemporary art practices – and in a positive way since the inclusive is transformed into a source of confusion, simple replication of the surrounding world? Does this change of sign constitute a driving force of the current art regime?*

My critique had two sides to it and tackled two forms of indistinctness. The first was what we find in critical art, where critical distance was erased of its own accord. What still claimed to have a purpose in understanding, in teaching awareness and in determining militant energy turned out to be just chasing its tail. The way I see it, what we get there is a version of Rousseau's criticism. The artist sets up images from advertising here, a billiard table there, a merry-go-round, a giant football table or a cabin with disco sounds and manga images to denounce consumerism and the entertainment industry. Along comes the critic and he says: all you've done is stick a billiard table here, a few images there, a merry-go-round over there, a little film and a few disco sounds – that's all you've done. You haven't produced condemnation of any kind.

There exists a second form of indistinctness that intervenes when the work of art again takes up a form of social intervention. That's the story of the Cuban artist restoring an old couple's house in a poor neighbourhood and then showing this intervention in a video in a museum. I'm not going to go back over this example because

---

[55] 'In their passage from the critical to the ludic register, these procedures of delegitimization have almost become indiscernible from those spun by the powers that be and the media or by the forms of presentation specific to commodities.' (*Aesthetics and Its Discontents* (Cambridge: Polity, 2009; translated by Steven Corcoran), p. 54.)

I've commented on it extensively elsewhere. I said then that there was a radical swing here from the artistic to the ethical which we could see as being parallel to a radical shift from politics to ethics – something that's overwhelming in any case in the whole politics of humanitarian interventions and the whole humanitarian ideology. At the time, I simply pointed out how a whole logic, the logic of critical art, ended up turning on itself and consequently lost all that made for its legitimization in a representative logic, namely, that you produce virtue by giving pleasure. I went on to examine the dead ends in this desire to make art over as social intervention, a desire itself caught up in a caricatural revival of something that was once a lot more powerful – the project of transforming art forms into forms of a new way of life, notably in post-1917 Russia. By that, I didn't in any way herald the end of the 'aesthetic regime' of art.

For me, it's a regime that can absorb anything into its contents, but that is at the same time, in its form, always on the ropes, on a knife-edge. In the 'aesthetic regime', so as not to turn into a simple social game, it's normal for art to be always on the point of falling back into some version of a representative logic or an openly ethical logic. The difference between *Aesthetics and Its Discontents* and *The Emancipated Spectator* is that, in the first case, I tried above all to dismantle that logic, which once again made politics and aesthetics converge in a vague ethics; and in *The Emancipated Spectator* I tried to show that what was overwhelmingly interpreted in ethical terms could be interpreted in aesthetic terms. That's a bit the sense of what I did on Alfredo Jar's installations on Rwanda or Sophie Ristelhueber's photos of Israeli roadblocks on Palestinian roads. Those are works that are easy to annex, because of their subject, in this configuration dominated by the tall shadow of Lanzmann: the art of disaster, of catastrophe, of the unrepresentable. I tried to say that when an artist encloses photos of the Rwanda massacre in boxes, that doesn't mean we're dealing with the unrepresentable. In fact, what he then puts on the photo box is the person's name and story. As a result, he's able to displace the issue, it's no longer about what is representable or not, what you can or can't show; it's about what kind of relationship the work assumes between the visible and the sayable, what status it gives the victims of genocide and in what ways genocide can be the subject of a work of art.

In the first case, I tried to contest the logic of the unrepresentable, and in the second case, which I'd already started working on in relation to *Shoah*, I wanted to show that works catalogued as belonging to an art of the unrepresentable, as referring to a kind of ethical absolute, could be thought of differently, within an aesthetic logic in which it's not a matter of withdrawing from the visible but of reconfiguring the relationships between the visible and the sayable. We're not obliged to bury the images of the victims of genocide; we can just exhibit them differently. That's an artistic decision and not a tendency immanent to the 'aesthetic regime'. And, on my part too, it's a theoretical decision to displace the dominant forms of interpretation in relation to such artworks.

Concretely, I'm not saying that the 'aesthetic regime' is the latest, I have no idea about that; it seems to me that we can see three major kinds of functioning and that what dominates today is a logic deriving from the third kind of functioning, inasmuch as it's an inclusive logic, unlike the other two – but by the same token there's the fact that inclusion can mean banalization, and that fighting against the latter is always directed towards restoring other logics. It's a question of limits – there is no beginning or end, just immanent limits.

The Dispersal of Images; Another Art Regime?

Let's stick to the issue of the new, but in relation to film and the image. You sometimes say that you are 'a homomyny labourer': you take a term and you unpack the various practices and associations it covers. You've carried out this labour of unpacking on cinema which, as you show, is both an art and entertainment. But more and more often now films are also shown in museums or in live stage shows. Yet we get the feeling with this example that the specificity of this or that mode of experiencing cinema has little importance in your thinking about the practice ...

Without deciding whether or not there is a way of experiencing cinema that's irreducibly linked to the movie theatre, it's clear that there is a very strong bond between three things: film as an art form, film as a form of entertainment, and a specific place, the movie theatre, whether we give that place a theoretical status or not. Cinema is in a sense the one art that has stuck to its essential apparatus, even if film today is digital and film screening is going digital, too – that's another issue. Cinema has stuck to its apparatus and, even if DVDs and television are the platforms on which we view films more and more now, there is nonetheless a specificity to cinema compared to many of the arts. Today the darkened cinema hall is tending to become, as I once said, a refuge for the specificity of the art, whereas the museum is becoming a place where the arts merge. We need to hold on to that point, and it refers us back to one other thing: in cinema there's an absolutely fundamental temporal reality, the temporal closure of the film. And that remains very powerful – even if we've gone way beyond the canonical ninety minutes, with a blowout in running times that's sometimes considerable. It's the entertainment structure that has imposed a certain kind of closure and that produces a form of artistic constancy.

But, besides that, there are all sorts of ways of showing cinema. It's a formula that covers very diverse realities, like the use of projections on stage as part of the theatre set which is becoming more and more prevalent and which can sometimes include the screening of film extracts. This is a use of something that belongs to one art in another art that finally tends towards the instrumental. Moving images have also moved into museums and their presence can be divided into at least three kinds. First and foremost there is video art, an art form that is primarily and overwhelmingly an art of space. There was a time when video was seen as being linked to its specific medium, all that Raymond Bellour talks about. That was a time when people thought there was a specificity to the pencil of light that would produce a specific kind of artwork, a specific unfurling of moving pictures. And then there was what happened, which is that video art has become more and more like fresco art or the art of sculpture. In museums, video art is projected more and more on several screens, on a whole series of monitors that provide a sculptural dimension. It's becoming an art of space, and not of time any more – all the more so as the spectator rarely sees everything. I'm not talking about Christina Marclay's Venice film, which is a film about time that's twenty-four hours long. But even if a film only lasts ten minutes, the spectator very rarely stays till the end, given that there are still a few dozen other video works to cast an eye over in the show. The video device is therefore often going to be primarily spatial. It's independent of the platform anyway. There are a certain number of films that get into museum spaces, exhibition spaces, and that can be in 35 mm. James Coleman's film, *Retake With Evidence*, which was shown in Kassel in 2007 and which is a film based on the figure of Oedipus, was in 35 mm shown on a very large screen in a cage. We're in a museum space, there's a pane of glass through which the spectator can see what's happening on the screen and, if he likes, he can go into the space through side doors and stand or sit on the floor. There is a whole apparatus which, whatever the film's platform, turns it into something that first and foremost occupies a space.

There are also museum installations by film-makers that are generally not as interesting as their films. I'm thinking, for instance, of the installations Chantal Akerman has done based on her films, especially the film *From the East*. That shows people queued up waiting for the bus for the entire length of the film, which may have a significance that the artist feels she's transposed by having multiple screens that capture the waiting crowd at different moments. But, for me, the tension of the image is stronger in the film's temporal device than it could possibly be when spread out like that in this device of having multiple screens that function a bit like crowd barriers the spectator has to wind their way around. I won't say anything about the Godard exhibition, which was for me a classic example of the considerable gap in the way someone can both think about cinema and practise it with the force we're familiar with as an art of collage or superimposition, and who gets it completely wrong when he's given a space to fit out and has to use the already traditional gadgets of installation art to furnish a space he can't quite furnish with his notion of cinema. That's the second kind of presence of cinema in the museum – the film-maker who turns himself into an installation artist.

There is a third kind, which is where the museum has an auditorium where they run films that never get shown, or very rarely, in the movie theatres. I've written about Bela Tarr's films for the Beaubourg retrospective. I first came across his films in a retrospective at MoMA (the Museum of Modern Art, New York) ten years ago. In a way, the presence of cinema outside the movie theatres, including in spaces like museums, is divided into at least three forms: with one of them, we could say that museums offer picture theatres where the cinema industry does not, with the museum thereby functioning as a place of artistic legitimization. In the two other cases, the museum is opened up to artworks based on moving images, but those images become one element in a spatial apparatus. We know that many video artists started off as visual artists, painters, sculptors, while a certain number come from dance and others are linked to performance art. It makes you think there has indeed been a fragmentation: under the same banner as art and with the same support surface, what we get in the end is a Lessingian distance between an art of time and an art of space.

Our question about the parsing of cinema referred to Serge Daney's definition of the 'postmodern' in the early 1980s as an increase in the number of image platforms. We were saying a moment ago that you are against the idea of art or images being divided into eras. But what do you think is the significance of this multiplying of platforms? Are they able to be absorbed into what you more broadly call the 'aesthetic regime' of the arts that we've mentioned several times already? Or should the contemporary dispersal of images be incorporated into a new kind of visibility and perhaps an art regime that heralds or anticipates the fragmented film experience whose dimensions you've just reminded us of?

We can perfectly well define elements that go to make particular time periods except that they don't necessarily always match up. And they don't necessarily confirm the expected schemas. It's abundantly clear, to take a perfect example, that the break the talkies represented doesn't have the sense some people claim it has. By giving cinema words, the talkies allowed it to give silence a role. Above all, the talkies freed film from the model of sign language, pantomime, a whole host of ways images were indexed to words that were very powerful between the end of the nineteenth century and the 1930s. In a sense, the talkies liberated the images and movement from having to be a language.

It's obvious, anyway, that changes in the equipment play a role too: if we can go in anywhere with a tiny camera, like Pedro Costa at Fontainhas (a shanty town in Lisbon), then we're no longer stuck in the oppositions between studio cinema and realist cinema. It's also obvious that with a Steadicam, Bela Tarr no longer has to choose between a shoulder camera and a great whopping machine, and so he can invent new ways of varying movement and freezing it, in dealing with bodies. There's a whole series of transformations that define the possibilities of the image at various levels. The mobile phone started out as something represented. As such, it allowed people to produce unprecedented forms of emotion like the 'i love u' and the 'delete' that, in Eric Khoo's film, *Be With Me*, fill the whole screen to express the end of a love affair. Now it's used for making films. There's a whole series of layers incorporating video and electronic images, if you think of Brian de Palma and the way, in *Redacted*, he reprocesses, in a film that remains a feature film, documentary images that have already circulated on the Internet but that also give the cinematographic image the look of a computer screen. All that certainly plays a role, since technology is no longer used so much in perfecting images as in a dispersal and a de-hierarchization of kinds of images, of the public and the private, of art and the circulation of information and messages. In this sense, it would confirm the aesthetic regime's capacity for accommodation, rather than signing off on the death of the image.

We also have to incorporate the issue of spaces. Obviously the disappearance of local cinemas marks a periodization of cinema that we need to take into account; it corresponds to a kind of formatting, since the multiplex is a film-formatting tool, given that film as an art

was a bit undecided about whether it was really art or just entertainment, so the multiplex serves to sort the wheat from the chaff. There
is also cinema's entry into the museum, and the *cinémathèque* or film
institute, which becomes an exhibition space – a whole series of
extremely important transformations among which is this distribution or dispersal of different forms of the moving image.

The hard thing, the thing that's impossible for me, is to find a way
of harmonizing all these transformations, if we're to avoid falling
back into the schemas: triumph versus death of the image, aestheti-
cization versus anaesthetization, etc. Before you decide if a new tool
is a decisive turning point in the history of images, you have to take
the time to look long and hard at the images it produces.

Popular Cultures

*Different forms of popular culture turn up in your research but
almost always via artists. For example, there is an essay on television
since the days of Fritz Lang in* Film Fables *and a reflection on 'entertainment' via Vincente Minnelli in* The Intervals of Cinema. *Doesn't
such an approach risk taking us back to an opposition between high
and low, the noble and the humble that you criticize elsewhere?
What is your relationship to television or to the variety shows you
sometimes talk about?*

I worked hard at a certain time on things that belong to what we
call popular culture, the whole issue of working-class poetry, or song
in the nineteenth century, theatre – the idea, which seemed to me to
matter, always being to focus on forms of cultural appropriation that
break down barriers, rather than getting interested in a domain
known as 'popular culture'. In the beginning, I worked from a critical
stance in relation to the divisive notion that the people have their
own culture. Well, everything begins with the fact that some of the
people who make up the people don't want to have the people's
culture. In any case, what has always interested me over and above
anything else is the issue of borders – either that people who are
destined in theory for popular culture want another culture, or that
a so-called noble culture takes shape by incorporating elements of a
so-called popular culture, like pantomime, the circus, song, popular
music and so on, as occurred within the 'aesthetic regime' of the arts
through a series of forms and processes.

A second point is that I write about two sorts of things, about
kinds of experiences that are meaningful in relation to the issue of
division, and I write about the things I love. I choose works that have

struck me through their intrinsic force and that at the same time reveal something about the distribution of the sensible. That is actually the case with *Madame Bovary* more than *Mysteries of Paris*, and the films of Pedro Costa more than various TV series. In the world of 'media studies' and 'film studies', once we get away from France a bit, people fall upon you demanding to know why you're talking about Minnelli or Fritz Lang and why you haven't done anything on *The Wire*. The number of people who are working on *The Wire* in the Germanic and anglophone world is absolutely phenomenal. There is this very strong idea that, if you're on the left and you're interested in politics, you have to work on things labelled 'popular culture' and that any work that stands on its own instead of simply being a statistical or symptomatic element is 'elitist'. But what I'm interested in are issues to do with borders and trying to get across, in another language, a certain kind of emotion that I might feel looking at works of art that also play around with this idea of borders.

What interested me in Flaubert was this moment when literature becomes autonomous by turning into the interpreter of ordinary people's aspirations of having a different culture, a sensible world that's different from the one destined for them. I think people have a tendency to confuse two completely different things: the opposition between the legitimate culture and the non-legitimate culture, and an internal hierarchy linked to a refinement peculiar to sensation. In all cultural domains, high or low, we know very well that, once a practice produces a refinement in sensation, there are things we can no longer listen to or look at. This happens to people who like comics or hip-hop every bit as much as to people who like so-called classical music or museum art. In so-called popular forms of culture, there are in fact degrees of appreciation that are completely hierarchical. Someone in museum culture, classical music or so-called art films might think that rap is always rap. For someone who lives in the world of rap, certain forms of rap are hopeless, unlistenable to, unbearable. We really have to distinguish between all that. The level of aesthetic competence at the heart of all appreciation of any cultural or artistic form whatever is independent of its high or low status on a general scale.

I've just spent a fortnight or three weeks writing a book about Bela Tarr. I had to break off and go and see Lars Von Trier's latest film (*Melancholia*). When you've spent three weeks on Bela Tarr, you can't look at a Lars Von Trier and yet Lars Von Trier is a canonical auteur, acclaimed. It's an exigency that functions at the sensible level; in all domains, there are things you can no longer bear. There are

people whose refinement in so-called popular cultures is infinitely
greater than that of people who go off to classical music concerts or
to the Venice Biennale. You can get interested in all forms, but you
absolutely must reject the notion that it's something you have to do.
Why force yourself to read or see things you can't bear? Above all,
you have to distinguish the aesthetic hierarchies produced by the
aesthetic experience from all classifications of art forms in terms of
high and low.

*The question didn't necessarily bear on the defence of 'popular
culture' but also in a way took up the problem of the new that we've
already asked you about. Do you see the new in a form that is not
produced by a canonical auteur?*

The problem is, quite simply, that the notion of a 'canonical auteur'
doesn't define any specificity. A classification is not an identity. And
the idea of the 'new' is itself problematic. Aesthetic pleasure is always
more or less a mixture of recognition and surprise. There are very
simple melodies that touch you in a variety song or an opera aria
because you feel like you've already heard them, because they tie in
with other sensations, with moments in your life. It might be the
timbre of a clarinet or a horn in Mozart or a chorus in Verdi that
brings back songs from holiday camps. That is the 'François le
Champi' effect Proust described. There are moments when, on the
contrary, you get the feeling that no one has ever filmed a body or
a place in that light, that kind of movement, at that pace ... It might
be the beginning of Mizoguchi's *Miss Oyu*, or the dialogue between
Mouchette and the poacher in *Mouchette*, or the peasants going into
the empty manor house in *Satantango* ...
     But it's also clear that the possibility of experiencing something as
new and embracing it is itself linked to a whole practice of immersion
that makes you tolerant or intolerant of a spectacle. And this practice
is also a practice which, without our realizing it, links the sensation
we feel in the face of new forms to childhood memories. You have
to have liked cheap romances about unhappy children and felt nostalgia in abandoned houses, and that has to be mixed with Bresson,
Mizoguchi and lots of others for you to appreciate 'aesthetically' the
novelty of *Satantango*. That's why all this stuff about elitist art and
popular art is so stupid and so bogus.
     Of course, it's also a question of personal synesthesia. I've spent
my life reading the same books over and over again. On the one
hand, that has made most books unreadable for me (in a manner of
speaking because, at the same time, it's allowed me to read them very
fast and in the end to see very quickly what could make them

interesting symptoms). On the other hand, it has no doubt allowed me to see as works of art a lot of films that, in the majority view, are works of pure popular consumerism, and to be sensibly moved by films that, in the same majority view, are boring exercises for intellectuals. The issue is one of using your time in a way that either allows you to take the time necessary for what can enhance your ability to feel or, conversely, to take just the time it takes to understand how certain things are made and what they are symptoms of.

Part Four

Present Tenses

Mapping Possibilities

You say here and there that your job is to map the present. You specify that it's more like 'mapping possibilities'. The expression brings us to two questions. The first has to do with the metaphor of mapping itself. We could defend a thesis about history whereby, in a period when criticism is on the wane or is attacked in positions like yours that involve 'criticism of criticism', thought often defines its task as a mapping operation. That was a trope of thought in the 1970s and it is an image you resurrect, one that presupposes a disorientation we might well need to define and discuss. The first question is whether the mapping operation itself, or the metaphor of mapping, poses the problem of a position differential between the speaker and what is spoken about, what you are mapping. If so, it would then be something that partly contravenes your thinking. Doesn't the mapping metaphor pose a problem from this point of view in relation to the whole of your approach? The second question touches on the definition of the possible referred to several times in your philosophy. You sometimes speak of a 'system of possibilities', and you say that politics is the thing that can turn this 'system of possibilities' on its head. Are the 'system of possibilities' and the 'system of places' the same thing? How do we explore the possibilities of an era? How do we draw a line between what's possible and what's impossible, given – and this is something you say very early on in your work – that what's possible is not simply a product of a utopian or unbridled imagination that would lead us to construct spaces that are simply unreal?

We might start with the simplest thing there and say that the word 'possibility' is used in my texts with varying degrees of rigour and not necessarily with a single meaning referring to a theory of the possible. I'd say two things, though. In general, 'possible', the way I've used it, is not opposed to 'real', and 'possible' is not so much opposed to 'impossible' as it is to 'necessary'. In other words, 'possible' doesn't define something waiting to be actualized but more a way of thinking about what is. I like revisiting Aristotle's comment, which is that what is real is in any case possible. When I talk about possibilities, these are always possibilities that have been achieved, that have been actualized, and the question is basically what the status of that actuality is. In that sense, 'possible' is opposed to 'necessary'. But both are modalities of reality, ways of conceptualizing it. The necessary is the reality that cannot *not* be. 'Possible' is what could well *not* be, what is not the consequence of a sequence of circumstances that precede it and predetermine it. By the same token it's what keeps space open for connections other than the ones produced by the necessary. If we're thinking in political terms, we can establish a divide between what we can think in terms of the necessary and what we can think in terms of what exists as the emergence of the possible, the emergence of something that could very well not be. That also means the emergence of a scene, of an actuality, an event, that we could think of as belonging to a different distribution of the sensible, a different system of coexistence than the normal system of the sequence of reasons.

'Possible' is never, for me, in the nature of the imagination in the sense in which the imagination precedes reality. The possible is not a utopia, in the sense of something waiting to be actualized. It is a reality, an existence that is not preformed within the conditions of its existence, it's an excess in relation to the conditions of its existence. And so, by the same token, it defines something like another possible world. In other words, we can relate certain events from the real world back to connections that are different in kind from the normal connections. The phenomenal uprisings, from May 1968 to 'the Arab Spring', and different movements of the kind, define possibilities that have appeared in situations that weren't made to accommodate them. Suddenly it appears that a world without hierarchies can exist along with forms of popular presence, of assembly, that don't chime with the dominant logics. A whole series of forms of connecting, appearing, demonstrating and joining together in solidarity, can come to be. Small segments of other possible worlds are given in any actuality. Basically, the whole issue every time is whether we interpret things according to a logic of the necessary or according to a logic of the possible and whether we think of the emergence of something like an insurrection as an effect of causes or as something that wasn't anticipated. The issue is whether what happened in 1968, for instance, was a fashion phenomenon linked to the behaviour of young people and to consumerism and all that people say about the Thirty Glorious Years following the Second World War and the rest, which weren't as glorious as all that anyway, or whether it's the emergence of a one-off event that paints a different picture of those same years. Redefining a universe of possibilities in the end comes down to putting the possible back into the real and doing away with the necessary. It's a question of extending and interpreting whatever emerges.

Which brings me to mapping. The important thing is not the idea of making a map in the sense of drawing the outlines of the territory and its divisions, but of pitting a model of distribution and coexistence against the models of exclusion entailed in a certain view of time. I've already mentioned the years I spent studying Feuerbach when I was young. He has concepts about time as excluding and about space as the medium of coexistence. In a way, I've remained faithful to that or, rather, I've stumbled upon that idea another way: not thinking of an actuality as the consequence of a temporal sequence, and not thinking that what *is* expresses what was before and is called on to be eliminated by what is to come, but thinking of it as a different mode of presence. There exist several modes of presence, several kinds of sensible presentation at one and the same time. The important thing for me is not the idea of making a map. I wasn't all that keen, in that Foucault–Deleuze interview, on the theme of the new cartographer. This thinking in terms of cartography or topography is more to do with a critique of historical necessity. The essential thing is the idea that there are always several different kinds of present, several different times in any one time.

Figures of the Present, Modalities of the 'Police'

There is a tension in your work between the construction and elaboration of your categories of thought, on the one hand, and, on the other, the fact that ever since Althusser's Lesson *or* Logical Revolts, *you've been very big on the notion of a* conjuncture *and on ideological debates about the present. That's why, if we read your œuvre as separate from these localized public discussions, we get the impression that, beyond such recurring categories, it offers characterizations of the present that change with the works. If we take the question of politics, for instance, and in particular the question of democracy, we've noted a certain number of successive notions that describe the contemporary age of what you call 'the police', or a certain state of contemporary democracy: you talk about 'consensual democracy', 'post-democracy', 'epistemocracy', but also 'oligarchy'. You also talk about 'de-symbolization' of the social order. In other words, there is a set of categories that definitely evoke slightly different problems or difficulties, but that are there to try to define the present-day 'police'. This raises the question first of notional compatibility, and correlatively poses the problem of metamorphoses in what you call 'the police' in your political thinking. How do we describe the 'police' at present? How do we determine its most characteristic features, and how do we distinguish these from the police of the 1930s or of the Thirty Glorious Years you just mentioned? Those are the two parts of the question: the internal compatibility of these successive descriptions of the contemporary 'police', and the problem of the historicity of different kinds of 'police' and ways of distinguishing between them.*

Let's start with the fact that you're right to talk about 'descriptions'. Descriptions are always differentiations. Talking about 'post-democracy' does not mean defining a concept of democracy in the age of the 'post'; it's a way of displacing what the declared present of democracy is. I started using that expression in the 1990s as a way of answering the question: what currently exists as a system of power operations and modes of representation going by the name of democracy? Calling it 'post-democracy', 'consensual democracy' or any other name is first a way of creating a split in the notion. At the time, it was a way of getting out of the usual division, which meant that either you believe in parliamentary democracy and the democratic values of free speech, or you believe that all that is just a superficial cover for exploitation, etc. There is an interplay of descriptions that tries every time to break down or shatter the closure of a notion such as it is given in public opinion, including in the opinion of those keen to criticize or denounce it. That's the first point: a noun is a performer of displacement, and the logics of displacement oblige us to follow the re-compositions in the dominant logic – for example, to see how the dominant logic goes from the democracy vs totalitarianism opposition to this schizophrenic discourse that pits democracy against itself.

The second point concerns the notion of 'police' which has a double inflection in my work. On the one hand, it's a differential notion that allows me to say that what we call politics or the political in fact covers distinct practices, operations and systems of representation that are not homogeneous; that it is strictly the meeting of two fundamentally opposed heterogeneous logics. That's an initial moment in response to a question that became the title of a 1991 symposium: 'What is Politics?' The second moment, which is part of the maturing of my own work, tries to construct the concepts of 'police' and 'politics' in terms of a 'distribution of the sensible'. In a second phase, I was keen to define the police as a mode of symbolizing the common order and not as a state apparatus, not as government practices or the disciplining of bodies. I then opposed a saturated structuring of the sensible order that places people and things in common according to a logic of places and identities with a logic that shatters that structure by opposing it with this supplement, this 'part of those who have no part' that has no place in it. From this structural point of view, you can define a radical heterogeneity, whereas, from the point of view of the analysis and polemical reconfiguration of the present, you're always dealing with certain forms of composition and their relationship. This creates a tension in the use of the word that sets off the simplifications of those who think I call the state apparatus 'police' and whatever contests it, 'politics'. That would be a pretty stupid way of putting the problems and solving them. There's always an overlap between deconstructing the political scene as it is given and positing concepts that can serve as operators in defining what's happening at any given moment or conjunction of what we call politics. It's not like we have the 'police' up to their usual tricks in their corner, and politics responding in its corner, opposite. There is a certain interplay in the middle of which state operations are defined, but also the whole media construction of the common world in which those operations occur, and then there are the forms of contesting this logic.

That said, if we try to think through a history of the 'police' – of the present disposition of the politics–police relationship, to be more precise – the concept of consensus may be an overarching concept. Consensus, as I've tried to redefine it, is based on a notion of common opinion that dates from the end of the 1980s, from during the Rocard government in France, when there was the idea that we were now about to define a national consensus. That was also the moment when the original socialist programme was finally liquidated, the moment when the ideological process that was Mitterrandism, this marriage between a limp left-wing ideology and the hard-line reactionary right, pulled off a fusion that, to cut a long story short, basically defined the ideology of *Esprit* in the 1990s. I started off with the word 'consensus', which characterized that particular conjunction, the moment when you realized that what the socialists wanted and what the RPR[56] wanted wasn't all that different, that it relied on common analyses and on programmes of forms of government that didn't have a lot of differences. I tried to turn this into something like the concept behind a specific relationship between politics and the 'police'.

Defining our age as the age of consensus means two things, in my view. Firstly, it designates a certain number of state practices, and the constitution of a relationship between government practices and forms of international and supranational government that are themselves linked to financial institutions. We could say that consensus consists in the construction of this globally common world, which is essentially structured by market forces and the rule of profit, with the construction of relationships between the state and supra-state institutions and of relationships between supra-state institutions and international financial institutions defining the share of the states and the way in which national governments reflect within the nation the consequences of the global order – in the destruction of systems of solidarity, protection and social security, in diminishing job security, and in the liquidation or privatization, when it's profitable, of what were public assets, the domain of the common. Consensus is primarily this redefinition of the common in terms of relationships between peoples and governments; it's the construction of an international, global logic of domination that never really existed. We could say that Europe means a certain capitalism that never really existed before. That's a primary aspect, this reconstruction of what is common space for singular peoples within this global space, the whole set of government operations that produce this reconfiguration.

Secondly, in terms of the 'distribution of the sensible', consensus is also and by the same token a sensible configuration of the common world as a world of necessity, and as the world of a necessity that eludes the power of those living within that necessity. If consensus is in a sense this whole set of government operations I was talking about, it's also the construction of obvious facts about the sensible world within which these operations can be carried out without too much trouble, in particular the intellectual, media construction

[56] The Rassemblement Pour la République is the main right-wing political party. *Translator's note.*

which intellectuals, historians, sociologists, university philosophers and television and newspaper journalists have all collaborated in. It's the construction of this world where we're faced with necessity, where no possibility exists, no choice, but only the choice of the best way to manage necessity. This also means the construction of a common world in which the dimension of conflict is essentially replaced by the relationship of knowledge to ignorance. Consensus includes this construction of the global system of information, of knowledge as a sort of triumph of the logic of education, of mindlessness, whereby every event, every thing that happens, must be presented as something that has to be interpreted. I've tried to describe this information system by saying it's not at all about drowning people in a flood of images, but the exact opposite: it's a matter of presenting everything that happens to them as something that's hidden from them, to which they have no access, and which has to be explained to them, or 'decoded', to use the expression that has now become their open sesame.

Consensus is the gradual putting in place of this practice by governments and intergovernmental agencies as well as this representation of the common world that plays up its opacity to those who are involved in it, at once both pushing the necessity of a government of experts and the necessity of being constantly handed the keys to what is happening. We could define this as being at the heart of the current police logic, with the fact that the current logic builds extremely wide margins and pushes back a whole host of populations, population movements, and forms of resistance which are more and more marginalized. In a way, the police order is constructed more and more like something to which there is no collective response, and in relation to which there can therefore only be the displacement and downward spiral of individuals. The police order is constructed as something that no longer has to face conflictual proceedings that are legitimate in the sense of legitimized by an analysis of situations, but only acts that are erratic, sick, criminal or whatever. The police order is rounded off by the fact that anything that isn't caught up in the system becomes a matter of marginality, migration, pathology, delinquency, terrorism and so on. By the same token, the consensual order is forced to endow itself with reinforced police tools to control the margins and the leaks that it necessarily never ceases creating.

We can clearly see the connection, in what you've just been saying, between consensus, epistemocracy and the de-symbolization of the social order – or, in any case, the absence of the work of symbolization that would otherwise allow these leaks, these margins, these

*individual skirmishes to constitute a different common world. Does
this also mean that in such descriptions or characterizations of the
present, there is a historical cause and effect? Or that they are above
all strategic, that they serve to shatter a current commonplace that
you seem to feel is detrimental to understanding the present? Perhaps
not all the descriptions have the same weight.*

Among those descriptions, some have a polemical role that's defined
by the configuration of whatever given needs to be called into question. It's a matter of breaking down a common notion and working
on it from the inside. Other descriptions define a single aspect of the
process. If we're talking about 'epistemocracy', we can clearly see
that we're defining one aspect of the process, namely, the growing
legitimization of forms of government by science, including in the
absurd situation where everyone can see that we're blindly conform-
ing to so-called scientific norms that are, we note, what's more,
ineffective and potentially manipulated by crooks. Anyone could see
that Sarkozy knew nothing about economics, that he relied on economic truths people thought were eternal ten years ago and that have
since collapsed; and that he struggled to hang on to a rating awarded
by agencies made up of financiers who were themselves largely
corrupt. 'Epistemocracy' designates this representation of power that
is necessary to its functioning, not the effectiveness of a government
run by science based on the Platonic model – or what a few techno-
crats still dream of that as being.

*The 'police' can also, in a way, be standardized according to this
scale of rights, equalities and different forms of access granted. You
sometimes say – it crops up throughout your work – that in a way
there are good and bad eras of policing. So, there must be certain
criteria that allow us to say one police is more or less favourable to
the population than another, surely?*

Yes, but once again only by avoiding substantializing the police and
politics. There is a state in the relationship between the police and
politics, a state in politics when it makes progress. That means the
conditions for a better life are better organized at one point than
they are at another. There are very simple criteria – we might think
of corruption. We know there are countries where you can't get
anything without paying the policeman or functionary concerned,
etc. The fact of living in countries where the administration is basically not systematically corrupt is extremely important. But that
doesn't define a 'good' police. It defines a national state that's favourable to relationships between contradictory logics, a system of

constraints on government practice. Whether the normal reaction when people go out on the streets is to fire on them, or the opposite, to not fire on them, is one criterion that allows us to distinguish the state of those relationships. We might recall that the law proposing to reform the universities[57] had to be buried in 1986 when hostile demonstrations ended in a death. I remember once taking a petition to the Élysée when Chirac was in power. We arrived at the little side door and then we went up and saw someone in the Cabinet. It doesn't matter who it was we saw or what happened to our petition. But *that*'s an important criterion, the fact that you don't have to be frightened of stepping inside the headquarters of the supreme government of the nation. Once again we can't dissociate the state of the police force from the state of political capacity.

Ruptures, Revolutions, Revolts

A lot has been said about revolutions regarding the events of 2011 in parts of the Arab world. When it comes to any historic rupture, choosing the right words is an intrinsically political challenge. What word do you prefer to use yourself? You've talked on several occasions about a 'collective capacity' in a bid to pinpoint this category of moments. Foucault gives the impression of preferring the term 'uprising' to 'revolution'. For his part, Deleuze tries to trash the idea that a revolution can be associated with a teleological representation, which is why he prefers the notion of 'becoming revolutionary' ...

I don't really have a good term to suggest for designating what is, after all, the mark of a break happening in the present, starting notably with the 'Arab Spring'. I've got nothing against the term 'revolution', but it's important to disconnect the link between revolutions and *the* revolution, between revolutionary events and conjunctures and the revolution as the fulfilment of a historic necessity, the radical transition from one mode of production to another, according to the Marxist mode. We've seen, in modern history, revolutions that have lasted three days, a few months, a few years.

---

[57] The Loi Devaquet provided most notably for a more competitive university selection process. Student protests against it ended in the death of a student, Malik Oussekine, in the Quartier Latin in December 1986. *Translator's note.*

What is a revolution for me? It's the moment when a whole order of the visible, the thinkable, the possible, finds itself abruptly sent packing and is replaced. If we think of the concrete sense of the word, what it's become, in the modern world, is the moment when the world starts to turn the other way, whereas the initial sense was a return to the starting point. Having done a lot of work on 1830, 1848 and 1871, I hold that we can speak of a revolution wherever there is a sudden interruption in a whole given symbolic order, and wherever things that were absolutely unthinkable appear to be possible, along with a popular actor who had no place on the preceding stage. The event of speech is the way this actor names himself by once more seizing on those excess words, 'liberty', 'equality' and so on. Something like that did indeed happen in Tunisia and in Egypt. We need to reject the argument that goes that, since none of that managed to bring about either the overthrow of state power or the end of capitalism, it wasn't a revolution. That argument is also applied to the revolutions of the past. People say that an interruption is not enough, that you have to organize yourself over the long haul to have a final and definitive revolution. But a revolution is a sequence of time in which the power relationships and the whole construction of the sensible and thinkable world we live in suddenly find themselves disrupted. That lasts for different lengths of time, but we can call any process of the kind a revolution. An 'uprising' designates the fact that people are on the move, but it doesn't designate the important process of transforming the scene of the possible. We need to be able to use the term 'revolution' again to describe upheavals, over a certain sequence of time, in power relationships and in the very representation of what places people in a community, with consequences over the short term, medium term or long term that can vary greatly.

Foucault said somewhere apropos of revolutions that the role of the intellectual 'should today be to re-establish for the image of revolution the same degree of desirability as existed in the nineteenth century'. What's your own role? What are your thoughts about intervening in the press?

I wouldn't talk about a role as an intellectual. I'd talk about my role as a researcher and writer. The thing that runs through all my writings, after all, is the idea of maintaining the desirability of those states of total subversion of power relationships and of all the systems of representation that make these power relationships acceptable, normal or inevitable. I don't know if that's the work of an intellectual. For thirty-five years, I've tried to keep a space open for thinking – which also means a space for effective power, for desirability

– about all that I've understood by the noun, emancipation. That work can, in certain circumstances, come down to the forum of an op-ed page. But the condition of an op-ed page is nevertheless to intervene wherever you can do something. Writing a column to say to the Tunisians 'that's really good, what you're doing' is not something I like doing. Writing a column about something that might concern France's illegal immigrants or the Romany people, something close to home that I have a handle on, the possibility of suggesting another mode of visibility – yes.

For me, there are really two kinds of work and of intervention: there are efforts that seek to constitute something like the sensible fabric of the possibility of a different world, and interventions that try to re-describe a situation. Basically, there is this twin effort. There is an attempt to shatter – as much at the level of conceptual, supposedly theoretical, analysis as at the level of ticking off current police watchwords – common notions that are most often shared by upholders of a certain order and those who think they're contesting that order. But these interventions are deployed against a certain backdrop, which is the work that constructs this sensible fabric and allows us to think that the people who are talking about emancipation are reasonable and that they are proposing desirable things.

We'd like to get a better idea of how you see the effects of political subjectivization. Can we differentiate these effects as a function of the benefits they procure, in other words, beyond the fact that they may well redefine the sharing or divisions of the social – effects in terms of law, or well-being, or inequalities, for example? Is it important to you that we set ourselves criteria for the effectiveness of political subjectivization, even if these criteria don't appear in Disagreement *or in the most canonical essays of your political thought?*

For me, there is one fundamental criterion for the effectiveness of political activity, and that is whether that activity creates, enables and extends the institutionalization of the conditions themselves for its being carried out. This means effectiveness is always subjective first of all: it's an increase in the power of the political subject as such. That said, this increase in power also shows up in the readjustment of the balance of power as it is registered in state institutions and social institutions. If a political movement, uprising or revolution – whatever you want to call it – results in the capacity for people to get together and demonstrate and to have elections where the vote isn't systematically rigged, then that's always an effect, even if it's included in an electoral system where the people endorse some oligarchy. We know very well that all rights are limited by the material possibility of benefiting by them, but the principal right is the right to be a political actor without fear. The fact that I can go down into the street with the idea in mind that the most probable risk is not that they'll shoot at me but that they might knock me around a bit and send me to gaol, is very important. Beyond the purely material aspect, the creation of conditions whereby the people are allowed to be present as such, as different from the people embodied in the state, is a fundamental criterion of political effectiveness.

There are also criteria for what a political struggle might produce in terms of equality in living standards. We can see this clearly today with the European endeavour to destroy all that once existed as a common fabric of solidarity: the fact that the poor could go to the same hospitals as the rich, that there was equality in living standards when it came to education, healthcare, public transport, etc. This is something that comes directly under the measurable effects of political struggle; sadly, it also comes directly under the measurable effects of the rout of the political. I'm not at all into the discourse of these people who say that all that is never anything more than a trap, that if there exist social rights, a welfare system, it's solely to railroad the working class and wipe out any resistance. That discourse is simply not interesting and in the end only shores up the present oligarchic offensive. Conversely, there has always been a correlation between these extensions of a fabric of relative equality and any extension of ways of exercising the capacity of each and every person. The effects of the political struggle can be seen simultaneously in such subjective growth and in the conditions for the equality of rights, and also a certain number of minimal conditions required for existence.

A New Internationalism?

You talk at the end of Disagreement *about a 'world police'. But when you talk about this 'world police', in which the humanitarian plays an important role, you challenge the idea that a world politics exists in your sense of the term. 'The "world" can get bigger. The universality of politics doesn't get any bigger.'[58] So, politics as you see it can't have the world as its scale or as its original setting, even if that is sometimes one of the presuppositions of globalization in its various forms. In Marxism or in the new globalization, there is often the idea of an original common humanity that we'll get back to at the end of the historic process. That's a big wrap for contemporary*

[58] *Disagreement, Politics and Philosophy* (Minneapolis, University of Minnesota Press, 1999; translated by Julie Rose), p. 139.

*globalization as a phenomenon that would finally give the process
of emancipation its true measure or scale. Without going into this
telos, the question is nonetheless how to interpret the constitution
of political scenes that are postnational, and can be supranational
for institutions, or transnational through social movements? How,
for instance, can the spaces of struggle that have been opened up
over the past thirty years, or, at least, opened up again after the
decline of working-class internationalism and the end of the Cold
War, be incorporated into your notion of the relationships between
the police and politics?*

There are two things here: the question of political subjectivization,
and the question of the perspective of humanity linked to it ('The
Earth belongs to mankind alone'). Let's start with the idea that
might connect them – internationalism. The Workers' Internationale, before becoming a simple tool of the Soviet state and Stalinist
power, was after all primarily a conjuncture of social movements
that were national. A national movement is not the same thing as
a nationalist movement. It's a movement that, starting with effective
social groups in a defined conjuncture of class struggle, is capable
of constructing ways of universalizing situations. This relationship
of the local to the capacity for universalization it enables is very
important for me in defining the political. These processes of universalization developed in opposition to nation-states that, here and
there, enforced the scaled-up application of a certain order of domination. Today, it's all too clear that internationalism of that kind
does not exist. What does exist, on the other hand, is a capitalist
internationale that's perfectly set up to impose its rule. The supranational structures that currently exist, starting with what's known
as Europe, are its creations and instruments. On the one hand, they
impose its rules on the various peoples of Europe through the
member states. On the other hand, they make the conditions for
struggle more difficult since they amount to an absent enemy, in
the face of which it's very hard to construct these processes for
universalizing the local that were once constructed in opposition
to a state or to an employer group. And the anti-globalization
movements and demonstrations like the ones in Seattle, Genoa and
elsewhere don't compensate for this loss. These movements say that,
since the stage is global, we have to act globally. But such action
is essentially symbolic action, attacking the organs of global governance wherever they periodically come together, and not where
they produce their destructive effects on jobs and on the social
fabric of this or that country. At the same time, those organs of

global governance are not the ones that cause order to prevail in our nations and societies. With this distribution of tasks, there is a split between struggles that take place at the local level and these symbolic global actions, which tend to be the actions of specialists of the international.

The gap between that and the perspective of emancipated humanity is obviously marked by the fact that the human issue is today also the business of specialists. With NGOs, we have a whole host of organizations located directly at points where the world order is suffering; they're there at all the points where that world order defines something that's more drastically intolerable than something else: refugees, the starving, the persecuted. I'm not one of those who say that that's just charity and not politics, which seems to me far too simple. We know that very often NGO activists are activists who fight the powers of the world government, on the ground, and help promote awareness and a way of organizing people who are victims around the place. With movements of the Avaaz kind trying to echo their action, we can clearly see that there's an effort to constitute a sort of international public opinion capable of bringing its weight to bear on whatever is intolerable in what's happening – in Syria, in Africa and other countries. That's important in redefining forms of sensitivity to the political and in constituting a new spirit of internationalism but, otherwise, none of these movements has the capacity to turn a unique situation into a universality. In fact, the philosopher who called for a new Internationale, namely Derrida, did so against a backdrop of suffering humanity – not humanity in the making. And it was Derrida, again, who actually completely disconnected politics, which he identified with sovereignty, from the figure of the other, the guest you host but also the one whose hostage you are. In brief, for Derrida, there is the same, who is of the order of the sovereign subject, and the radically other, who is the human being inhabited by the power of the inhuman. This comes down to excluding the very figure of the political subject as a power for change in the order of identity. For me, it's only by reconstituting social movements that can fight here and there in concrete forms of rallying against equally concrete enemies that we can hope to resurrect a true sense of the emancipation of humanity.

Migrant Bodies, Suffering Bodies

You've often been appealed to on behalf of illegal immigrants. You also recently referred to the fate of the Romany in Europe. Foucault

*spoke of boat people as 'an omen of the future'. What is the place
of the influx of migrants in your work?*

We could try and start again and say that I'd like to separate the
issue of the migrant influx from a certain pathos to do with that
section of humanity that's doomed to the condition of being refugees,
the idea that contemporary man is a man of the camps. There is a
pathos surrounding refugees, camp-dwellers, as a signifier of contemporary existence. I think we need to get back to the fact that
migrants today are first and foremost people who move so they can
gain the means of having a better life. There are, of course, different
phenomena, people who are parked in camps after massacres, forced
displacements of populations. But we need to start with the fact that
migrants are people who move the way we move in the job market,
to try and get to places where they think they'll be able to earn a
living, send for their families, or set up a circuit to send money home.
We must not start out, from the word 'go', by putting the migrant
issue in the same basket as some ontological condition, or as a scene
of political division. In a way, migrants seek to cross borders; they
encounter this dual logic of the system we were talking about earlier,
whereby for capital to circulate freely, what you have to do, on the
other hand, is to stop people from circulating freely. On the one
hand, we tell people that if they want to keep their job, they can do
so only on condition of agreeing to go and work in Malaysia or
China; on the other hand, we have to be able to stop at the border
people who are not from Malaysia or China but from Kurdistan,
Ethiopia, Ghana or some other country in Africa or the Middle East.
Here we get something like a violent clash between the simple possibility of living and the international order, such as it's structured.
Even where we need immigrants, we first need to control their flow.
I recently saw Sylvain George's film, *Qu'ils reposent en révolte (Let
Them Rest in Revolt)* on the Calais jungle, in which we can clearly
see that that's a situation no one can manage to construct politically.
The support activity is always a bit out of whack, since those people
are there primarily to get to somewhere else. What they're looking
for in any situation, including in relationships with the police and
with the wire fences stopping them, is how to get through. They're
not there as political subjects. It's different from the situation, whether
in France or elsewhere, where people work for five or ten years but
still aren't made legal, aren't given the necessary papers. That is a
genuinely political situation, meaning that we've got people there
who are both included and excluded at the same time and who can
objectify, in the form of the different illegal-immigrant movements

we've seen, this relationship between exclusion and inclusion. We can clearly see, in the tension between what's happening at the borders and what's happening at the centre, how the political space is torn apart, with the migrant being two things at once. He is solely a migrant who has to deal with an order of policing that blocks anyone from getting through, but he is also a potential political subject the moment he claims the right to live exactly where he is, the way everyone else does. This tension is extremely hard to resolve and that's when you realize that we don't have internationalism, in the sense in which anything to do with the flow of immigrants is constantly divided between a scene of confrontation between police and individuals and a genuinely political scene involving the assertion of a part of those who have no part.

From that point of view, the right of foreigners to vote is fundamental to the reconfiguration of the scene.

It is indeed fundamental to the inclusion of this part of those who have no part in a much bigger political universality. It's certainly criminal on the part of the official left always to have been so lukewarm on the problem and to have accepted the abject argument that the French weren't capable of dealing with it. It's not hard to see what's behind the anti-politics practised by the so-called political parties of excluding precisely what constitutes the very possibility of a political scene. That's not to say that the participation of foreigners in municipal elections will change much; that's not the problem, but it matters at the level of the reconfiguration of common space, of the very idea of identity, of what it means to be French, to be a citizen of a country. What ties the two things together is the overall construction of a limited membership. For an ideal political scene, we'd need to tie several things together: the rights of migrants, the rights of immigrants, of those who've settled here, and then the issue of the general instability of existence, which is coming increasingly under threat. Some people are familiar with precariousness on the economic level which can go from having the most menial jobs to the problem of all these postdoctoral students all over Europe who are still out of work at thirty or forty years of age. There is a general condition of precariousness that goes from economic marginality to the actual impossibility of getting going, via the denial of rights, and this overall precariousness today probably forms the basis of a possible subjectivization; it may well be the thing most readily turned into a universal, but at the same time it's kept compartmentalized. We get this gap, then, between these rallies of jobless graduates which people immediately describe as being nothing more than movements of yuppies, of petit-bourgeois hipsters, and the situation of these migrants who burn their fingers so they can't be identified by the European police.

Humans, Non-Humans: On Political Ecology

Political ecology keeps evolving and being beefed-up and made more complex as an intellectual tradition. It seems to us that we could reread it with the conceptual tools you offer, perhaps by forcing the issue, which is something you would no doubt not agree with. Anti-specism is one part of extreme ecology – to which we could possibly add the ecological thinking of Bruno Latour around the idea that we could get 'non-humans' to talk in a 'parliament of things' – and it implicitly uses a criterion of the political similar to yours. After all, it's a matter of reconfiguring parties and parts, of making visible subjects or objects that are not normally seen, such as animals and sometimes even things that are part of our daily lives: in short, giving a voice to what would otherwise be just noise. It seems to us, though, that this possible extension poses a difficulty. Indeed, your definition of the political almost always implies the idea of language, of a political animality defined as 'literary animality' – so much so that you would presumably not grant the possibility of political subjectivization to 'non-humans'. How do you evaluate this tension, this incompatibility that's sort of split between the mode of thinking of a section of radical political ecology and your own thinking?

There is a decisive point of difference for me. Politics has always been defined in terms of a polemic about the human, about the distribution of human groups, the capacities they're acknowledged to have, about the capacity for speech they're granted. Politics for me has always played out around these questions: are these humans true humans, do they belong to humanity, or are they half-human or falsely human? Are these people, who are making a noise with their mouths, speaking or not speaking? Politics has always been defined within a political relationship in which the dividing up of human beings is called into question, starting with the capacity of uncounted humans to get themselves counted by themselves declaring their membership and their capacity. I don't think you can have politics without the possibility of subjectivizing the 'part of those who have no part'. Subjectivization happens through a declaration that reconfigures the division between human beings. What lies beyond that? Of course there exists a theory of equality that goes beyond the political scene and in which the acknowledged or asserted capacities of humans are redistributed; and there is a concern for equality that says there has to be equal consideration for all living things, or that says negatively that a proper human community is a community that sets itself limits and declares itself not capable of anything and everything.

Once we've said that, there remains a whole host of problems straight out of the fables of La Fontaine: are we going to represent wolves or lambs? We're familiar with all the brawls over biological diversity, namely, that it's all very well to put wolves back in the mountains, but it's not quite so nice for the sheep and, anyway, the shepherds can speak for the sheep. That's where we basically fall back on this problem: the representatives of animals, of nature, of the Earth and of things, are always going to be humans, which means human interests. If the shepherds or breeders did a different job, they'd be less keen on the conservation of sheep – that's the first problem.

The second problem is that the idea that wolves are useful in biodiversity and that biodiversity is useful in saving the planet is an idea peddled by people who pose as specialists of the bigger picture, holders of a knowledge lacking in people who are locked into their relationship with their land and their livestock. Even if there are tensions within the ecological conglomerate, the premise of ecology takes us back to a certain model of politics as defending common interests with the aid of science. Once again we come up against the idea that, for there to be politics, we need there to be management of the planet, of natural resources, and that this can't be done by just anyone. There is a tension within ecology between what we might call support for radical egalitarianism and support for technocracy, a technocracy that validates government by scientists. You'll tell me that there is a radical ecology that's very different, but there is nonetheless this very strong meshing of ecology and the rule of science, with all that this implies. The most widespread ecological discourse is the one that says that the poor don't know how to warm themselves, dress themselves, build houses or protect their environment, and that they're the ones who are stuffing up the planet. I don't think we humans can define subjectivization for non-humans, or otherwise we are necessarily going to give people the capacity to represent things. When Latour says 'we represent humans, and we represent things every bit as much', the difference is nonetheless that humans can challenge those who represent them, like the Indignant of Madrid who said 'you don't represent us'. Things, wolves or sheep, can never divest humans of the representativeness they've given themselves.

The question of representation you've just raised is not absent from the universe of the unadulteratedly human either: the problem of delegating, of having spokesmen, of power, and the asymmetries in capacities all these involve are always present.

There is the question of what makes politics possible in general. It's the possibility for anyone at all to get up and declare their capacity. This self-declaration is furthermore what gives potential legitimacy to all forms of representation at the end of the day. Wherever this capacity is absent, representation becomes a lot more dubious. The empirical argument that objects are never going to take action and defeat their representatives at the elections may seem derisory, but it refers us to something more fundamental, which is the presupposition of a shared capacity that can manifest itself in its own voice.

We might agree with what you were saying about ecology as leaning towards the government of science. But there is also a tendency towards radical democracy in this current of thinking, with Arne Naess or Isabelle Stengers. In these examples, there is an idea that's common to your thinking, which is that any authority based on science remains problematic ...

The democratization of science comprises two things, the idea that the laboratory is everywhere and that science is shared. But, once again, it's shared by humans. At the centre of the democratization of science we find the idea of a capacity shared by both patients and doctors. There again, in spite of everything, we remain within the sphere of human capacity. The democratization of science is defined by a human capacity to think and speak, and whenever it extends to animals, it is as an object of concern and not as an entity that's going to interrupt you.

A World That Has Lost All Sense of Reality: How Do We Inform Ourselves?

In The Emanicipated Spectator, *you put forward a strong thesis that takes up an idea found in various forms in Virilio and in Baudrillard but the other way round – that an indistinct flow of images leads to the loss of a sense of the world's reality. We are not suffering, you say, from an overflow of images – quite the contrary, we're faced with strategies for withholding information that select and order images and eliminate from them 'anything that might exceed the simple superfluous illustration of their meaning'.[59] In this*

---

[59] *The Emancipated Spectator* (London: Verso, 2009; translated by Gregory Elliott), p. 96.

sidestepping of the dominant anti-media discourse, what protocols do you propose, not for decoding information, but for orienting ourselves, informing ourselves amidst this proliferation of images and data that file across our screens, the press, the Internet?

I don't have any specific strategy for dealing with information. There's what we glean from the Internet. There's news coming at you from left and right if you know people who are more especially tied up in what might be happening in the demonstrations in Tahrir Square, or in some movement for occupying a university or the main square in some state in America, what might be happening at a border or has happened in the suburbs of London. There's a whole heap of news that's channelled through activist relays. We all know people linked to a squat, to a group of illegal immigrants or to people who have a relationship, through the Cimade[60] or RESF, to the situation of illegal immigrants, or to detention centres, or enforced escorting of refugees back to the border. We all more or less know people who come from Palestine or from this or that Maghreb country, who bring their own news and bits of information. We know there are also lots of artists who, in the last ten years, have brought us political news. The first time I heard talk of the American process of 'extraordinary rendition', it was at a performance lecture given by (media artist) Walid Raad in Beirut. I'd never heard of it before that. Artists sort of cover the territory, they're on the ground everywhere, and they produce more or less militant documentary work or even more sophisticated work, to describe differently situations that are otherwise framed by the media; they tell us about situations outside that frame.

We try to work our way through these channels, knowing that information always reaches us filtered, through spokespeople. On YouTube you can see people talking from Tahrir Square or any other square without really being able to take the measure of these people and work out what they represent, whether or not they're sincere in what they say, who they're speaking for.

We have a whole host of elements that allow us to sort of burst open the straitjacket of information such as it is, limited and over-interpreted from the outset, but it's hard to have a decent strategy, and our informers also bring us their analysis at the same time and that might be Marxist, Negrist, Agambian, even Rancierian at times.

---

[60] The Cimade is a French NGO formed by Christian activists in the Second World War to assist all those displaced by the war and Jewish refugees in hiding; it continues that work today, especially supporting undocumented immigrants. *Translator's note.*

The issue is what we ourselves want to do with this information. We know that, when all's said and done, no political assessment is ever based on totalizing information and checking it exhaustively. Such assessment works through configurations of the situation in which you have to decide, regardless, whether you see Ben Ali or Assad as defenders of secularism and women's rights or as bloodthirsty tyrants, and whether the people who rally in the streets against them are freedom fighters, Islamists, or poor manipulated stooges.

It's no accident that you bring up artists as mediators working towards an information transfer and a critique of the way informa-tion reaches us ...

Yes, obviously what artists offer us is not information that's been amended but modes of sensible presentation that shatter the very frameworks of representation. I've talked about this on several occa-sions in relation to the Middle East and the important role there of artists who've made it their business to demolish the image of people as victims, which we see in Lebanon with the fictions and fake archives of The Atlas Group; and the films of Joana Hadjithomas and Jalil Khoreige, who shift the perspective by talking about disap-pearance – of people, of places, of images themselves – instead of presenting images of the horrors of war; and the performances of Lina Saleh and Rabih Mroué, who show us how we can also laugh at the situation; and plenty of others ... The important thing is in these manœuvres of reconfiguration: showing things we didn't see before, changing the way bodies are present and represented in front of us, the way their power or powerlessness is shown.

The *Fait Divers*, Ordinary Lives, Investigation

Since we're talking about news and current affairs, we may as well talk about the news in brief, which you've written about several times. You say that with the news in brief, the fait divers, 'causality is plunged into the world of ordinary life'. [61] *In* Aisthesis, *there is a chapter on Stendhal and* The Red and the Black *in which you mention the way Stendhal worked through the* Gazette des tribun-aux, *the newspaper that reported from the law courts, to try and capture 'the dangerous energy and intelligence of the children of the*

---

[61] 'Poetique du faits divers', Jacques Rancière interviewed by Hervé Aubron and Cyril Neyrat, in *Vertigo*, July, 2004; reprinted in *Et tant pis pour les gens fatigués* (Paris, Amsterdam, 2009), p. 398.

people'.[62] *Are you sensitive to the contemporary* fait divers *despite the fairly dreadful media coverage, which seems to strip it of the power you give it? Do you strive to restore the energy and intelligence of ordinary lives?*

I think the glory days of the *fait divers* are behind us. In actual fact, I only talked about the *fait divers* because I was asked to do so by the review *Vertigo* for a special issue. That allowed me to think of the irruption of the *fait divers* as being linked to this dual phenomenon of the appearance of these energies, at once intellectual and emotional, possessed by the people, and the breaking of the bonds of traditional causality that occurred at the same time. I analysed the moment the *fait divers* appeared as the moment when the people became present also in the form of appalling crimes, improbable aspirations, incomprehensible acts, the moment when the individuals who make up the people showed themselves to be capable of anything. The *Gazette des tribunaux* first appeared in 1827. It was a way of popularizing trials that was very different in form from the literature of lament and the usual leaflets. I don't know if Stendhal was himself a great reader of the *Gazette*, but the story of Julien Sorel's crime which appeared three years later was actually constructed by merging two such reported crimes. I once said that we could establish a clear link between *Madame Bovary* and the creation of the Worker's Internationale as two ways in which the event of the right to speak entered the lives of ordinary people. There is a much more direct link in Stendhal with this moment when the people appear, which was marked by the revolution of 1830, but also with the attention that was suddenly paid to the way popular energies were expended on crime. What's interesting in the *Gazette des tribunaux* is that you can see the dual treatment of the people at work: there are reports of crimes that touch on the conflicts and deviancies of everyday life, in which we're shown morons who turn up without being able to talk or understand what's happening to them; and then there are the complex crimes, well-planned crimes, involving lower-class individuals who no longer take the form of the village idiot of comedy, but represent the intrusion of this dangerous being who is now capable of anything. There was a great age of the *fait divers*, which was also the great age of revolutions and the novel.

Of course, we're no longer in that powerful paradigm; we've moved on to another phase of the *fait divers*, which began fifty years

---

[62] 'The Plebeian Heaven', in *Aisthesis: Scenes From the Aesthetic Regime of Art* (London: Verso, 2013; translated by Zakir Paul), pp. 43–4.

after Stendhal. If you think of *The Red and the Black*, for me its counterpart in the 1880s would be Maupassant, in particular his *Little Louise Roque*, the tale of the rape of a little girl by the honourable village worthy. That's the moment when the *fait divers*, which used to mean dangerous energy on the part of members of the people, starts to mean something else, an animality, an inhumanity, that subtends this civilization that believes in progress, this varnish over civilization that covers the brutal beast within. That's the *fait divers* of the age of Nietzsche and Lombroso.

There are sort of two traditions of the *fait divers*, a tradition of popular capacity, and another tradition of watchful animality. There is a moment when the symptomatic function of the *fait divers* varies and takes on different values. The *fait divers* is always interpreted as a sickness of civilization, but that sickness can mean the promotion of the children of the people, or simply the evil that is always lying in wait behind the normal order of things. The *fait divers* was thereby to turn into an instrument of pathologization. These days, it's clear that it's essentially sex crimes and especially stories of paedophiles that make up the bulk of the *fait divers*. When I was young, in the 1950s, the typical *fait divers* was known as a 'crime of passion': these were jealous husbands or wives who killed the lover or mistress, and that gave rise to great oratorical jousting sessions in the law courts. Nowadays the essential *fait divers* is the rape of a little boy or little girl. The criminal has overwhelmingly turned into a sick person. This means that ordinary life doesn't have a lot of room any more for invention. Since the days of Maupassant, all the doctors, psychiatrists, psychoanalysts and educators have latched on to it. As soon as ordinary life is shaken up, as soon as it stops being ordinary, it is automatically interpreted and medicalized.

This chimes in with what we were saying earlier, namely, that we are in worlds where disobedience takes the form of deviancy, the downward spiral of the individual, terrorism, criminality, and most especially a residual criminality that can't be switched off, since we know full well that, if there are crimes for which different types of rehabilitation or penal strategies have never done a thing, those crimes are sex crimes. The fact that this is what always appears in the foreground is like a sign of the disappearance of popular subversion behind the simple incurable sickness of civilization.

The nineteenth century you talk about, in which the fait divers *becomes important, is also the inaugural age of the detective novel. Behind the* fait divers *and the detective novel lies the investigation. What is the structure of the detective novel? What allows us to see what's really going on in the* fait divers? *It's the investigation, which is also furthermore the virtue you were attributing a moment ago to artists when they unpack the news. If we insist here on the theme of the investigation, it's to get back to the issue of political subjectiviza-tion and broaden the discussion. Some philosophers – we're thinking here of Dewey – see democracy as an opening up of the practice of the investigation, and others, following Marx, think of emancipation as participation in collective investigations. So there would seem to be a connection between the democratic revolution, the elucidation produced by common sense, which is also a theme in your work, and the investigation as a practice. How do you situate this link? We also have a different theme in mind, one not so far removed – Foucault's discourse on* parrhesia *and 'truth-telling'. There, political subjectivi-zation would consist in telling the truth to power. Those are elements that aren't immediately mobilized in your definition of politics or democracy, but we can easily see that asserting equality may well not be a matter of figuration, but also of 'truth-telling' and investigating. How do you situate these practices?*

Let's start with the fact that the investigation designates things that are completely different. In the tradition of the detective novel, the investigation is opposed to the logic of the *fait divers*, since the detec-tive novel has been the great salvaging operation of causality in the age of literature. The fictional detective investigation has been this re-rationalization or over-rationalization, something that goes against the logic of the novel and even against the logics of pathology I men-tioned a second ago. In a sense, Dostoevsky signs off on the ruin of the police investigation ahead of the event. Porphyre doesn't conduct an investigation, he waits for the criminal's sickness to take him to the criminal. The rationality of the *fait divers* is thereby completely dif-ferent from this rationality which the detective novel develops and which people like Henry James or Jorge Luis Borges then get all nos-talgic about. What you define by investigation is very different; it's something like the development of popular militant expertise. It is part of democracy, the constitution of a whole space of expertise that is a counter-expertise in relation to the expert machinery of power and the scientific machinery enlisted by the powers that be.

I've never been all that wild about this overblown theme of *par-rhesia*. It doesn't really seem to be part of Foucault's essential con-tribution. I understand that he may have needed at a certain moment to grapple with the issue of the truth again, no doubt feeling that the Nietzschean tradition he'd more or less been heir to had let him down. I don't have anything against the fact that you reinvest in the truth, but this translation of the truth Diogenes came up with when confronted by Alexander into a political virtue – I don't really believe in it. There's also the fact that 'truth-telling' in politics has been pretty much compromised since the 1980s, when 'truth-telling' became the buzzword of both the right and the left for the return of lucidity, of looking at things head-on, which ultimately meant seeing them according to the logic of power and the logic of the official economics, the logic of consensus about 'what is'. But, above all, you don't 'tell' the truth 'to power'. You develop forms of investigation, of information, of knowledge, that will then reconfigure the situation in relation to the configuration of things that power imposes. Power has no truck with the truth; it deals with a whole host of ways of constructing situations that then define forms of 'truth-telling' – though that doesn't mean that the truth is relative ... The question always comes back ultimately to knowing where the truth is happening and how it circulates, how it constitutes a common fabric and a form of constructing the common world. The investigation aims both at broadening the field of what belongs to a situation and also the world of those who are qualified to talk about it and to contribute knowledge.

Precarious and Popular Arts of Living

Let's press on with 'ordinary lives' from the point of view of what you call in the last chapter of Aisthesis *'the art of living', 'an art beyond art' that meets up with the horizon of the historic avant-gardes. You say from this viewpoint that* Aisthesis *can also be read as a counterpoint to* The Nights of Labour.[63] *How does this popular art of living manifest itself today? What is the evidence of it around you?*

One thing's for sure and that is that *The Nights of Labour* talked about how discovering an art of living or a lifestyle was an important element in the dynamics of working-class emancipation. That chapter in *Aisthesis* refers to the wrench James Agee felt over the fact that the art of living he discovered in the dwellings, clothing and gestures of the sharecroppers of Alabama is something they couldn't possibly appropriate for themselves as their power. I don't have a lot to say about what the art of living is today for those who occupy the place of artisans in *The Nights of Labour* or for the sharecroppers of the

---

[63] 'The radical break is to stop living in the world of the enemy.' (Jacques Rancière interviewed by Eric Loret, in *Libération*, 17 November 2011.)

heartland of America. To have something to say about all that, you'd have to do the work in the form of an investigation and I no longer have the energy or am the right age to come up with forms of investigation that would have the same intensity and the same significance for me as *The Nights of Labour*.

So I'll limit myself to two empirical considerations that touch on this condition of precariousness we were talking about and that run through the different levels of culture. As a teacher, I've known quite a few people who are sort of lifelong students, people who now live between several worlds, worlds of study, the world of a paid job that might be as a night watchman, a carpenter or a gardener, and taking part in a world of art practices. There are heaps of lives that play out between several worlds, that are built on the art of living both within the precariousness of a particular set of conditions and within the luxury of thought at the same time. Just the other day, I was in Brussels and I ran into a friend – the Croatian translator of *The Ignorant Schoolmaster* – who'd come from Zagreb, where he lives off little jobs at the radio and things like that. The first thing he did when he arrived in Brussels was to go and buy *Aisthesis* because you can't get it in Zagreb. He has very little to live on, but it's a luxury for him to be able to create this relationship between a completely precarious life and investment in things to do with the mind. He's translated I don't know how many of my unpublished essays, and he's happy to have translated them; he doesn't make any effort to do anything with them. That's something I also notice in the world of the musicians my son surrounds himself with: they try to construct an art of living for themselves that involves focusing on looking after their money and being absolutely rigorous in the work – whether paid or unpaid – they've chosen to do in their desire to live well. It's also translated into forms of sharing and solidarity and sociability that are pretty different from the forms of sociability that existed among Marxists of my generation. Something that amounts to various policies for living is being woven, modern equivalents of those cenobitic economies I talked about in reference to Gauny. I also remember this student, a 'Badiouist', who, in the middle of a strike at Paris VIII over the problems created by a hike in university fees, angrily interrupted people arguing in support of the struggle: 'The problem isn't money, it's doing philosophy. This is what I've got to live on', he said, and it really wasn't much. 'But that doesn't interest me. What interests me is doing philosophy.'

There are these arts of living that I see around me, along with the arts of living that exist in the so-called popular universe and that are made palatable to us by artists. I'm thinking of Pedro Costa, whom

I've already mentioned. If you look at the way Costa devotes himself to the immigrants or reformed druggies he follows around, first in the shanty town, then in the dazzling white apartments they've been rehoused in, you can see that he's trying to capture a capacity these people have, even though they live in misery, in precariousness, including psychological precariousness – the capacity to tell their story, to find forms of expression that help them hold their heads up a bit and deal with their fate. We were talking a moment ago about Sylvain George's film on Calais, on the people who spend years on the road suffering the worst brutalities, miseries, humiliations. Those people are capable of doing what they do and reasoning about their fate and thinking through what they do in relation to what they might eventually be able to offer their little brothers or their children by way of a life. Burning your fingers so you don't have identifiable fingerprints any more is part of an art of living for yourself within the police order, but also of preparing a better life for those who come after you. So that's what I'm able to say today and it's more in the nature of impressions that I've picked up looking around me over the last twenty years, and what certain artists reconstruct for us in their bid to track the capacity to think, speak and live that belongs to people who are in principle the most downtrodden and the most destitute.

We're touching here on a phase in your thinking that we've already tackled, an ethical phase, whose status in your overall edifice doesn't seem to us to be completely clear. We could see it coming since the art issue, but this ethical dimension is, we think, somewhat politically ambivalent. We're not thinking here of what, in some of your essays, you call 'the ethical turn of politics', or 'the ethical turn of aesthetics'. This ethical aspect seems to have a double meaning in your work. It can act as an obstacle to political subjectivization, or it can play out as a condition of this latter, as you've just underlined in relation to precariousness. We might have brought up the concept of parrhesia *a bit too soon. Well, parrhesia isn't just about the issue of discourse or 'truth-telling', but also the issue of 'the courage of the truth'. Foucault was more broadly interested in ethical training or spiritual exercises that make it possible to 'tell the truth'. Shouldn't we be thinking, in the same vein, about what could or should prepare us for political subjectivization as you understand it? It would not simply depend on a labour of symbolization, or figuration, or investigation as discussed, but also on 'arts of living'. The possibility of political subjectivization depends on the work done on the* ethos. *From this point of view, we might ask ourselves if the people you talk about who are living precariously aren't in a situation comparable to a historic figure we're already familiar with, that of the artistic and literary bohemia of the nineteenth century, even if their anti-bourgeois ethos was not all that politically productive?*

I don't think the kind of attitude I was talking about, which is linked both to the condition of precariousness and to an ethical and militant commitment, has anything to do with the bohemia of the nineteenth century. It's not about shocking the bourgeois. When you've been teaching philosophy for a very long time to people who know they won't be able to do anything with it professionally, what you see in them is a desire to live with dignity and in solidarity with others, and to be as independent as possible of the conditions the dominant order imposes on you. That's very different from the bohemia of the years between 1830 and 1840. It's more like what I saw in the different forms of working-class emancipation.

Emancipation is firstly the constitution of a certain kind of independence that is achieved through various strategies of subsistence; the cenobitic economy is one, militant collectives that collect food through farmers' circuits are another. There are ways of cutting down, living in a group, a whole host of behaviours that define forms of withdrawal in relation to the economic constraints, and the ideological constraints, of the dominant order. Of course, these conditions are very often like the preconditions of political subjectivization, but that's also the ambiguity of emancipation. Emancipation is always also a way of living differently in the world as it is. In a way, there is always, at the heart of the nineteenth-century working-class processes of emancipation such as I've studied them, the possibility of contenting yourself with the current emancipation, because you can live in a way that's different from the one prescribed by the system. The conditions that make you likely to fight against a system are the same as those that make you likely to support it, to uphold it. This is where the meshing of politics and ethics that interests me comes in, and not in those visions where politics is recast as a matter of cyborgs, ghosts or dead people ...

The Distribution of the Sensible and Contemporary Art

Let's talk now about the present, or presents, plural, in terms of the way you characterize them. We stumbled on a sentence at the beginning of the foreword to 'Distribution of the Sensible', the first chapter in The Politics of Aesthetics, *in which you flag a form of historic relaying between the field of politics and the field of aesthetics. You say that 'a battle fought yesterday over the promises of emancipation and the illusions and disillusions of history continues today on aesthetic terrain'.*[64] *We'd like to invite you to extend that sentence so as to grasp why you oppose 'today' and 'yesterday' here. Why do you say that it's in aesthetics that something that was of the order of emancipation and the unkept promises of history in the nineteenth century is now being pursued? Does this mean that there has been a sort of 'relieving' of politics by aesthetics? If so, that would seem to us incompatible with other claims made in your work.*

The expression may well create a misunderstanding. That essay is from the end of the 1990s and it doesn't at all refer to any sort of overall view of modernity, of the relationship between aesthetic revolution and political revolution; it referred to a much more specific conjuncture. It didn't refer to the history of revolution and emancipation, but to a much more localized history – the history of the liquidation of the age of revolution as that liquidation was crowed about in the 1980s and 1990s. All I said was that the discourse on art, its post-life, its end, the 'conspiracy' behind it, that whole discourse that flourished in France in those years, was a repetition of what we'd heard on the subject of politics ten years earlier. I'm talking about the claim that Marxism, utopias, politics, history, had reached their use-by date, along with all that had tried to orient the movement of history towards emancipation, etc. What we saw in the polemics on the 'end of art' at the close of the 1990s was an extension of that lament, or attack. People went from condemning the legacy of 'master thinkers', fathers of totalitarianism, following Glucksmann, to condemning the complicity of the pictorial avant-gardes in the same totalitarianism, following Jean Clair, or 'the art conspiracy', following Baudrillard. What I said didn't involve a whole analysis of the overall relationships between an aesthetic revolution and a political revolution, just the relationship between two different declarations about the liquidation of this revolution.

That said, even from this point of view, that sentence wasn't accurate. When I was working again recently on the history of the transformations of the modernist paradigm on a purely aesthetic level, I realized that Greenberg was a pioneer in relation to the whole

---

[64] Jacques Rancière, Foreword to 'The Distribution of the Sensible', in *The Politics of Aesthetics* (Continuum: London and New York, 2004; translated by Gabriel Rockhill), p. 3. (This translation covers only part of *Le Partage du sensible* (Paris: La Fabrique, 2000). *Translator's note.*)

contemporary discourse on consumerist democracy. He was the first person to say that what high art and revolution were threatened by was popular culture, the culture born of consumerism, of the fact that the sons of peasants and workers had turned into petits bourgeois and wanted their own culture. In a sense, that whole discourse on consumerist democracy and mass individualism was something Greenberg and Adorno were conducting, in their own way, well before Baudrillard, Guy Debord and Christopher Lasch followed their lead in the 1980s.

In contemporary art, particularly with exhibition curators, part of your work is used in a way that leads to absolutization of the category of 'dissensus'. It then becomes a matter of assiduously anticipating which artworks will be able to create a 'dissensus' to conform to your diagnostic of present-day art. That makes no sense in relation to the principle of indeterminacy you propose. Similarly, what you call the 'distribution of the sensible' is immediately associated with distance, rupture, whereas you work the stereotypical element of the commonplace, of consensus, every bit as much. As you've reminded us here, consensus is an established 'distribution of the sensible'. So we get the feeling that 'distribution of the sensible' has turned into an odd catch phrase in the world of contemporary art.

I don't quite know how to answer you since what all the people who read *The Politics of Aesthetics*, and quote it and use it, really understand by 'distribution of the sensible' remains relatively obscure to me. I think there are several interpretations. There is a certain lyricism of the sensible, and sometimes there's a crossover between that and an education marked by phenomenology, which is pretty meaningful in some of these circles. People sometimes have the idea that politics resides in the sensible, anyway, and so art is directly involved in politics. I have to say I don't have much control any more over how people read or interpret my books or over their effects. I get letters all the time from people organizing biennales which, they say, are designed according to my principles, which is why I should come. As I can't go everywhere, I can't know. There are a thousand ways to interpret the term, either in the sense that we're involved in politics, anyway, or in the sense that it has once again been proven that art has a political job to do, and this means that that job can be tackled in the traditional forms of art criticism or art activism.

And sometimes the message gets through, regardless, that we need to rethink both the idea of art as being at the service of politics and the idea that there are apparatuses that automatically produce political effects. The principle of indeterminacy you mention is not a principle of indifference. It entails the effort of directors and curators to construct spatial circuits that amount to no more than possible histories, leaving the spectator the chance to construct his own history based on that. After all, I get the impression that that's something that can be visualized by some of the people who've read me or heard me talk. That's what I pick up in the work of Manoel Borja-Villel, in his conception of space at the museum he's the director of, the Reina Sofia in Madrid. I also noticed it at work once at the Moderna Museet in Stockholm where the director, Daniel Birnbaum, who was also the curator of a Venice Biennale that centred around the title, *Fare Mondi* (*Making Worlds*), was trying to call into question once again the policies and educational support systems at work in museum exhibitions, so as to open up a space full of possibilities, involving a reorganization of spaces and a rereading of histories, leaving the spectator his role to play.

Without wanting to give myself too much importance, I get the impression I've managed to get something across. One of the things the 'distribution of the sensible' theme has served to do in this milieu is, after all, to overcome the stultifying effects of the kind of thinking that goes, 'art equals the market, anyway, so there's nothing we can do'; or else, 'art is what the institution says it is, so anything goes', which is an overwhelming, debilitating discourse. *The Distribution of the Sensible* contributed to giving people back the ability to think through spaces so that they are not already predetermined by a given, implacable, relationship between art, the institution and the market. It's important to loosen up this relationship between art, the market and politics; and to say that, despite all we know about the institutions and the market, we can nonetheless suggest different ways of making different realms today. At the same time, this has to be done a bit modestly. It's something certain people are intent on, despite all the constraints they otherwise have to put up with due to the fact that all these institutions have to both grow according to market forces and to cover themselves, regarding the public authorities and intellectual opinion, through a whole system of legitimizations based on the radical opposition of the culture to the market. Obviously, these people live in a universe full of pretty overwhelming constraints and their possibilities for loosening things up are limited. It seems to me to be not uninteresting to have managed, nonetheless, to construct a bit of free space in this somewhat over-regulated game. On top of that, as we know, there are a whole host of artists and curators who think of one thing only – getting a supposedly hip philosopher for their catalogue. And a curator or director in quest of legitimacy will always find one, whether it's Rancière,

Didi-Huberman, Virilio or someone else. It's an individual affair, defending yourself against these peripheral effects.

The Future of Socialism

Does the word 'socialism', as you have revisited it and enlarged on it in your early works, still seem to you to have any significance today? Could that significance be recharged symbolically? If so, how do we then redefine and appropriate it? And, if that's what it's all about, does the 'principle of equality' suffice to define this brand of socialism? Or would we have to add additional clauses that would either parse the principle – that's also sort of why we were talking about practical maxims a moment ago – or, on the contrary, finalize it according to the sectors of activity? Or should we also arm ourselves with other slogans that have cropped up in socialism's long history – words like 'association', which you've been interested in, or the words 'abolition of private property'?

There are several ways of understanding what's central to the socialist idea. In the more global sense, we can say that the idea of socialism is the idea of a world that doesn't have private interest as its organizing principle. And since we know that private interest isn't, as they say, in everybody's interest, but just the interest of a small group of individuals, this boils down to saying that the idea of socialism is the idea of a world that isn't structured by the principle of seeking the maximum return on capital. And that, in my view, includes two things. On the one hand, the idea of socialism is the idea of a world where the common commodities everybody needs to live are as much as possible the property of the community and have a use in relation to the greatest number. It's a world where water, land, the means of production, education, health and communications are as much as possible at the service of the greatest number. That also means – and experience has demonstrated this after all – that they're the *property* of the greatest number. That's a primary principle, one that's perceptible to us, conversely, by what we've been seeing over the last twenty or thirty years, which is that everything that was once considered to be the property of the greatest number has been more and more completely privatized and subjected to a logic of profit. The second thing that is at the heart of socialism is the idea of association. This means that what is common, shared, is managed as much as possible in ways that are forms of exercising a power that belongs to each and every person, or a power that belongs to the greatest number. Socialism thereby defines a social fabric in which the forms of industrial production, as well as a series of economic forms and forms of life that are involved in education, health and communication, are managed in an associative and democratic way to the maximum. In the idea of socialism there is a sort of idea that what is necessary for everybody is common property; and, secondly, there is the idea of an optimal exercising of the capacity of anyone at all in associative forms.

We can think of it in a minimal or a maximal way; it can go from a certain maximal vision of a classless society entirely in the hands of producers, etc., to a minimal vision a bit like what we've seen with the system of what is called – maliciously and out of a desire to destroy it – 'the welfare state'. That system actually means an 'egalitarian social fabric', which is not after all quite the same thing. What we might call 'socialism' is this double aspect of what concerns the greatest number as being common property, and of the participation of the greatest number in the management of this common property. It's something that keeps its topicality, including currently, when we are seeing all of it recede, a bit like the boat Winckelmann talks about at the end of his *History of Art* and which is taking a loved figure of the community far away. But it still has a meaning. That said, we need to see that on top of all that, the word 'socialist' is the generic name for those who, in different ways, have never ceased betraying what the idea of socialism once stood for. We are in this conjuncture where the word 'socialism' can still define a certain powerful notion about common ownership and common capacity; and, at the same time, it defines a political configuration – of people who have lived only to endlessly betray everything the idea of socialism stood for.

Political Economics

At different points in your work on Gauny, of whom we've already spoken, you refer to the idea of a 'counter-economy'. This counter-economy is described in detail, then immediately captured in the egalitarian principle. Elsewhere, you've attacked the strategic notion of suspending economic activity or blocking supply in social and political struggles. You have also declared that what is happening currently is the collapse of a system and you foresee new forms of organizing the economic world.[65] How do you link the economic

[65] 'The debate about the financial economy and the real economy is certainly not enough, but it bears witness to the fact that a certain figure of the economy, one that was identified with the whole evolution of society,

dimension with your notion of politics? Do all economic issues get swallowed up in equality?

We actually have to start with the fact that, in the modern era, the economy has always meant several things at once. It designates the sector of production of the means of existence, but at the same time economics has always referred to a certain idea of the world, to hierarchies. When people say, for instance, 'you're talking politics and not economics', it's easy to see that this doesn't mean that you don't take enough interest in economic mechanisms, but that you're interested in the surface and not in the depths. 'The economy' has become the name of the final cause, the final instance, the thing that needs to be replaced in order for something to change. And it's clear that when people say that if we don't overhaul the economy, nothing will change, what they mean is that if we don't overhaul the final cause, nothing will change. Since they're more or less unruffled about the fact that we'll never touch the final cause, they can carry on with their denunciatory discourse *ad vitam aeternam*. The primacy of economics, in a sense, also means the eternal reign of domination. The discourse on economics chimes with what I was referring to a moment ago and which consists in saying: democracy, capitalism, economics or consumption – it's all the same thing. Economics is then the kind of Nietzschean state of civilization, the civilization of the 'last man', that we are living in. There is also the tactic that tries to replace economics with ecology by saying that, behind the means of production and of existence, there is the planet, and it's the planet we now have to worry about. Whatever the case, the idea of economics is associated with an idea of knowledge of necessity.

What I react to first and foremost is the position of economics as this final cause that we need to change but never will change. I'm also opposed to identifying economics with politics in the form of the multitudes, seen as this sort of global subjectivity that is immediately both economic and political at the same time. What's left after that? What's left is the overwhelming fact that today we can no longer say that economics is the world of truth that's behind politics. The law of economics and the law of politics tend to be

has nonetheless been put to rout. The good thing about the financial crisis is precisely that it liberates us from "economics" as an unequivocal reality and as an unavoidable law.' (In 'Construire les lieux du politique', Jacques Rancière interviewed by Le Sabot, reprinted in *Et tant pis pour les gens fatigués* (Paris, Amsterdam, 2009)), p. 674.

seen as identical. You can see how the real question is not whether
the government should accept free-market competition or not, since
the government doesn't just accept it, it imposes it. Once upon a
time there were the famous 'iron-clad laws' of economics which
governments were supposed to work with, or which they had to
remedy. But today a number of these economic laws are being
constitutionalized. There is an interlocking of political and economic
domination to a point never before seen. Marx used to say governments were the agents of Capital. But what governments did for
Capital at the time consisted most especially in making sure that
order, in the form of the police in the strict sense of the term, was
respected, and in preventing things from changing. Today, governments do more than prevent things from changing; they impose
certain economic dogmas as the law itself. We're in a situation
where domination by the state and by economics merge, tending
to become the same thing. And we get this double-dealing whereby,
at the same time, our governments present this fusion as a necessity
they're forced to bow to. It's a way of declaring the impotence and
incapacity for all. Our governments have turned themselves into
the agents of worldwide economic necessity and thereby into agents
who produce the conditions of a general incapacity – all the more
so as yesterday's economic counter-forces, like the big trade-union
organizations, have been decimated.

So what's left? A central question is left: is there anything we can
do, or is there nothing we can do, and what are the ways we can do
something? And there remains an obvious fact that's more powerful
than ever: the economic issue can't be separated from the issue of
reasserting the capacity and power of anyone at all, at all levels. It
can't be separated from the idea that the power of anyone at all
should be able to be exercised as much in relation to supposedly
ecological issues as in relation to labour and its forms of organization
or manifestation in the public arena. On the one hand, we can say
that the precondition for all action on the economy is the reconstitution of effective people power. On the other hand, it's clear that such
power itself presupposes a capacity to act on all the places where
economic domination is in play, and to do so in the form of the public
struggle against the transformation of the laws of the official science
of economics into laws of the state, as well as in the form of resistance to new forms of exploitation of labour or in the form of the
creation of alternative forms of economic organization. Clearly, there
can be no democracy, no socialism, without forms of economic
organization that are also forms of exercising the power of all, within
whatever space those forms can be integrated.

Unfortunately, we can't say much for the moment except that we need to rethink the issue of economics based on this interconnection of state power and economic power, which is at a maximum today and which imposes the precondition of an equally global reconstitution of a form of people power that no longer makes any distinction between economics and politics. Today, we can no longer say something like, 'let's take the factories and then the rest will follow', because the factories have been pulled down, they've been packed off elsewhere. We're in an unprecedented situation that probably necessitates what we mentioned earlier, the creation of a new Internationale, but that's over the long haul. In a way, we tell ourselves that maybe we need to wait for a conjuncture between the movements of those whose jobs have been taken over here, and those who've been made to live elsewhere in factory production conditions. For the moment, we're really at a point where we can't do much in terms of prediction and predication. All we can do is reassert this global gap between people power and global economico-state power.

Interviews and Dialogue

You've granted a lot of interviews, to very different people and for various print media – militant revues with more or less small print runs, high-circulation magazines, and books made up of interviews like the one we're putting together here. How do you organize your written work, on the one hand, and this significant investment in the spoken word? Do interviews have a value that's independent of their relationship to your writing, to the construction of thought? And, if so, would that value be distinct from the value of other forms of interlocution, of philosophical transmission, such as what you've worked on through the figure of Jacotot, but also dialogue insofar as the dialogue is a cardinal figure in philosophy?

Let's start with the empirical fact that for a very long time I didn't do interviews because no one asked me to, so for a long time I didn't have to divide my time between writing and interviews. That said, one of the paradoxes of the situation is that people started asking me a lot for interviews only after the publication of a work that was just an interview to begin with, and that was *The Distribution of the Sensible*[66] (the first part of *The Politics of Aesthetics*). That's the

---

[66] *Le Partage du sensible* was partly translated into English as *The Politics of Aesthetics* (Continuum: London and New York, 2004; translated by Gabriel Rockhill). *Translator's note.*

first point. The interview is not a constant figure in my work, but, starting from the moment I acquired a certain notoriety, for whatever reason, right or wrong, I saw a whole host of requests come my way. First point, to begin with, for me, interviews are outside of work. Someone comes and asks you to retranslate whatever's been constructed within the research-writing binomial in a form that will allow your work to register in the normal space of knowledge transfer, of information transfer, or, more clearly still, of political debate. There's a whole conversion exercise that has this negative side of converting into general propositions the work of research, which is always work involving the relationship between thought and what it thinks, the thinkable. All of a sudden, they ask you to explain your thinking by taking it out of its direct relationship with what it's trying to think, with what it's exerted on. There's a considerable risk there of converting yourself into your own populizer, your own journalist.

Otherwise there is, of course, the fact that if you write, if you're not happy just to study and transcribe your research for your own purposes, if you publish something, you feel in a way that it's sort of legitimate for people to ask you to account for what you've published. Even if that sometimes involves an enormous expenditure of energy, it seems only normal to me to respond to the demands of people who are trying to come to grips with what you've said, with what I've said, with this endless meshing between what is supposed to be of the order of thought and what appears to be of the order of description, narration, empiricism.

There's a third side to this, which is that the exercise of translation can itself have the effect of making you think differently. There are moments when the interview formula can lead you to a certain number of formulations you've been skirting around. A classic example of a successful interview is the one that led to *The Distribution of the Sensible (in The Politics of Aesthetics)*. There were very short questions, based on which I was able to pull off a synthesis of something I'd been skirting around. Afterwards, the problem is that people ask you for interviews about the interview you did; they ask you to rehash it, to make accessible to a bigger audience what you've already said in an interview that has turned into a book. But there's the fact that this can lead you to think what you weren't thinking, to respond to some provocation. In the interviews I've reread, I sometimes say to myself: 'Really? I said that?' I've forgotten what I said. That means that something happened that I didn't have control over in advance and that wasn't predictable as the answer Jacques Rancière gives to the questions people put to him about his aesthetics or his politics. So, there is this value sometimes, which is essentially a value as provocation. A good interview is one in which all of a sudden you say things that weren't expected, that are not only new, have never yet been said, but that wouldn't have been said if there hadn't been this specific kind of provocation. There is the work of writing, which is a response to a certain provocation, to the way research subjects provoke you. There is the kind of writing that produces. And then, potentially, there is this provocation that comes to you when what you've written comes back at you.

The notion of a 'dialogue' poses a different problem. I don't believe in the virtue of dialogue in the form of: here's a thinker, here's another thinker, they're going to debate amongst themselves and that's going to produce something. My idea is that it's always books that enter into dialogue and not people; consequently, responding to what someone else has to say to you is something you do in the form of a written work. This means that the dialogue always happens afterwards. If you ask me questions, it's an interview; but if, in our interview, there's a subject that is more especially yours, one that attests to a specific and independent interest, it can then play the role of a provocation and involve this afterthought that is dialogue. Dialogue is never, for me, what it appears to be, which is something like the lightning flash of an encounter, a live exchange. No, dialogue is always something that happens with time, with a lapse of time; it's dialogue from work to work and not from person to person, from individual to individual. And then there is the case where the dialogue appears to be hidden inside the interview and you try to be a part of it after the event, by reworking it. Because the initial response to an interview always – well, maybe not always – has something self-protective about it. You give the response that protects you. After that – possibly in the moment, but most often afterwards – the dialogue dimension appears in the sense that something has been said which you haven't replied to and you have to reply.

You sometimes talk on radio and we've seen you at least once on television. Do you think about these external conditions of speaking in terms of what you want to say? Since people always also virtually address a public that differs for each occasion.

The question has several layers. Let's say first off that I don't control the places I'm asked to speak in, from the solemn lecture theatre to the tacky premises of certain contemporary art spaces, from the lectern of Anglo-American lecturers to the armchairs of some relaxed discussion. I adapt, that's all. This comes down to the fact that, if I have a public voice, it's very rarely on my own initiative. My

interventions – spoken or written – in the public arena, of the kind
involving an article on current affairs or a word or two on radio or
TV, or possibly at conferences, debates, round tables, or discussions,
are most of the time things I'm asked for and very rarely things I've
initiated. I take the initiative when I take up my pen and find someone
who'll publish me, when I get the feeling there's something to say
that no one else, for various reasons, can say. When I get the feeling
there's an intellectual consensus and that it will win the match
because no one is answering back, because people are afraid of
getting egg on their faces by answering back, or because they don't
feel the need to answer, then I might decide to intervene, as I did
with *Hatred of Democracy* where I had to make up my mind to do
it because, apparently, no one else felt they had the strength or the
desire to say certain things. I thought I could say them and I said
them. That's also how I've intervened on my own initiative around
issues of racisim, 'the extreme right', etc. – not because nobody else
wanted to talk about those things, but because people's reactions
seemed to me to accept the enemy's presuppositions. But these vol-
untary interventions are rare. Most of the time, they're requests from
outside, and I try to work out where I stand in relation to the request
and possibly to challenge the position of the philosopher who comes
along to talk to politicians and journalists, etc., or the position of
the man who's come to be an expert on the situation, to say *ex officio*
what philosophy has to say on this or that subject. In relation to that,
my second principle is to take practically no notice of whoever it is
I'm talking to. I adopted that principle fairly early on in the piece.

*In relation to the journalists interviewing you, or in relation to
an audience?*

In relation to the audience; with journalists, it's a bit different. I try
to apply the principle of equality of intelligence – the fact that in a
way everyone is capable of understanding something of what I say
and making something of it. This capacity that we can assume in
others is independent of the cultural level we might assume them to
have. If some association is organizing cultural debates in a small
country town and they invite me, I'd say the same thing as I'd say in
a supposedly prestigious university. I think the fundamental question
is whether I have something to say or not, and then to try and say
it as well as I can. The thing an audience always senses is if someone
has something to say or not. In the first case, they'll take the time
to think about it. The business is more complicated when you're
dealing with journalists. In our society, the journalist has become
the figure of the mind-numbing educator. He's the ultimate educator

who starts getting into a tizz as soon as he sees you coming, and tells you, 'You know you're not dealing with intellectuals, etc. You can't talk for long, and you have to use very simple words.' That's an attitude that comes with the job. It's the same thing if the job is filled by *normaliens* (graduates of the École Normale) with university degrees, etc. It's the very principle of the job to assume you're talking to morons. I have a rule which is that I'm not talking to morons, I'm talking to human beings who have the same intelligence as I do, and I say what I have to say, and that's it. In general, I've always turned down radio or TV debates where you're there to play a role, to adopt a position: to play the role of a leftie by debating with Finkielkraut, or with Gauchet, or whoever. I once found myself in a situation where there were two blokes from the extreme right on the set; so I only turned up on set the moment I was called, and I said what I had to say in one go and kept my mouth shut after that.

You managed to take control of the conditions, after all.

There's a way of controlling conditions when it comes to the media, but that's mainly certain kinds of radio or TV confrontations where you have to play the role of the philosopher, the guy on the left, etc., though that's relatively limited. In those cases, I try to control the conditions.

Is it an opportunity for you to put your own thinking differently? When we talk about conditions, they are of course external conditions, with journalists and technical interventions, but those conditions also allow the possibility of inventing a discourse that functions differently than in books or articles, just as it does in interviews ...

I've made it a duty to myself, even if I don't always manage to live up to it, not to get bored. After all, I'm often asked to talk about things I've talked about a lot, and written about a lot, and there's the overwhelming threat of saturation. So I try to seize on the word or question that will allow me to put what I have to say differently so I don't bore myself. It's a very demanding requirement and I can't always meet it. The bookshop discussion format has this advantage: it's incredibly hard to make one lecture different from another lecture; it's much easier, when you don't have a bit of paper in front of you, no compulsory format, to find an opening for saying things differently and shifting the emphasis in what you've said. For me, that's essential. Without it you die.

Index